P9-CPV-428

Differentiating Instruction and Assessment for English Language Learners

A Guide for K–12 Teachers

Shelley Fairbairn

Stephaney Jones-Vo

Caslon Publishing
Philadelphia

Dedication

To Scott and Nora.
—S.F.

To Vinh.
—S.J.V.

And to our wonderful students
from around the world who
continue to teach us.

Copyright © Caslon, Inc. 2010

All rights reserved. Except for the quotation of short passages for the purposes of criticism and review, no part of the publication may be reproduced, stored in a retrieval system, or transmitted in any form or by any means, electronic, mechanical, photocopying, recording, or otherwise without prior written permission of the publisher.

Caslon, Inc.
P.O. Box 3248
Philadelphia, PA 19130

Caslonpublishing.com

9 8 7 6 5 4 3

Library of Congress Cataloging-in-Publication Data
Fairbairn, Shelley.
   Differentiating instruction and assessment for English language learners : a guide for K/12 teachers / Shelley Fairbairn, Stephaney Jones-Vo.
      p. cm.
   Includes bibliographical references.
   ISBN 978-1-934000-02-1 (soft cover)
   1. English language—Study and teaching—Foreign speakers.
2. Multicultural education.   3. Mainstreaming in education.   4. Language acquisition.   I. Jones-Vo, Stephaney.   II. Title.
   PE1128.A2F245 2010
   428.2'4—dc22

Foreword

Over the past few years several books and articles have come out on the topic of differentiating *instruction* for students with various needs. Many of these works have been helpful and teachers are more aware than ever before of the need to develop differentiated learning environments for students who are not well served by the mainstream school experience. And yet the topic of differentiating instruction as it pertains to *academic language development* for English language learners (ELLs) is still scarcely addressed and poorly understood at a time when the number of ELLs has surpassed 5 million across the United States.

Research has demonstrated that ELLs, like all students, need access to the same challenging academic skills and content to maximize their opportunities to learn. However, access to grade-level content is only meaningful if teachers have the skills to recognize where ELLs are on the continuum of language development and to differentiate the instruction and assessment in ways that ensure understanding and active participation. This is a tall order, especially when we consider that, for the most part, only the English as a second language and bilingual teachers have received training that includes an extensive acknowledgment of the needs of ELLs and strategies for meeting those needs. Within most language support programs, ELLs spend a fraction of the day with the ESL or bilingual teacher and most of the day in content area classes with the teachers whose professional development has included little or no information about meeting ELLs' needs.

Hence my excitement when I read Shelley Fairbairn and Stephaney Jones-Vo's guide written for all teachers who work with ELLs. I have been hoping someone would take the time to write a resource for teachers that clearly articulates the many needs ELLs have, but more importantly, goes the extra step and provides examples that teachers can follow as they differentiate language expectations in diverse classroom settings. *Differentiating Instruction and Assessment for English Language Learners* is an important resource for teachers precisely because it provides charts and activities that are easy to understand and return to long after an initial reading. At WIDA we talk often about illustrating the *linguistic pathways* ELLs need to be successful in all their academic subjects. This guide makes a significant contribution to recognizing and differentiating for ELLs' growth along a path from the beginning through the more advanced levels of proficiency. The most striking features are prose that is thorough yet "readable," the true-to-life scenarios of students and teachers, the focus on classroom assessment strategies, and the connections throughout to TESOL's and WIDA's English language proficiency standards that illustrate the language demands of core content area classrooms.

The notion that we must explicitly teach academic language within all school classrooms is gaining ground today. Gone are the assumptions of language learning "by osmosis" or that a specialized language arts curriculum alone can provide what ELLs need. Even under the best of classroom circumstances where teachers use a variety of student-centered methodologies, there is still a role for developing meta-awareness of academic *languages.* To engage students in this kind of intellectual work, teachers have to develop awareness of language and the ways that language is uniquely employed within their class and across differing academic subjects. Such attention to academic language helps ELLs access the core school curriculum, but it also supports any learner who struggles with the discourses of school. This guide is packed with ideas for purposeful and differentiated language instruction and assessment that can be applied throughout most content classrooms. It provides a guide for any teacher who is eager to assure that students are learning deeply. I predict this text will be as popular with teachers already facing the daily challenges of educating ELLs as it will be in university teacher preservice programs. As teachers read it and make use of the strategies, they will begin to share the excitement I felt at finally seeing a guide that addresses language differentiation for ELLs.

Tim Boals, Ph.D.
Executive Director
WIDA Consortium
Wisconsin Center for Education Research

Preface

The Need for This Book and Chart

Demographics in America's classrooms are rapidly changing, ushering in the inarguable necessity of every teacher embracing the responsibility to educate every student in the classroom. Despite the compelling fact that new and diverse learners come from a variety of experiential, educational, cultural, and linguistic backgrounds, some teachers in schools across the United States have continued to employ pedagogy addressing only the needs of "mainstream" homogeneous students. At the same time, the number of English language learners (ELLs) increased 57% between 1995–96 and 2005–06, to more than 5 million students nationwide, or 10% of the nation's preK–12 students in 2006 (Office of English Language Acquisition, 2007).

Interestingly, the largest proportion of ELLs in the United States were born in the United States (Capps et al., 2005). In 2007, 75% of school-age children who spoke a non-English language at home and who spoke English with difficulty were speakers of Spanish, while 12% spoke Asian/Pacific Islander languages, 10% were speakers of Indo-European languages, and 3% spoke yet other languages (National Center for Education Statistics, n.d., ¶ 5).

U.S. classrooms include a significant number of U.S.-born and immigrant children from families who have immigrated from Mexico, Central America, and South America, as well as a multiplicity of other countries around the globe. Often, the working-class parents of these students may have brought them here when seeking better jobs and improved opportunities for their children. In addition to specific educational, linguistic, and cultural needs, these ELLs may also have needs related to their socioeconomic status. Implementing a variety of support strategies can offer teachers, school districts, and communities a multitude of opportunities to enhance the success of ELLs and their families.

A subgroup of K–12 ELLs includes children of professionals who have come to work or study in the United States. These students may well be on grade level and ready to immediately participate and perform in U.S. classrooms. They often possess highly developed literacy skills in their first languages that will serve them well as they acquire English.

Many other ELLs in U.S. classrooms are refugees from troubled areas around the world, a group that is often overlooked and is in need of special consideration. In a display of exemplary humanitarianism, the United States resettles more international refugees than the rest of the world's countries combined (Patrick, 2004). Many of these displaced persons were born in or living in stark and dangerous refugee camps for many years. Such school-age newcomers often arrive in U.S. classrooms having developed a very specific knowledge base that might have little relevance to U.S. school expectations in terms of academic preparation, classroom behavior, grade-level achievement, socialization skills, and more. Further, these newcomer students present an array of socioeconomic implications that teachers must consider.

An additional group of English learners cannot be overlooked: U.S.-born native speakers of English whose language development does not lend itself to immediate academic applications. In addition to ELLs, these students will also benefit from the incremental, differentiated approach outlined in this book. Like their ELL classmates, such native English speakers, or "standard English learners" (Freeman & Freeman, 2009), will advance their proficiency in English and in the content areas with appropriate instruction, differentiated according to their linguistic needs.

Instruction using specific strategies that meet the linguistic and cultural needs of the students in one's classroom is neither optional nor supplemental; it is imperative. While teachers must address the needs of this growing diversity of students, many are underprepared to do so (Fitzgerald & Graves, 2004; Harper & de Jong, 2004; Kouritzin, 2004). In fact, as of 2008–09, only three states required that prospective teachers demonstrate competence in the instruction of ELLs (Education Week, 2009).

This book has been developed in response to K–12 teachers' requests for guidance in how to differentiate instruction and assignments/assessment for ELLs in their classrooms. These teachers understand that, in accordance with *Lau v. Nichols* (1974), providing ELLs only with instruction identical to that designed for native speakers of "standard" English is not sufficient. Further, such teachers realize that the key to students understanding content and acquiring the English language simultaneously is through implementing differentiated instruction that takes into account levels of language proficiency.

The Development of This Work

The chart that accompanies this book was the genesis for this work. Development of the chart was an authentic combination of the authors' experiences as veteran teachers of ELLs in many contexts, their research-based professional development and practice, and their strong desire to contribute to the successful instruction and assessment of ELLs across the state of Iowa. The first iteration of the chart appeared in *Educating Iowa's English Language Learners: A Handbook for Administrators and Teachers* (Iowa Department of Education, 2007) when the authors added teacher and assessment strategies to a "Language Acquisition Chart" adapted from Grognet, Jameson, Franco, & Derrick-Mescua (2000). Later revisions of the chart were distributed to various educators at workshops conducted by the authors.

The final version of the chart accompanying this book evolved from earlier iterations through a lengthy process of rewriting and refinement as the authors developed increased insight into effective differentiated assessment and instruction for ELLs through the reading of educational research literature, the practical application of information and strategies, and discussion with a variety of stakeholders in the educational process. The student descriptors, formerly focusing on Iowa definitions of proficiency, were rewritten for listening, speaking, reading, and writing, aligning with the Teachers of English to Speakers of Other Languages (TESOL) *PreK–12 English Language Proficiency Standards* (Gottlieb, Carnuccio, Ernst-Slavit, Katz, & Snow, 2006). Both the instructional and assignment/assessment strategies were also expanded to target the language domains of listening, speaking, reading, and writing in order to more comprehensively address the needs of ELLs. Research and best practice informed this process.

A Word About English Language Proficiency Levels in Different States

As stated previously, the five English language proficiency levels described in this book and its accompanying chart are based on TESOL's national English language proficiency standards. Since these standards are an augmentation of the WIDA (World-Class Instructional Design and Assessment) English language proficiency standards, teachers in WIDA states and teachers in those states whose language proficiency levels are based on TESOL's national standards will find clear alignment between the student descriptors and guidance for instruction and assessment herein and the English language proficiency standards with which they are familiar. However, educators in states that have made use of proficiency levels not closely aligned with the TESOL or WIDA standards may need to make adjustments when implementing the guidance presented in the book and on the chart. For instance, a given state's definition of a Level 3 student may more closely align with our description of a Level 2 student. Readers are urged to determine how the language proficiency levels used in their states align with the student descriptors described here and to implement the direction provided in the book and chart accordingly.

The Organization of the Book and Chart

The first two chapters of the book lay a foundation for the remainder of the volume by enumerating the student factors that teachers of ELLs must consider, explaining both the value of knowing one's students and ways to accomplish that goal, detailing general guidelines for working with ELLs, outlining the language acquisition process, discussing perspectives on culture that inform the information presented, and elucidating the general instructional and assignment/assessment strategies listed on the chart.[1] Following the model of backward lesson design

---

[1] Note that the instructional and assignment/assessment strategies presented on the chart and in the book are not intended to be an exhaustive list, but rather, a starting point for teachers to use in differentiating assignments/assessments and instruction for ELLs at different proficiency levels.

(Wiggins & McTighe, 2006) where assignments/assessments are planned prior to the development of lesson plans, Chapters 3 through 7 describe students at each of the five proficiency levels with scenarios based on real students and discussion rooted in the student descriptors found on the chart. (Note that the student descriptors on the chart and in the book are general in nature and must be taken in grade-level context.) After describing two students at a given proficiency level,[2] Chapters 3 through 7 each provide a sample assignment differentiated for students at that chapter's focal proficiency level, using a "mini-template" based on the full assignment/assessment differentiation template presented in Chapter 8. The mini-templates also include descriptions of types of scaffolding and support that would be appropriate for students at specific proficiency levels in order to successfully complete the task. Further, the mini-templates in Chapters 3 through 7 contain guidance regarding appropriate expectations and scaffolding and support for students at the next level of proficiency as a reminder to teachers that they must continually push ELLs to higher levels of achievement.

Following the template-based sample assignments, each chapter enumerates specific, accessible standards-based assignment/assessment strategies that can be used to assess ELLs at that given proficiency level. Finally, each chapter explains a range of ways that teachers can provide comprehensible instruction that ensures that students are able to meet the expectations of differentiated assignments and assessments.[3] The last chapter in the book brings all this information together by assisting readers in thinking about students at all five proficiency levels simultaneously. This purpose is accomplished through the use of student-focused classroom scenarios at the elementary, middle, and high school levels (again, drawn from real student examples in the authors' experience) and through the use of the full assignment/assessment differentiation template to design differentiated assignments/assessments and instruction at all five levels of English language proficiency. Though the topic of collaboration among educators who serve ELLs is addressed throughout the book, the final chapter provides additional guidance in this regard, as well as discussing the scoring of differentiated assignments/assessments.

How to Use the Book and Chart

Educators are urged to read the book through from start to finish in order to understand how to effectively implement the information presented

---

[2] One student in each chapter has received limited formal schooling, while the other is more or less on grade level in his or her sending country.

[3] Note that some of the strategies listed within a given level of proficiency may also be appropriate for other levels of proficiency. When this is the case, different examples are provided for those strategies in chapters that focus on subsequent proficiency levels. The repetition of strategies in multiple proficiency levels both on the chart and in the book is by design because of the utility of those strategies with students at more than one proficiency level and based on the recognition that some teachers may use the chart and book to focus only on particular proficiency levels.

on the chart; the use of the two documents in tandem will empower teachers to differentiate assignments/assessment and the corresponding instruction for culturally and linguistically diverse students in their classrooms. The use of both resources together is critical, particularly since the book provides extensive description and a wide range of specific examples regarding how to implement the strategies listed on the chart. We do, however, recognize that, based on individual needs, some teachers may elect to only read certain chapters because they work with students who only represent certain proficiency levels. In these cases, we recommend that readers begin with Chapters 1 and 2 before proceeding to the chapters that focus on the specific language proficiency levels of interest. The foundational information presented in those chapters is essential to the differentiation process, and many important concepts and strategies are presented therein. Readers are also guided to make use of the end-of-chapter professional development activities and resources and the templates found throughout the book. The activities, resources, and templates offer teachers practical ways to put the information and recommendations from the chart and book into practice. Further, as teachers read the book and refer to the chart, we recommend that they always be thinking in terms of how to apply the information to the needs of specific students in their own contexts. Once teachers have grasped the depth and breadth of the information represented by the chart through reading the book, the chart is meant to be posted in their classrooms as a ready reference for the creation of appropriately differentiated assignments/assessments and lesson plans.

This book does not aim to provide guidance in exactly how to set up lesson plans. Many fine resources already in existence address that endeavor very capably (e.g., Echevarria, Vogt, & Short's *SIOP Model*, 2008). We fully support the importance of building background knowledge and experiences for students, ensuring that input is comprehensible, using effective strategies, creating opportunities for interaction, and other facets of lesson planning addressed in the *SIOP Model* and other resources. What this book and the accompanying chart uniquely offer is explicit guidance in how to differentiate expectations for students at each proficiency level, based on a firm understanding of student capabilities at each level of language proficiency. (This differentiation is addressed in the form of language objectives in many settings.) This guidance comes from the student descriptors for each proficiency level, from the strategies for instruction and assignments/assessment at each proficiency level, and from the template used for individual levels of proficiency in Chapters 3 through 7 and across all five levels of proficiency in Chapter eight. This template enables teachers to operationalize appropriate expectations for students at all levels of proficiency and to scaffold instruction, ensuring that students can meet those expectations. We urge readers to apply their learning from this book to whatever format for lesson planning that they find most useful.

We hope that the chart will serve as a daily classroom reference guide for teachers of ELLs in need of practical instructional and assignment/assessment support. Welcoming newcomers into their classrooms, these educators can make a world of difference in the lives of English language learners.

Contents

Chapter **4**   **Differentiation Strategies for Level 2 Students**   **127**

Chapter **5**   **Differentiation Strategies for Level 3 Students**   **163**

Chapter **6**   **Differentiation Strategies for Level 4 Students**   **195**

1

Differentiation for English Language Learners: Key Considerations

Teachers have the potential to be the gatekeepers of students' futures.
When they have high expectations and recognize the potential
and uniqueness of each student, they honor not only students'
cultural and linguistic characteristics,
but also become partners in their successes.

—Dr. Carmen P. Sosa

This chapter outlines essential topics related to effectively differentiating instruction and assessment for English language learners (ELLs). After introducing the reader to the notion of differentiation of ELLs and the importance of working collaboratively to meet students' needs, we discuss eight student factors that impact the teaching and learning process. Next, we address the need to know each student and outline ways in which teachers can accomplish this important objective. We end the chapter with a description of crucial steps in the ELL differentiation process.

The Critical Role of the General Education Teacher

Teacher Scenarios

Ms. Harris is a first-year teacher who was surprised to learn that she will have four ELLs in her classroom. Her teacher education program did not require her to take a course focusing on how to work with ELLs, so she is feeling somewhat nervous. A friend who has also just begun teaching reminds her, however, that they were both taught about the concept of differentiation. The friend assures Ms. Harris that she will be fine if she simply applies those concepts.

Mrs. Turner is not new to teaching, nor to working with ELLs. She feels comfortable about her work with a colleague in special education that has served her special needs students well in the past few years, but she is troubled with increasing levels of anxiety about how to best meet the needs of the ELLs in her classroom. Although she has only served one or two very studious ELLs each of the past few years, this year she has six students from a range of educational, cultural, and linguistic backgrounds in her room. At times, she feels overwhelmed by the challenge of working with these students and disheartened because she is unsure of how to meet their needs.

The notion of differentiated instruction has gained currency and credibility as an effective and powerful means to meet the needs of diverse learners in today's classrooms. This approach allows teachers to take into consideration the readiness of each learner while facilitating instruction and assessment rooted in the same content standards for all students. However, the philosophy of differentiation itself does not explicitly tell teachers how to enact differentiation for ELLs, a reality that Ms. Harris will very soon discover and one that Mrs. Turner is already keenly aware of. Without ELL-specific knowledge, even the most willing and eager teacher will struggle needlessly with understanding how to implement differentiation for ELLs. This differentiation process requires knowing and understanding key cultural and linguistic factors that profoundly and predictably impact each student's learning and language acquisition, information that will serve as a lifeline for Ms. Harris and Mrs. Turner and teachers like them.

Effective differentiation for ELLs cannot take place without first knowing the basics of both intercultural communication and the language acquisition process, including the characteristics of each stage of language development, essential for the teachers we have described. Purposefully matching these predictable stages of language acquisition with specific instructional and assessment strategies will result in meaningful input that discretely scaffolds the learning of ELLs in order to maximize their achievement in the content areas. As a result of this mindful pedagogy, students benefit from learning content and language simultaneously; ELLs are afforded parity in terms of access to the curriculum. The development of this kind of data-based linguistic differentiation of both instruction and assessment is a necessity for teachers like Ms. Harris and Mrs. Turner and is the aim of this book.

The Need for Shared Responsibility and Collaboration

In order to ensure that diverse learners enjoy equal access to the curriculum and, therefore, an equal opportunity to realize their maximum potential, every teacher must embrace the notion that she or he is responsible for the learning of each of her or his students. In other words, the learning of the English language learner is the full responsibility of the classroom/content teacher as well as the responsibility of the English as a second language (ESL) or bilingual education teacher. All classroom/content teachers need to tailor their instruction and assessment so that they are appropriate for the ELLs in their classrooms. Mimicking the architectural notion of universal design that, from inception of the design, creates an environment accessible to every individual regardless of abilities, this sort of universally designed instruction (CAST, 2008) is created to be accessible to all students from the beginning, rather than through attempts to retrofit unsuitable instruction and assessment for diverse learners. With this approach, variations in student needs are anticipated and planned for, rather than perceived as an aberration or a problem. Therefore, teachers, whether novice or veteran, must be prepared to make the curriculum meaningful according to the student's current level of content knowledge, skills, abilities, and, importantly, the current level of English language proficiency. This book and the accompanying chart aspire to make this work possible.

Classroom/content teachers such as Ms. Harris and Mrs. Turner can use the book and chart to prepare content lessons that are differentiated to meet the needs of ELLs and to ensure that assignments and assessments are in line with the language proficiency levels of these students. ESL and Bilingual education teachers can also use the chart to tailor their instruction and assessment to the needs of students at different levels of language proficiency. Further, and perhaps most importantly, these two groups of teachers can collaborate while using the book and chart in order to meet the linguistic and cultural needs of ELLs in the content classroom. This type of collaborative work on behalf of ELLs is the ideal approach, merging the expertise of both kinds of teachers in order to ensure that English language learners receive high-quality instruction and assessment that is attentive to their linguistic and cultural needs.

This merging of teacher expertise requires that teachers work together to build an atmosphere that fosters the sharing of pedagogical insights and skills. For instance, many ESL/bilingual teachers may not be experts across all content areas. Likewise, many classroom/content teachers, such as Ms. Harris and Mrs. Turner, have not received "cross-training" to deepen their expertise in the myriad issues associated with teaching ELLs. We define "cross-training" as professional development in which teachers with one kind of expertise (e.g., classroom/content teachers) gain expertise about another area (e.g., ELL teaching and assessment strategies). In order to maximize the efficacy of both classroom/content and ESL/bilingual teachers, we advocate that these two types of teachers partner in order to share expertise for the benefit of their students. Though this kind of "reciprocal mentoring" (Jones-Vo et al., 2007) will be discussed in detail in Chapter 8, we urge teachers to enter into collaborative relationships from the outset of their reading of this book. Such mutually beneficial partnerships can expand and enrich teaching capacity, resulting in improved instructional and assessment practices that better serve all students in the classroom. Through such purposeful collaboration, teachers are better able to seamlessly blend appropriate strategies for both instruction and assessment and to set the stage for increased student achievement.

As colleagues embrace the need to share responsibility for the learning and academic success of all students in the classroom, there are a variety of ways to team up with a common vision, depending on the resources and needs of the district. Following, we offer a few specific examples of ways in which teachers might collaborate, based on our experience:

- *Pull-out.* In terms of collaboration, pull-out can be a useful delivery model, particularly at the earliest stages of language acquisition. During such time, the ESL teacher can focus on targeted instruction for specific students to build the oral language of ELLs in small groups in a separate setting. The pull-out time can be utilized to support vocabulary development in thematic ways (linked to curricular topics where possible) and to build a foundation on which to develop proficiency. Pull-out should not be favored indefinitely, however, as it tends to isolate ELLs from more capable peers who provide modeling, authentic opportunities to interact and practice language. Benefits of such support of ELLs by native-English-speakers should not be underestimated.

- *Push-in.* The second model suggested for teaming, the push-in model, occurs when a trained and, ideally, bilingual professional joins the teacher in a classroom to provide support to ELLs. In this model, the professional who "pushes in" could be another teacher, an experienced paraprofessional, or even a volunteer who offers instructional support and resources. If the individual is bilingual, the first language can be used to clarify instruction and to support learning through the completion of assignments and assessments. The expanded support of this model allows for making sure that all students comprehend and are producing according to their English language proficiency levels across the curriculum, while targeting the next higher level of proficiency.

- *Teacher Leader: One Cross-Trained Educator Plans for All.* Another way to embrace shared responsibility for all students is the teacher leader model: one teacher who is trained in both math (for example) and in ESL strategies is designated the ELL/math teacher leader. This expert understands and is familiar with the entire grade-level math curriculum and has the responsibility to break it down into weekly instructional units. In addition, the ELL/math teacher leader identifies key math vocabulary, devises strategies, and designs and procures manipulatives, relevant math games, and other materials. Finally, at weekly grade-level planning meetings, the ELL/math teacher leader shares the math goals, strategies, and all materials with all grade-level teachers of math. This approach ensures that all students receive similar, consistent instruction and the same high-quality, hands-on materials to enhance comprehension. Further, through the teacher leader model, math instruction is linked consistently to the district math curriculum.

    If teachers notice that a student is falling behind or has difficulty with a math concept, the pull-out model can also be implemented for enrichment and further instruction. Such a pinpointed response can result in growth of all ELLs in terms of math achievement.

    One caveat: When implementing a collaboration model such as the teacher leader model, it is incumbent upon districts to embed dedicated planning time for teachers into the school day on a regular and sustained basis.

- *Collaboratively Plan Lessons During Embedded and Dedicated Time.* A fourth way to collaborate and build capacity to meet the needs of all learners is meeting weekly to co-plan lessons. In this model, the classroom/content teacher and the ESL/bilingual teacher meet to identify goals, content and language objectives, key terms, instructional and assessment strategies, and so on. In this way, the ESL teacher can enhance language instruction through actual classroom content material, making the language learning authentic and meaningful. Both teachers share and exchange their expertise and apply it to their individual contexts. As a result, classroom/content teachers can better utilize recommended ELL strategies, and ESL/bilingual teachers become more familiar with the classroom material and expectations and can better support content learning. The result will be increased student learning.

- *Co-teach.* Finally, a fifth way for teachers to share responsibility for all students is to coteach. In this model, two experts with different backgrounds, such as ESL and 3rd grade or special education and math, actually teach a class together. When observing this type of partnership, one might not recognize which teacher is actually the "teacher of record." Through both co-planning and co-delivering the content, students receive the benefit of both teacher perspectives and both types of expertise. The co-teachers require dedicated planning time and are mutually responsible for the learning of all students in the class.

While we have offered a brief overview of a few collaborative models here, teachers are reminded that there are unlimited ways to collaborate. We encourage teachers to engage in conversations and develop collaborative models that best suit their own contexts.

Relevant Student Factors

There are a number of important issues to consider when teaching and assessing English language learners. These include educational background, immigrant and refugee status, cultural background, prior difficult experiences, age, language distance, social distance, and psychological distance.

Educational Background

> **Tam**, an Amerasian student from Vietnam, arrives at high school with no formal education. He is unable to read or write in his first language and is not familiar with school protocols such as sitting in a desk or holding a pencil. His teachers mistakenly assume that this lack of skills is due to a cognitive impairment.

Svetlana, a student from Ukraine, arrives at the same high school having attended school in Kiev consistently through grade 11. She is on grade level in her native language and able to immediately participate in some classes based on her first language background knowledge and skills.

Increasingly, U.S. schools are welcoming students from a wide variety of educational backgrounds and experiences. For example, while some ELLs arrive with comprehensive educational backgrounds, some may arrive having missed critical educational development in formal settings for a variety of reasons such as political unrest, poor economic conditions, racial, ethnic, and sexist issues. Other students may have been migrants or moved frequently, possibly resulting in below-grade-level performance. Yet other students may have studied in places where the curriculum or teaching methods are so different from expectations in U.S. schools that the students arrive off grade level. Still others, like Tam, may have never had the benefit of any formal education. Nevertheless, each of these students arrives with a highly developed bank of background knowledge and experiences. Though this knowledge may not carry much currency in traditional K–12 classrooms, teachers must recognize the depth and value of these "funds of knowledge" (Moll, 1992) and embed opportunities for students to relate them to classroom-based content and curriculum.

Of course, some ELLs, such as Svetlana, arrive with grade-level skills in their first languages. These students may be accompanying parents who are enrolled at institutions of higher education or are working in various contexts. Similar to the students with limited formal schooling experiences, learners with uninterrupted schooling benefit from instructional practices that acknowledge and capitalize upon their first cultures and languages. Teachers are encouraged to tap into the expertise that their ELLs bring to the classroom, regardless of their educational backgrounds.

Cummins (2001) points out that academic language knowledge, skills, and abilities can be transferred from one language to another. In so doing, he clarifies the difference in challenges faced by Tam and Svetlana and by the two types of ELLs that they represent. Students with interrupted or limited formal schooling face a much larger task in acquiring academic language and content than their peers with uninterrupted schooling. The latter are likely able to transfer previous learning to English-language contexts, while the former have little to draw upon in terms of academic knowledge and language. Their differences in literacy development also present unique challenges.

The instructional importance for ELLs to possess literacy skills prior to learning English cannot be overstated. Such a foundation provides a reference point that can accelerate second language learning. Having once learned basic tenets of literacy such as the relationship between sounds and print, directionality, and features of text, the ELL is far more easily disposed to transfer these skills to learning English literacy skills, despite discrete variations that might occur between the first language and English.

To understand the impact of first language literacy development, imagine an ELL with the first language of Arabic. This student arrives in his 3rd grade classroom already reading at a third-grade level in Arabic. He will need to learn that books in English are read from left to right and that what he considers to be the front of a book is actually the back of a book written in English. After meaningful literacy instruction, this student will relate that both English and Arabic print have order and progression, and that, in reading, both languages are represented by sounds (although it is likely the student has not heard or articulated some of the sounds in English). Further, this student will be able to grasp that written language is represented by words and governed by a system of grammar. Because this student has already developed a systematic understanding of such reading concepts, he will likely be able to derive meaning from English text with relative ease, when compared to a same-language peer who has not had the opportunity to develop first language reading skills.

In contrast, imagine that a Sudanese student from a refugee camp in Kenya has appeared in the same 3rd grade classroom. This newcomer has never experienced formal schooling and does not possess understanding of literacy in his first language, a tribal language rich in oral tradition. This lack of literacy awareness and skill inhibits his understanding of the written word. It is essential to note that this sort of difference in language development does not indicate that the student is lacking cognitive ability or other communication skills. Neither does it necessarily indicate a need for entitlement into a special education setting, as some teachers suspected in the case of Tam. Teachers and other stakeholders in the educational process must understand that neither a lack of exposure to educational opportunities nor obvious cultural differences (such as behavioral differences) are themselves alone indicators for identification of students for special education.

While the Sudanese student described here would benefit from literacy instruction in his first language to lay the groundwork for the development of literacy in English, pragmatic concerns often dictate the efficiency of instructing students from multiple language backgrounds using English as the common instructional medium. As a result, the program model of ESL or ESOL (English for speakers of other languages) is frequently the model of choice for economic and other reasons.

Regardless of the model used for language development, students with and without strong first language reading skills must be provided with vigorous, comprehensible, and meaningful reading instruction that will enable them to gain access to the content curriculum. School districts in the United States would do well to follow the lead of our neighbors to the north regarding the placement of and services for English language learners. In Canada, students who have not yet developed literacy in the first language (L1) are afforded instruction that meets them at their L1 literacy level, thus providing an improved opportunity for the development of literacy in English and access to the mainstream curriculum. Their L1 literate counterparts are provided different instruction that is appropriate to their needs. Unfortunately, ELLs in the United States with and without L1 literacy are frequently not distinguished from one other for placement and service purposes. As a result, many ELLs across grade spans are at risk of being instructed by teachers who might not recognize their deep, underlying instructional needs or how to address their disadvantaging and "inconvenient" lack of literacy. Preliterate ELLs such as these are less likely to reach grade-level achievement, graduate, or otherwise reach their greatest potential. Such an outcome is patently unacceptable, yet currently contributes to an alarming dropout rate among ELLs in the United States.

Accordingly, the aim of this book and its accompanying chart is to ensure that teachers understand ways in which to differentiate instruction and assessment for ELLs at different proficiency levels and with different educational backgrounds. Guidance in how to tailor instruction for students both with and without strong educational backgrounds will be addressed throughout the remainder of the text.

Immigrant and Refugee Status

> **Juan**, the son of a professional multinational company employee, enrolls in middle school in 8th grade. His father's company in Venezuela has transferred the family to the United States. The family resides in a wealthy suburb.

> **David**, an unaccompanied minor from Liberia, enrolls in 8th grade in the same middle school. As a child, he witnessed the rape of his grandmother during a war. He still has nightmares about that event.

Fortunately, for the sake of teachers and administrators, schools are not charged with determining the citizenship status of students arriving from other locales (*Plyler v. Doe,* 1982). Nevertheless, knowing details about each student's background contributes greatly to the quality and appropriateness of support provided to individual students and families.

Whereas the term *immigrant* often refers to individuals who have permanently moved to a new country of their own accord, the term *refugee* is defined as

> a person who is outside his or her country of nationality or habitual residence; has a well-founded fear of persecution because of his or her race, religion, nationality, membership of a particular social group or political opinion; and is unable or unwilling to avail himself or herself of the protection of that country, or to return there, for fear of persecution. (UNHCR, 2007, p. 6)

Although many immigrant families face incredible challenges, refugees, by definition, have often experienced extreme situations requiring teachers to exercise the utmost awareness and sensitivity. When teachers make the necessary effort to learn about their individual students, these issues often come to light. Ways in which to develop understanding of student background experiences will be addressed in the following pages, and ways to honor and capitalize on the students' experiences and knowledge bases will be explicated throughout the book.

Cultural Background

> **Brigitta**, a student from Germany, exhibits many behaviors similar to her U.S.-born counterparts. She has a strong sense of personal identity and is not afraid of competition. Further, she shows initiative in individual class projects.
>
> **María**, a student from Ecuador, is quite different from Brigitta in her cultural orientation. She consistently strives to work with others and shies away from individual recognition. (Teachers have misinterpreted her checking her work against peers as cheating.) She lives with her extended family of 13 people.

The more that teachers know about students' individual cultures, the better equipped they are to interact in meaningful and productive ways with their students and their families. Teachers must bear in mind that their job is not to make students become similar to themselves but to respectfully facilitate their students' ongoing negotiation of cultural differences so they can be successful in various cultural contexts. For example, María complains that she feels pressure from her parents to maintain her heritage culture. Yet, at the same time, she feels the tension of peer pressure calling her to be an "American" teenager. Culturally responsive teachers can help María to negotiate this difficult time by respecting her first culture while objectively informing her about the new culture.

Though there are many definitions of culture, it is essential to bear in mind that culture is much more than easily visible external trappings (e.g., attire, food, music). Rather, the deeper, more meaningful underpinnings of a given group's way of life are what comprise the foundation of culture. Ting-Toomey (1999, p. 10) defines culture as "a complex frame of reference that consists of patterns of traditions, beliefs, values, norms, symbols, and meanings that are shared to varying degrees by interacting members of a community."

To be culturally competent, then, is to develop the ability to respectfully maintain one's own cultural stance while honoring the perspectives of another. That is, one does not need to abandon his or her own belief system. Rather, a culturally competent person must become informed about and sensitive to the belief systems and experiences of others. For teachers, this combination of knowledge and skills can be applied in order to understand, encourage, and support all students, particularly those that are least able to ask for assistance.

Though an in-depth discussion of individual cultures is beyond the scope of this book, one useful paradigm for understanding cultural differences is the continuum spanning individualism to collectivism (Ting-Toomey, 1999). While all cultures fall somewhere along this continuum, some are noted for promoting more individualistic attitudes, as in Brigitta's case, while others are more collectivistic in nature, as is the case for María.

Some teachers may notice that students from individualistic cultures tend to emphasize "self-efficiency, individual responsibilities, and personal autonomy" and that their personal identity, rights, and needs take precedence over those of the group (Ting-Toomey, 1999, p. 67). Hofstede (1991, p. 51) points out that individualistic cultures are "societies in which ties between individuals are loose: everyone is expected to look after himself or herself and his or her immediate family." For example, Brigitta is not especially interested in cooperative group work, but, rather, prefers individual academic tasks. She seeks personal recognition for her individual efforts and takes pride in her accomplishments and achievements.

María, in contrast, exemplifies a more collectivistic culture. She prefers working with a group and receiving recognition for group-based achievements. Ting-Toomey clarifies that collectivistic cultures emphasize group-based identity, rights, and needs. She further asserts that collectivistic cultures stress "relational interdependence, in-group harmony, and in-group collaborative spirit" (Ting-Toomey, 1999, p. 67). Hofstede states that collectivistic cultures are "societies in which people from birth onwards are integrated into strong, cohesive in-groups, which throughout people's lifetime continue to protect them in exchange for unquestioning loyalty" (1991, p. 51).

While many educators have likely recognized differences in living arrangements of families from different countries, they may not realize that these practices are culturally bound and can be explained, at least in part, by the individualism-collectivism continuum. While most people in the world come from more collectivistic countries (Hofstede, 1991), the United States is considered to exemplify individualistic culture (Hofstede, 1951, as cited in Ting-Toomey, 1999, p. 67). Consequently, the differences in behavior of many ELLs may stand out in the context of a U.S. school. Since U.S. schools often operate within the framework of the "mainstream" U.S. culture of individualism, students from collectivistic cultures often need explicit instruction about how to function within the dominant school "culture of power" (Delpit, 1995). Delpit's five-part explanation of this cultural reality helps teachers from "mainstream" culture to understand how differences in classroom culture and student culture can be reconciled (p. 24):

1. Issues of power are enacted in classrooms.

2. There are codes or rules for participating in power; that is, there is a "culture of power."

3. The rules of the culture of power are a reflection of the rules of the culture of those who have power.

4. If you are not already a participant in the culture of power, being

told explicitly the rules of that culture makes acquiring power easier.

5. Those with power are frequently least aware of—or least willing to acknowledge—its existence. Those with less power are often most aware of its existence.

We have seen the need for explicit teaching about the culture of power played out in our own classrooms; students who have different ways of interacting with teachers (e.g., snapping fingers to get the teacher's attention) need only be informed of other, more culturally appropriate ways to initiate conversation in order to be able to take advantage of and participate in the power structure in U.S. classrooms. In this way, different points on the cultural continuum can be bridged by teachers, who consciously enhance their roles as cultural informants and brokers.

In Table 1.1 is a list of countries found by Hofstede (1991, p. 53) to be largely individualistic and largely collectivistic. (These lists are drawn from a list of 50 countries that were ranked along the individualism-collectivism continuum.) Hofstede points out that, in general, countries that are more individualistic are wealthier.

Other points of interest relate to the languages most commonly spoken by ELLs in U.S. schools: Spanish, Vietnamese, Hmong, Korean, and Arabic (National Clearinghouse for English Language Acquisition [NCELA], 2007). To round out the list, we provide additional insights about Mexico, South Korea, and Arab countries (Hofstede, 1991, p. 53):

- In terms of Spanish-speakers, Mexico is listed toward the middle of the individualistic-collectivistic continuum of countries, but on the collectivistic side.

- Regarding speakers of Korean, South Korea is the 11th most collectivistic country.

- With reference to speakers of Arabic, Arab countries are listed in the middle of the individualism-collectivism continuum.

Based on our own insights gained from living and working with individuals from Southeast Asia, both Vietnamese and Hmong cultures are highly collectivistic. These two language groups complete the list of top languages spoken by ELLs in the United States (NCELA, 2007).

Table 1.1 Individualistic and collectivistic countries

Most Individualistic Countries (in descending order)	*Most Collectivistic Countries (in descending order)*
United States	Guatemala
Australia	Ecuador
Great Britain	Panama
Canada and the Netherlands (tied in the study)	Venezuela
	Colombia
New Zealand	Indonesia and Pakistan (tied in the study)
Italy	
Belgium	Costa Rica
Denmark	Peru

Prior Difficult Experiences

Laura, a student from Mexico, shares with her class that she arrived in the United States with her mother after a long separation from her father and brother, who came first. She describes the abject poverty in her hometown that precipitated the family's move to the United States.

Dariou, a student from Sudan, experienced significant, life-altering trauma prior to arriving in the United States when his right arm was amputated by rebel soldiers. In addition, he does not know what happened to members of his immediate family and is living here with an uncle.

Laura came to the United States unwillingly. She left behind a network of friends and her grandmother, to whom she was very close. She cries nearly every night because she misses her grandmother so much. Laura continues to blame her parents for uprooting her and has displayed a poor attitude at school. Her teachers struggle with how to help her to become motivated to engage in school activities.

Though Dariou's injury was sustained years earlier, he is still traumatized by mental health symptoms associated with post-traumatic stress disorder. These issues, together with his physical impairment, family situation, academic deficits due to interrupted schooling, and lack of academic language skills, frame his extensive needs as a learner.

The realities of both these students illustrate their different but profound needs. The importance of teachers knowing and understanding each student's background cannot be overemphasized. Teachers who exercise cultural competence and make concerted efforts to meet the entire range of a student's needs can make all the difference in the life of that student. These efforts may include collaborating with other professionals within the school system (e.g., guidance counselors, school psychologists), connecting students with community agencies that can provide support (e.g., mentoring programs), and ensuring that students are getting needed medical care (e.g., connecting students with free clinics, soliciting funds from civic groups to pay for such care, making appointments for students, and arranging transportation for appointments). In the absence of formalized programs designed to meet these needs, teachers have been known to demonstrate extreme creativity in forging relationships with community and faith-based organizations to meet various students' needs. We have found that "going the extra mile" in these ways can be vital for students and families and critical to positioning students to take advantage of academic opportunities. In addition, providing this type of essential support to students can be very rewarding. Teachers have to ask themselves, "If I don't do this for my student, who will?"

Age

Sol, a kindergarten student from Brazil, is developmentally close to her peers' levels of instructional needs. While she will benefit from focused vocabulary instruction and activities that develop her ability to distinguish among and produce sounds in English, her academic needs are not entirely unlike those of her peers. She is able to pronounce new sounds fairly easily when given appropriate instruction and support.

Krystian, a 10th grade student from Poland, is able to draw upon the content and academic language (both learned in Polish) that he brings with him to the United States. However, he has more ground to cover in catching up with his grade-level peers than a younger student, so it takes him longer to achieve grade-level performance than Sol.

In the field of second language acquisition, there is much discussion of whether there is a "critical period" for learning a second language. While many studies have focused on accent, finding that older learners often retain some pronunciation features of their native languages (Lightbown & Spada, 1999), studies focusing on other language features also find that there are advantages to beginning second language learning early in life. For instance, Patkowski's (1980, as cited in Lightbown & Spada, 1999) study focused on language proficiency devoid of accent by having trained native-English-speaker judges rate transcripts of ELL interviews on a scale of 0 (no language) to 5 (educated native speaker proficiency). This study found that learners who began to learn English prior to puberty far outscored those who began learning later. In another study reported by Lightbown and Spada (1999), Johnson and Newport (1989) found that younger students outperformed older ones in indentifying the grammaticality of sentences.

In contrast, Snow and Hoefnagel-Höhle (1978, as cited in Lightbown & Spada, 1999) found that adolescents were better learners than young children or adults on a wide range of tasks. However, the difficulty of some of the tasks inherent in the study may have been at least a partial reason for this finding. In light of all of these findings, Lightbown and Spada (1999) assert that if nativelike proficiency is desired (as it is for ELLs in U.S. schools), the earlier that a child can begin to acquire the language, the better. Older learners can draw upon a broader range of life experiences and learning strategies in the acquisition of a second language (as can Krystian), but there seems to be a benefit from beginning the language learning process at a younger age (as is the case for Sol).

Another consideration in this equation is also essential; older ELLs have more ground to cover in catching up with their native English-speaking peers in comparison with younger ELLs. The significance of this difference in terms of the demands of both language and content learning should not be underestimated.

Language Distance

Gabriel, a high school student from Colombia, is able to read aloud with seeming proficiency. The teacher soon realizes that Gabriel's comprehension is below what the oral reading proficiency might indicate. However, Gabriel can identify the meanings of some words, particularly those (cognates) that are nearly the same in Spanish and English (e.g., *computadora* and *computer*).

Rahila, a high school student from Afghanistan, struggles with reading in English. She has had to learn a new script, since the written form of her native language, Farsi, does not use the English alphabet. In addition, the directionality of her first language on the page is different from that of written English (i.e., Farsi is read from right to left). Further, she has difficulty capitalizing on cognate knowledge, since her language is so different from English.

Language distance is defined as "the extent to which languages differ from each other" (Chiswick & Miller, 2005, p. 1). Chiswick and Miller, citing the work of Hart-Gonzalez and Lindemann (1993), list linguistic scores of a wide range of languages, ranging from 3.0 (easy to learn) to 1.0 (difficult to learn). These language scores were found to correspond to eventual fluency of immigrants to the United States and Canada included in the study; speakers of languages that are harder to learn were much less likely to gain conversational fluency in the second language even after 15 years in country when compared to speakers of languages that were easier to learn, as defined by Hart-Gonzalez and Lindemann (1993, as cited in Chiswick & Miller, 2005). The inverses of the language scores listed by Hart-Gonzalez and Lindemann (1993) were defined by Chiswick and Miller to be indices of linguistic difference. The language distances for the various languages mentioned in Table 1 of the Chiswick and Miller (2005) study are summarized in Table 1.2.

From this table, teachers can understand that students who speak languages with smaller linguistic difference indices (e.g., Afrikaans and Norwegian) will likely learn English more easily than students who speak languages with larger linguistic difference indices (e.g., Japanese and Korean).

Social Distance

Dražen, a student from Croatia, is part of a family that has quickly become self-sufficient in their new community. They are homeowners in a new housing development that is home to few other immigrant families and none from Croatia. Further, Dräžn's best friends are native speakers of English who grew up in the United States. He enjoys a status of social equality with his U.S.-born peers.

Miguel, a student from Mexico, lives in a Mexican neighborhood where English is not a necessity for daily living. Residents have access to a number of Mexican stores and rely on one another for friendship and support. Miguel plans to work at one of the businesses in his community and does not see the relevance of graduating from an English-speaking high school.

Social distance is a key student factor described by Schumann (1978). Schumann lists eight questions to consider in determining the extent to which a given group of language learners might learn (or not learn) a second language (p. 77):

Table 1.2 Language distances from English for selected languages

Language Distance Index	.33	.36	.4	.44	.5	.57	.67	.8	1.0
Level of Language Difficulty	Easy to learn (Similar to English) →							Difficult to learn (Different from English)	
Language	Afrikaans	Dutch	French	Danish	Indonesian	Bengali	Lao	Cantonese	Japanese
	Norwegian	Malay	Italian	German	Amharic	Burmese	Vietnamese		Korean
	Rumanian	Swahili	Portuguese	Spanish	Bulgarian	Greek	Arabic		
	Swedish			Russian	Czech	Hindi	Mandarin		
					Dari	Nepali			
					Farsi	Sinhala			
					Finnish				
					Hebrew				
					Hungarian				
					Cambodian				
					Mongolian				
					Polish				
					Serbo-Croatian				
					Tagalog				
					Thai				
					Turkish				

1. In relation to the TL [target language] group, is the 2LL [second language learner] group politically, culturally, technically or economically *dominant, nondominant,* or *subordinate?*

2. Is the integration pattern of the 2LL group *assimilation, acculturation,* or *preservation?*

3. What is the 2LL group's degree of *enclosure?*

4. Is the 2LL group *cohesive?*

5. What is the *size* of the 2LL group?

6. Are the cultures of the two groups *congruent?*

7. What are the *attitudes* of the two groups toward each other?

8. What is the 2LL group's *intended length of residence* in the target language area?

In order to foster language acquisition, the social distance must be small between the target language group (in the case of ELLs, English-speakers) and the second language learner group (ELLs). According to Schumann, small social distance occurs when ELLs

1. are on equal footing with native-English-speakers (nondominant),

2. set assimilation or acculturation as a goal,

3. integrate readily with native speakers across contexts,

4. do not focus on intragroup cohesiveness,

5. are small in number,

6. share cultural similarities with native speakers,

7. view native speakers in a positive light (and vice versa), and

8. intend to stay in the U.S. for a long time.

Examination of these various aspects of social distance will assist teachers in understanding the language learning patterns of their students; low social distance between ELLs and native speakers of English will facilitate the language acquisition process.

Psychological Distance

Schumann (1978) also points out that individuals can respond to learning situations in different ways. He ascribes this variation to psychological distance between the language learner and the target language group. Though Schumann's work in this area focuses primarily on adults rather than school-age children, this information provides food for thought for teachers in the K–12 setting. Specifically, Schumann lists "language shock, culture shock and culture stress, [and] integrative versus instrumental motivation" (1978, p. 87) as key aspects of this psychological distance. These factors may resonate with teachers who work with ELLs.

Language shock is associated with feelings of discomfort stemming from inability to conceptualize and use the new language, as well as fear of appearing silly. Culture shock is discomfort related to lack of ability to operate within a new culture; this drains the energy of newcomers (Larsen & Smalley, 1972, as cited in Schumann, 1978). Culture stress refers to the long-term impact of dealing with cultural differences, and Schumann points out that learning the new language is key to overcoming this. However, both culture shock and culture stress can hinder this process (Smalley, 1972, as cited in Schumann, 1978), as the language learner rejects the new country and its people and even herself or himself and her or his heritage culture (Schuman, 1978). What a student in this tenuous state needs is "a small community of sympathetic people who will help [her or him] in [this] difficult period" (Larson & Smalley, 1972, p. 46, as cited in Schumann, 1978). This is, without a doubt, the role of the school community in welcoming and supporting ELLs. Without the ability to surpass the challenges of language and culture shock, ELLs will maintain an unhealthy psychological distance from their new community and will be less able to acquire English (Schumann, 1978).

The area of motivation also impacts the second language learning process. Schumann (1978) clarifies that individuals with integrative motivation desire to get to know native speakers of the language, and this desire motivates them to learn the new language. In contrast, ELLs with instrumental motivation desire to learn the language for personal gains other than developing relationships with native speakers (e.g., getting a job). Individuals with integrative motivation are more likely to feel psychologically connected to native speakers of English and are, therefore, more likely to learn English at a faster pace than their otherwise-motivated counterparts.

Resource 1.1 at the end of the chapter provides a template to use in collecting information about these relevant student factors for individual students. Collecting this information may be particularly illuminating when working with challenging students.

Knowing Your Individual Students

Comer (1995) sums up a key facet of knowing one's students by stating that "no significant learning occurs without a significant relationship" (as cited in Payne, 2008, p. 48).

Knowing Student Backgrounds

Classroom teachers must not underestimate the importance of becoming familiar with the background profile of each ELL prior to beginning classroom instruction. The unique cultures and languages of ELLs will provide a wealth of information that can shed light on behaviors, literacy practices, and the like (see, for example, Flaitz, 2006). Such "research" on students should be considered a prerequisite to lesson planning; it is most essential in order to provide culturally responsive instruction.

As previously mentioned, two very useful pieces of background information that can inform and help drive classroom instruction are the ELL's previous educational history and the ELL's current literacy level in his or her first language. Knowing this biographical information will assist the teacher in setting realistic expectations for academic performance and contribute to formulating a program of meaningful differentiation.

Understanding the student's background, recognizing its role in the learning process, and tailoring instruction to meet the student's needs are necessities if the student is to feel comfortable in his or her new setting. The interaction of a welcoming and supportive teacher and a comfortable student results in the development of the student's linguistic and academic knowledge, skills, and abilities, as illustrated in Figure 1.1.

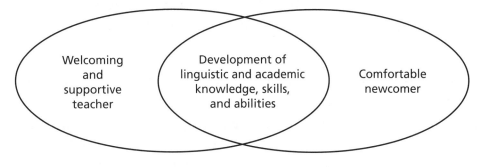

Figure 1.1 Key components in facilitating ELLs' learning

Note that only when the teacher and student interact under conditions of understanding and lowered anxiety can learning take place. Building these kinds of positive and productive relationships can be one of the most rewarding parts of working with ELLs and their families. This reciprocal process empowers teachers to better meet the needs of their students, and students and families to better understand and participate in the educational process. Further, it moves everyone forward along the continuum of cultural competence. Knowing one's students can be facilitated through checking students' cumulative folders, measuring what students know and can do in multiple ways, communicating directly with students, gaining insights from all teachers and para-educators who work with the student, and conducting home visits. These strategies will be discussed in the following sections. (See Resource 1.2 for a helpful checklist to use in gathering information about students.)

Documentation in the Cumulative Folder

The cumulative folders of ELLs are an often underutilized resource that teachers should regularly consult to gather information to inform their instruction. English language proficiency test results, information about previous education, and other background information may all be found in a student's cumulative folder. Some schools may also include information about students' content knowledge, skills, and abilities based on innovative testing practices during the enrollment process or on exemplary artifacts. All teachers can derive meaningful insight and information from the cumulative folder, which can assist them in tailoring their instruction and assessment to match students' individual levels of language proficiency and content mastery. As a result, every teacher should explicitly seek out information in student cumulative folders as a prerequisite to beginning instruction and assessment.

Multiple Measures of Students' Knowledge, Skills, and Abilities

While individual data points can provide a glimpse of a student's knowledge, skills, and abilities, the importance of using multiple measures for ELLs should not be understated. Teachers must realize that large-scale standardized academic achievement tests (in contrast with English language proficiency tests) are often an ineffective means of gaining understanding about what ELLs know and can do, because of their linguistic and cultural demands (Fairbairn & Fox, 2009). Alternative assessments are essential in order to gauge the learning of ELLs. For instance, some schools maintain collections of student work over time in portfolios. These collections can include all sorts of differentiated assignments and assessments that are designed to allow students to demonstrate learning while developing language mastery. Teachers are "accorded full permission" and, in fact, urged to design authentic, culturally and linguistically appropriate assessments of student learning. (Examples are provided in upcoming chapters.)

Communicating with Students Directly

Teachers must not forget to ask students themselves about their background knowledge and experiences, their interests, their activities, and so on. Asking such questions may require the assistance of a bilingual paraeducator, but who better to inform you about students than the students themselves? These conversations not only should be conducted upon enrollment, but also can be part of ongoing relationship development designed to reduce anxiety and increase confidence. Such conversations and the resulting information can serve as a springboard for a variety of teaching/learning and assessment opportunities.

Input from Colleagues

A variety of school personnel can share insights regarding the best way to work with an individual student. For instance, a given teacher may have experience with students from the same country. In another example, bilingual personnel may be able to share linguistic and cultural insights. Teachers are urged to make connections with others in order to gain a better understanding of who their students are and how to best serve them.

Home Visits

An additional and very important way to accomplish the goal of knowing a student is through the home visit. DeOliviera and Athanases (2007) point out that home visits are a key form of advocacy on the part of teachers, both novice and expert. These visits are a means to building relationships with families and promoting educational parity for families unfamiliar with the various ways in which U.S. schools "work," including the notion of parent involvement. In addition, home visits should be considered in light of various situations, such as birth of a child, celebration of citizenship, illness, death in the family, and other momentous occasions.

Expectations of the Visitor

There are numerous factors to bear in mind when visiting the home of a student whose culture does not match one's own. For instance, gift-giving is an expectation in some cultures. As the visitor, you can learn about these expectations from cultural brokers in the community (e.g., your students, community leaders, school personnel from the given culture). Stephaney took coffee beans and chocolate to the home of a grieving Eastern European family that had experienced a death in the family. She learned of the necessity of these particular gifts from a bilingual paraeducator. While living in Indonesia, Shelley provided coconut milk to an Indonesian acquaintance after a car accident. She learned of this traditional expectation from Indonesian colleagues and friends. In addition to expectations for specific situations, a small token given during an initial home visit can convey the teacher's good intentions (dependent upon the appropriateness of the gift). Note the importance of knowing what constitutes an appropriate gift. For example, while yellow flowers might seem to be an indication of positive intentions and friendship to many individuals born in the United States, this same gift is construed as a symbol of ill will by some Middle Eastern individuals (Dresser, 2005). To learn more about such intricacies, interested readers are directed to *Multicultural Manners: Essential Rules of Etiquette for the 21st Century* (Dresser, 2005).

After arriving at a student's home, a teacher can completely avoid many cultural missteps through simple observation. For example, whether to remove shoes can be understood by noting if your host is wearing shoes in the home. If not, err on the side of caution and leave your shoes with other shoes near the door. Follow your host's lead regarding where to sit during the visit. This precaution can prevent an embarrassing faux pas such as sitting in the position reserved for the head of the home. *Ges-*

tures: The Do's and Taboos of Body Language Around the World (Axtell, 1997) offers guidance in this regard.

Refreshments are often served at these home visits. Watch others to learn the "protocol" for eating or drinking all of your serving. Also, take sparing portions of new foods initially to prevent waste and in case you do not care for them. (Of course, you need to respectfully eat at least a portion of what you take.) In addition, some cultures mandate the appearance of extreme generosity with food; sometimes three refusals are required before the host can stop offering additional portions. Consider the fact that a flat refusal of any food or drink offered likely indicates a lack of openness to the culture and, therefore, the family. Shelley recalls a situation wherein she prepared a cultural meal of typical U.S. foods for her students while living in Asia. She was dismayed when one student could not even bear to try his apple crisp; she found herself thinking, "It's just apples, sugar, butter, and oatmeal!" She later realized that this must have been the same reaction of an Asian host who had served her tripe soup, which she struggled even to appear to eat. That host must have been thinking about the familiar ingredients of the dish, thinking "It's only tripe, vegetables, water, and spices!" Put yourself in the situation of your hosts when partaking of refreshments and recall that your goal is to build bridges with families.

In addition, consider the purpose of your visit when planning the length of stay, bearing in mind that a 10-minute "quick and to the point" initial visit may be viewed as rude. If the purpose is to meet the family and extend the invitation for family participation in the educational process, plan accordingly and take along materials for some meaningful activities and discussions. Stephaney routinely visited new families prior to their enrollment in school, along with one of the district's bilingual paraeducators. Together, they delivered a welcoming message, combined with pertinent school information (e.g., registration forms, immunization requirements). Further, through relationships built with civic and community organizations, they provided each new student with grade-level-appropriate school supplies tucked into a new backpack. As a result, students were outfitted to fully participate in school the first day they appeared. In addition, the relationship between home and school was established; phone numbers were exchanged between family members and the bilingual paraeducator, setting up a mechanism for successful first-language communication between home and school.

In another example, one excellent ESL educator uses home visit opportunities to share meaningful picture books and engage the whole family in learning games (Bonfils, 2009). This teacher recommends books such as *Whoever You Are* (Fox, 1997), *We Share One World* (Hoffelt, n.d.), *And Here's to You!* (Elliott, 2004), and *Is There Really a Human Race?* (Curtis, 2006). Games recommended by this teacher include hands-on activities related to counting, sorting, estimating, comparing, and describing (e.g., determining which jar brought by the teacher contains the most objects). These are games that could be continued in families without the presence of the teacher and do not require fluency in English. (Students had played these games before in the classroom, so they were familiar with the activity and could assist other family members in playing.)

Two additional considerations pertaining to home visits include possible lulls in activity and environmental distractions. Bear in mind that pauses in discussion or periods of silence need not be interpreted as indicators of a problem or a desire for the end of the visit. Again, observe your hosts to understand the meaning of these pauses; sometimes, these transitions prompt further and deeper engagement. Stephaney recalls an experience when attending a wake for the father of a student from Afghanistan. After removing her shoes and entering the home, she was greeted by a man who informed her that the other men seated on the floor needed to finish reading the Qur'an. Her student's son received the basket of fruit that she had taken and served her a drink. Observing the environment and the large number of men and women gathered, Stephaney sat on the sofa, noting that there was no conversation in the room. The point seemed to be that all gathered were expressing their sympathy and communal grief simply by being present and sharing the moment. She sensed her privilege in being accepted into this circle and remained in silence until the reading of the prayers was completed and all had shared in the prepared meal. This particular home visit proved especially valuable in strengthening the relationship between teacher and student; Stephaney could never have learned as much by simply hearing or reading about Afghan traditions. She came away with broad understandings that could be applied to a wide variety of cultural contexts.

While extended periods of silence can be viewed as an environmental distraction, normal home activities can also seem distracting to a visitor. It is possible that the television may not be turned off, children may "interrupt" the discussions and activities, and so on. Visitors should not be dissuaded from continuing a productive visit. A good rule of thumb might be, again, to observe your hosts; if situations do not seem a distraction to them, do not take offense or let these "distractions" disrupt your visit.

Individualistic and Collectivistic Cultural Expectations

As mentioned earlier, people in individualistic cultures tend to strive for individual achievement and recognition. In contrast, people in collectivistic cultures tend to promote the welfare of their entire group and view achievement and recognition as valuable to the extent that they benefit this group as a whole. Communication styles reflect these cultural orientations. For example, speakers from individualistic cultures are often very clear, direct, and linear in their style of communication; speakers must provide "straight talk" and "communicate clearly" so that the message is easily understood by the listener (Ting-Toomey, 1999, pp. 100–101). At the other end of the spectrum, speakers from collectivistic cultures tend to focus on the needs of the group, using an indirect, spiral communication style marked by "self-effacing talk, non-verbal subtleties, and interpreter-sensitive values (i.e., the receiver or interpreter of the message assumes the responsibility to infer the hidden or contextual meanings of the message)" (Ting-Toomey, 1999, p. 101). When individuals from each end of this communication spectrum interact, there are possibilities for confusion. These differences in communication style must be considered when speaking to those from cultural backgrounds different from one's own.

As an educator taking into account less direct and more direct interaction styles, it is often more productive to abandon strict adherence to either style. That is, a "give and take" approach to communication is a necessity. According to the situation, speakers move along a continuum and constantly adjust their communication styles. A general rule for improved communication with individuals from other cultures is to soften direct communication that can be perceived as rude in favor of more tentative and indirect language, particularly when asking about personal information. Further, educators will benefit from realizing that communication from individuals from less direct cultures needs to be interpreted in order to be understood. For instance, a parent's seemingly casual comment about not having a car may indicate a request for a ride to a school event.

As teachers bear in mind that they are guests during a home visit and behave accordingly, they must exhibit similar respect when interviewing parents in terms of sensitively posing their questions. As mentioned previously, softening of this communication may be needed because of cultural expectations regarding communication style *and* what constitutes typical topics of communication between an educator and a student's family. That is, parents from other cultures may not only expect a less direct questioning style, but may also be surprised by some of the topics raised by teachers that might never be addressed in the heritage culture (e.g., questions regarding family situations, strict focus on the child's cognitive development). Parents and teachers may have very different ideas about what are the most important topics for a parent-teacher interaction (e.g., student deportment versus cognitive development; Trumbull, Rothstein-Fisch, Greenfield, & Quiroz, 2001), so these communicative expectations must also be considered.

To implement more culturally competent communication when working with those from collectivistic cultures, teachers can consider the examples shown in Table 1.3, based on those found in Trumbull et al. (2001).

Table 1.3 Individualistic and collectivistic approaches to communication

Direct Approach (more individualistic)	Indirect Approach (more collectivistic)
I'm glad you made it. We need to discuss five aspects of your child's learning today. (The teacher has been charged with following a specific format for conferences and is under a limited timeframe.)	Welcome to my classroom . . . (followed by a bit of small talk). Some parents have questions or concerns about their students' school performance. (Gauge next statement or question based on parental response—this approach is likely to open the door for a question or comment by the parent that will direct the conversation.)
What problems is your student experiencing in school? (The teacher is attempting to broaden her or his understanding of the challenges of being a newcomer in the school.)	Some parents say that their students have problems in school. (Gauge next statement or question based on parental response—this approach is likely to open the door for a question or comment by the parent that will direct the conversation.)
Does your family need assistance in finding community resources? (The teacher has noted that the student comes to school in the same clothes every day.)	Some families like to learn more about community resources. Here is some information about a few that may be helpful.

Using appropriate interaction techniques is an important way to open up respectful communication between the school and the family. During a home visit, take the opportunity to conduct an informal environmental scan in order to better understand the realities of your student. For example, note whether the student has dedicated space in which to study with adequate light.

Be aware that cultures differ on the value of private space. For instance, the Chinese words that are closest in meaning to *privacy* are *secretive* or *selfishness* (Ting-Toomey, 1999, p. 134), while the best synonym for *privacy* in Arabic is *loneliness* (Nydell, 1996, p. 29, as cited in Ting-Toomey, 1999, p. 134).

Also, take note of any visible reading or print materials in the home (e.g., books on shelves, magazines, lists on the refrigerator). Such observations will assist you in gaining insight into the importance of reading in the family's daily activities.

Another point to consider is the number of individuals living in the home; it is not uncommon in many cultures for extended families to live in one home. Further, notice the general surroundings, including cultural artifacts (e.g., religious symbols and items, handmade textiles, pictures from the "home" country). One additional advantage of the home visit will be the opportunity to discern the family power structure. This can be ascertained by paying careful attention to which family member assumes a lead role during the visit, as well as which individuals participate and which others remain silent. Some teachers mistakenly assume that it is appropriate to direct conversation equally to either parent, whereas cultures might be more patriarchal or more matriarchal, rather than egalitarian, in this respect. Understanding the importance and visible indicators of cultural values within a given family will assist you in meeting your student "where he or she is."

Business to Be Conducted During a Home Visit

Home visits can be a productive time for completing necessary tasks prior to a student's actual attendance at school, provided that teachers are aware of students' upcoming school start dates. For instance, when visiting the home, teachers and bilingual paraeducators should consider the efficiency of collecting as much information as possible while the opportunity is ripe. (Of course, this effort calls for cultural sensitivity, as discussed in the previous section, in terms of lines of questioning.) Examples of the types of information that could be collected include

- Accurate and detailed contact information

- Enrollment forms, including

  - Registration forms

  - Immunization documentation

  - Free or reduced-cost lunch application forms (as needed, in appropriate languages when possible)

Also, as mentioned before, consider providing grade-level-appropriate school supplies. Many community and civic organizations may be interested in providing support by making donations of needed items. For example, Stephaney collaborated with an active member of the local Lioness Club and the United Methodist Women. Both groups adopted the ESL program as a service project, annually providing grade-level-specific school supplies and backpacks ready for delivery during home visits. Many organizations (e.g., Rotary International, Kiwanis, Lions Club, Optimist Club) may appreciate opportunities to develop these and other types of collaboration (e.g., support for medical needs, volunteers to read with young ELLs).

Another essential consideration when communicating with ELLs' families is that educators must not insist that parents speak English to their children. Doing so can cause breakdowns in family communication when children learn to speak English more quickly than their parents, leaving parents at a distinct disadvantage when interacting with their children (Wong-Fillmore, 2000). Wong-Fillmore points out that, taken to the extreme, this practice can result in a total loss of family communication. Instead, teachers must encourage students and their families to maintain their heritage languages and cultures, thus supporting students in maintaining appropriate dynamics in parent-child interactions.

Steps for Differentiating

There are a variety of perspectives on differentiation. While content, process, and product are all areas for consideration (Tomlinson, 2005), when focusing on English language learners, we emphasize the critical need for teachers to make changes to process and product, based on students' language proficiency levels. At times, content must also be differentiated, with prominence given to key "essential learnings" (Wiggins & McTighe, 2006). (For instance, many ELLs do not have the background in American history that students who have grown up attending U.S. schools may have. Their learning may need to focus on more basic information than on the extensive detail associated with extension activities.)

When differentiating for ELLs, backward lesson design (Wiggins & McTighe, 2006) can be helpful. By designing assignments/assessments for students at different levels of proficiency before creating lesson plans, teachers can focus on differentiating instruction in order to facilitate success in achieving the content and language objectives represented by those assignments/assessments. The steps in implementing differentiated instruction and assessment using backward lesson design are as follows:

1. **Get to know your students.** This topic has been discussed previously and will be expanded throughout the book. Important considerations include

   a. the English language proficiency levels of the students in listening, speaking, reading, and writing;

   b. the background knowledge and experiences of students (including their previous formal schooling);

   c. the cultural values, norms, beliefs, and practices of the students;

   d. additional relevant student factors (immigrant and refugee status, language distance, and social distance);

   e. "special" needs of the students pertaining to giftedness and cognitive or behavioral disabilities; and

   f. student interests.

   By understanding these considerations, teachers can design meaningful instruction that is matched to students' needs and that will facilitate optimal learning. Assessments that take these factors into account will allow students to fully reflect their knowledge, skills, and abilities in the content areas.

2. **Determine long-range learning goals, and set corresponding content and language objectives.** In keeping with the backward-

lesson-design approach of Wiggins and McTighe (2006), teachers must think about eventual goals and create standards-based content objectives in clear, specific, and measurable terms that reflect the ways in which students will demonstrate their achievement of those objectives. Further, in keeping with the sheltered instruction approach to teaching (including Echevarria, Vogt, & Short's [2008] *SIOP Model*), lesson plans for ELLs must include language objectives. These objectives clarify how students will use language in all four domains (listening, speaking, reading, and writing) to achieve the content objectives. The student descriptors and assignment/assessment strategies on the chart and described in this text clearly direct teachers in how to set reasonable linguistic expectations for students at all five levels of proficiency. Further, relying on daily explicit language objectives, in addition to content objectives, ensures the simultaneous development of both language proficiency and content knowledge, skills, and abilities.

3. **Design assignments/assessments.** These measures of student achievement should be based on the content and language objectives set forth for a given lesson, set of lessons, unit, or longer period of instruction. They must account for the range of student factors listed previously in such a way as to prevent those factors from confounding assignment/assessment scores unnecessarily (e.g., students' differing background knowledge hindering their achievement on a reading comprehension test because they are reading passages about unfamiliar topics). Further, the scoring criteria for these assignments/assessments must take into account students' English language proficiency levels, in particular, so that the expectations of students at different levels are in keeping with the test data available for each student. (Guidance in how to accomplish this purpose will be given in Chapter 8.)

4. **Design lesson plans.** Lesson plans should be set up in such a way that they enable students to learn the content and language necessary to achieve the instructional objectives of each lesson. Strategies listed on the chart and described herein will facilitate the alignment of instruction with the lesson's language and content objectives. In this way, students will be prepared to successfully demonstrate learning on the predesigned assignments/assessments. Teachers must not think of this sort of planning as "teaching to the test" in its negative connotation. Rather, this consti-

tutes high quality instruction; it is focused on the precise knowledge, skills, and abilities that are set forth in standards as necessary for all students. In this way, teachers set up students for success in achieving the objectives of each lesson.

5. **Teach and assess, adjusting as necessary.** Even when teachers carefully create assignments/assessments and choose strategies, their work may still require adjustment as a result of the unpredictable nature of the educational process. Further, information gleaned from the assessment process will necessarily inform future instruction.

Conclusion

The implementation of differentiated lesson planning and assessment is a challenging endeavor. This chapter has discussed key introductory information, relevant student factors, the importance of knowing one's students and how to go about gaining this knowledge, and steps for differentiating instruction for ELLs. Chapter 2 will build on this foundation by describing general guidelines for teaching and assessing ELLs, providing background regarding the second language acquisition process, and enumerating important assignment/assessment and instructional strategies that are suitable for ELLs at all proficiency levels.

Professional Development Activities

Activity 1.1   Application of Relevant Student Factors

Based on what you know about a given student, make notes according to the following categories. (Feel free to refer to relevant chapter sections as you do this.)

Then hypothesize how the factors described on the sheet may impact the student's learning. (If you are not currently working with ELLs, work with a partner who is to complete this activity.)

Student Name: _____

Student Factor	*Data*	*Hypothesized Impact on Learning*
Educational Background (What kind of schooling? Where? How long?)		
Immigrant or Refugee Status:	Country of origin: Country/ies of domicile (prior to arriving in the U.S.): ____ Immigrant ____ Refugee	
Cultural Background (place the student on the continuum with an *x*)	**Individualistic** **Collectivistic** ⟵—————————⟶	
Prior Difficult Experiences		
Age		
Language Distance (relative ease in learning English) (place the student on the continuum with an *x*)	**Easy** (First language similar to English) **Difficult** (First language different from English) ⟵—————————⟶	
Social Distance (between the student's cultural group and native speakers of English) (place the student on the continuum with an *x*)	**Small** **Large** ⟵—————————⟶	
Psychological Distance (between the student and native speakers of English)	**Small** **Large** ⟵—————————⟶	

Copyright © 2010. Caslon, Inc. All rights reserved. The first purchaser may photocopy this page for classroom and personal use.

Activity 1.2 Application of Student Data Collection Checklist

Referring to the Student Data Collection Checklist (Resource 1.2, which follows), reflect upon the following questions:

1. Why is it important to collect this information?

2. How can this information inform your teaching?

3. Who can help you to collect this information?

4. What are potential barriers to collecting this information?

5. How can you overcome them?

6. What is the name of the first student that you will collect this information for? Why?

Professional Development Resources

Resource 1.1 Student Background Information Sheet

This document is designed to be used to summarize information related to relevant student factors that impact learning. Some of the information may be collected through the use of the Student Data Collection Checklist (Resource 1.2), but can be summarized here for your own records and for sharing with other educators. This sheet may be particularly helpful in guiding work with challenging students.

Student Name: _____   **Photo:**

Student Factor	Data	Hypothesized Impact on Learning
Educational Background (What kind of schooling? Where? How long?)		
Immigrant or Refugee Status:	Country of origin: Country or countries of domicile (prior to arriving in the United States): ____ Immigrant ____ Refugee	
Cultural Background (place the student on the continuum with an x) (refer to "Cultural Background" section in Chapter 1)	**Individualistic** **Collectivistic** ←——————————————→	
Prior Difficult Experiences (e.g., civil war, religious persecution)		
Age		
Language Distance (relative ease in learning English) (place the student on the continuum with an x) (refer to Table 1.2)	**Easy** **Difficult** (First language (First language similar to different from English) English) ←——————————————→	
Social Distance (between the student's cultural group and native speakers of English) (place the student on the continuum with an x) (refer to the "Social Distance" section in Chapter 1)	**Small** **Large** ←——————————————→	
Psychological Distance (between the student and native speakers of English) (refer to the "Psychological Distance" section in Chapter 1)	**Small** **Large** ←——————————————→	

Copyright © 2010. Caslon, Inc. All rights reserved. The first purchaser may photocopy this page for classroom and personal use.

CUMULATIVE FOLDER	
Student Name and Photo	
Assessment Results	
English language proficiency test results	
Academic achievement test results	
Information About Previous Schooling	
Schooling in Non-U.S. Schools	
Literacy in L1	_____Yes_____No
Transcripts	_____Yes_____No
Do transcripts need to be translated?	_____Yes_____No
Report cards	_____Yes_____No
Do report cards need to be translated?	_____Yes_____No
Other information	
Schooling in U.S. Schools	
Transcripts	_____Yes_____No
Report cards	_____Yes_____No
Immunization records	_____Yes_____No
Information about program placement and services received	_____Yes_____No
Other information	
Information from multiple measures	
CONVERSATIONS WITH THE STUDENT	

Copyright © 2010. Caslon, Inc. All rights reserved. The first purchaser may photocopy this page for classroom and personal use.

TEACHER AND PARAEDUCATOR INPUT	
Other Relevant Information About the Student (e.g., linguistic or cultural background information, family information)	

HOME VISIT	

Date(s) of home visit(s):

Informal Environmental Scan	**(Notes)**
Dedicated study space	_____Yes_____No
Literacy materials in the home	
Family situation (number of family members in the home [Do extended family members live in the home?])	
Environmental realities (cultural norms, artifacts, etc.)	
Family power structure (Who is doing the talking during the visit?)	
Contact Information	
Home telephone number	
Home address	
Work telephone number	
Work address	
E-mail address	

Copyright © 2010. Caslon, Inc. All rights reserved. The first purchaser may photocopy this page for classroom and personal use.

Information About Previous Schooling	
Schooling in Non-U.S. Schools	
Are transcripts from previous schools available?	_____Yes_____No
Do transcripts need to be translated?	_____Yes_____No
Are report cards from previous schools available?	_____Yes_____No
Do report cards need to be translated?	_____Yes_____No
Do parents have other information to share about schooling in non-U.S. schooling?	_____Yes_____No
Schooling in U.S. Schools	
Are transcripts available?	_____Yes_____No
Are report cards available?	_____Yes_____No
Are immunization records available?	_____Yes_____No
Is information about program placement and services received available?	_____Yes_____No
Do parents have other information to share about schooling in the United States?	_____Yes_____No
Forms to Be Filled Out	
School registration	
Immunization records	
Free or reduced-cost lunch forms (in the appropriate language)	
Other forms	
Materials to be Given to the Family or Student (think in terms of what the student needs on the first day of school)	
Backpack	
Grade-level-appropriate school supplies	
Other items	
Additional Notes on the Home Visit	

Copyright © 2010. Caslon, Inc. All rights reserved. The first purchaser may photocopy this page for classroom and personal use.

2

General Principles of English Language Learner Assessment and Instruction

Every student can learn,
just not on the same day,
or in the same way.
　　　　　—George Evans

This chapter begins by laying a foundation for the general assignment/ assessment and instructional strategies that follow by offering five general guidelines for teaching and assessing English language learners (ELLs) that are grounded in research and best practice. We then outline key aspects of the second language acquisition process before enumerating a wide range of strategies appropriate for ELLs at all five proficiency levels.

General Guidelines

Teacher
Scenarios

> **Mr. Tate** is in his third year of teaching but is new to serving ELLs, as is his school district. In fact, since the district does not have a plan for serving ELLs in place, they enrolled an 11-year-old ELL in his 2nd grade classroom, claiming that this placement would support the child's early language development. Mr. Tate recognizes that a number of his students (not only the ELLs) have gaps in their content understanding, but he is not sure how to fill in those gaps without deviating from the district's required curriculum. Further, he is afraid to ask for help or to implement some of the innovative teaching practices that he has learned about through his own professional reading, since he is still in his probationary period as a new teacher.

Mrs. Allen is a veteran teacher who was taught to "aim for the middle" in her teaching. She is struggling with the changing clientele in her school, yet she firmly believes that "good teaching is good teaching" and that the needs of all students should be met if she uses a variety of activities and assignment types. Further, she senses that strict routines with swift consequences for infractions will provide her increasingly diverse students with the structure that they need. She has an "English-only" rule in her classroom as a way of encouraging her ELLs to expand their language proficiency.

Before discussing specific strategies for assessing and teaching ELLs across the proficiency levels, we outline five important guidelines related to these processes that are born of research and best practice. These focus on grade-level placement, reducing student anxiety, the nature of appropriate scaffolding for ELLs, the relevance of teacher-created assessments and creative instruction, and the use of students' first languages in the classroom.

Placing Students in an Age-Appropriate Grade

An important first step in effectively meeting the needs of ELLs is to ensure that they are placed in the appropriate grade. Despite the fact that older students may have minimal literacy skills in any language, districts must resist the urge to place them in inappropriately low grade levels in order to shore up these skills, as Mr. Tate's district chose to do. It is recommended that students be placed in a grade with those of the same age or within two years of that grade level, when justifiable. For example, one parent advocated for placing her adopted daughter who arrived midyear in 5th grade rather than 6th grade, at the age of 12. Her reasoning was that finishing the school year at the elementary level would support early language and social skill development, allowing the student to start at the middle school the next school year with a social network and basic communication skills in place.

Older students who arrive at high school with incomplete transcripts or no transcripts are necessarily enrolled in 9th grade. However, much older students can feel demeaned by a designation of "freshman." Districts can and should exercise sensitivity in designating the level of new enrollees. For example, one 18-year-old student who subsequently graduated when 21 (as the law allowed) was initially enrolled as a sophomore. Since the number of credits is more critical than a designation of freshman or sophomore, this student remained a "sophomore" for two years as she accumulated credits, affording her some dignity according to her age.

Putting Students at Ease

It is imperative that teachers create environments that help newcomers to feel at ease. As illustrated in Figure 1.1, teachers must be welcoming and supportive in order to help students to feel comfortable so that they can ultimately acquire the linguistic and academic knowledge, skills, and abilities that they need to be successful. Krashen (1982) describes the notion of an "affective filter" that must be lowered in order for students to be able to acquire language. Positive attitudes and a welcoming environment help this filter to be lowered so that students feel sufficiently able to attend to the input that they are receiving and to ultimately learn both language and content. The relationship between the student's comfort level and depth of learning as impacted by the affective filter is shown in Figure 2.1.

Teachers who work to ensure that students feel comfortable in the classroom set these students up for success in this regard. Mrs. Allen's strict routines and swift consequences for infractions may work against creating an initial comfort level in newcomers who may struggle to make sense of the routines. While routines are certainly helpful for ELLs,

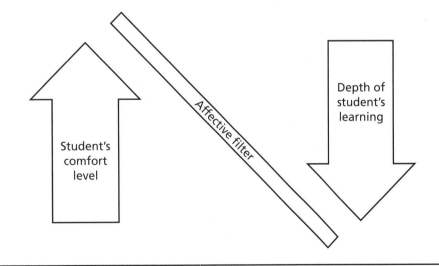

Figure 2.1 The relationship of the affective filter and depth of learning

teachers are cautioned to provide students with clear guidance regarding how to participate in such routines and to allow students time to understand and practice them before imposing consequences for infractions.

Graduated, Incremental Scaffolding

In order to facilitate successful student learning and demonstration of that learning, teachers must provide graduated, incremental scaffolding for students at each of the five language proficiency levels. Educators must make informed decisions about the kinds of necessary scaffolding for individual students based not only on curricular requirements, but also on test data focused on both language proficiency and on students' levels of knowledge, skills, and abilities in the content areas. That is, teachers may need to "shore up" student learning in order to engage them in required curricular tasks, and they must not be afraid to work in this way to ensure that students can successfully attain standards-based objectives. (Mr. Tate needs to take this student-centered approach in order to facilitate learning for all of his students.) Tasks that require levels of linguistic, cultural, and content knowledge, skills, and abilities slightly beyond a student's current level of proficiency call for meaningful and achievable growth, but necessarily require support from a teacher, paraeducator, volunteer, or peer tutor. Once students begin to gain independence with that level of support, this scaffolding should focus on facilitating student achievement at a slightly higher level of proficiency. That is, teachers must not allow students to "stagnate" at a certain proficiency level, but must always push them to the next level. This is a process that requires vigilance and finesse; teachers must not overwhelm students, but must make possible their achievement at increasingly higher levels of proficiency. It is feasible to achieve this purpose through knowing students well and through appropriately applying relevant strategies listed on the chart and described herein.

Teacher-Created Assessments and Creative Instruction

One of the most effective ways that teachers can provide differentiation is by developing assessments that are sensitive to the needs of their own students. In the case of ELLs, teachers must apply an understanding of the abilities of students at different levels of proficiency and must take into account the cultural backgrounds of these individual students in order to get the best "read" on their skills. The assessment tool itself should not prevent students from demonstrating what they know and can do. Instead, teachers must ensure that the tools that they use to gather information on student progress and mastery of content are "biased for the best" (Swain, 1985, as cited in Bachman and Palmer, 1996, p. 81). That is, the assessment process must be set up in a way that allows students to best demonstrate their knowledge, skills, and abilities. Creativity can and should be exercised in relating content knowledge to the student's language proficiency level. Teachers (including Mr. Tate) should not be afraid to exercise innovative practices in their classrooms; rather, they are encouraged to "think outside the box" in creating assessments that afford students the means to show what they know and can do in the content areas without being hindered by varying levels of language proficiency or lack of familiarity with assessment formats. A content assessment of an ELL should seek to separate conceptual understanding from language development (as long as the language of the content area is not part of what is being assessed). Teachers must realize that test results for ELLs are often confounded because of the influence of students' lack of language proficiency. Accordingly, teachers must do their best to strip assessments of any unnecessary "language load," thereby allowing students to show in a variety of ways that they are learning.

Creative instruction goes hand-in-hand with the development and use of innovative assessments. Once teachers have developed procedures for ascertaining ELLs' content knowledge and skills without extensive reliance upon language, they must craft instruction that facilitates learning of predetermined content and language objectives without full language proficiency. This type of instruction goes beyond the "one-size-fits-all" approach characterized by some curricula. Teachers, such as Mr. Tate, should not be afraid to seek assistance in formulating plans for such differentiated teaching. This teaching is the only kind that will facilitate the learning of students with diverse needs. Specific guidance about these kinds of creative, yet educationally sound, assessment and instruction of ELLs is offered throughout the remainder of this book and can be readily referenced on the chart.

Using Students' First Languages to Support Learning

On the path to developing proficiency in English, using the students' first languages can be an invaluable support. Teachers should encourage the development and maintenance of the first language whenever possible, in contrast with Mrs. Allen's "English-only" rule. Research bears out the power of transfer of language and literacy skills from the first language to the second (Lapp, Fisher, Flood, & Cabello, 2001; Snow, Burns, & Griffin, 1998). Thus the first language can be a useful tool in instruction and assessment. For example, using the first language can be far more efficient to explain or clarify a concept than using extensive charades, drawings, and explanations in simplified English. Teachers can also use the first language as a springboard to grade-level assignments by allowing students who share a first language to discuss content or an assignment, or by allowing a bilingual paraeducator to provide clarification about concepts or expectations to a student. In short, rather than forbidding students to use their first languages in the classroom, teachers are urged to support students in using this all-important tool to facilitate learning.

The Second Language Acquisition Process

Before teachers can begin the process of differentiating assignments/ assessments and instruction for ELLs, they must gain a general understanding of the ways in which these students acquire English. Teachers can feel overwhelmed in working with students who are beginning to acquire the English language. These educators may suffer anxiety as a result of beliefs often born of previous training and experience or lack of either. They may think that all students must achieve the academic standards in exactly the same way (or nearly the same way), using the same or very similar instructional materials and assessments. Their anxiety is further exacerbated when students' rates of growth in language proficiency seem slower than teachers might expect.

The student descriptors outlined in the chart and described in this volume recognize that the language acquisition process is incremental, taking place over time in somewhat predictable stages (e.g., Krashen & Terrell, 1983). Research further bears out the claim that students progress more quickly in their language acquisition at lower levels of proficiency and more slowly as they approach full proficiency (Cook, 2008). Taking this step-by-step nature of language learning into account, the chart and book clarify suggested instructional and assessment strategies matched to each of the language proficiency levels of an individual student. Using these references based in the educational literature, classroom/content and ESL/bilingual/dual language teachers can know what their students are capable of understanding and producing. As a result, these educators can apply the guidance on the chart and in the book both when planning instruction and when assessing learning; they can implement the strategies individually or use them when collaborating to serve ELLs in grade-level mainstream settings. Specifically, knowing the student's language proficiency level and individual background, teachers can reference the matching level on the chart and act accordingly.

The five levels described in the chart reflect those presented in the TESOL national *PreK–12 English Language Proficiency Standards* (Gottlieb, Carnuccio, Ernst-Slavit, Katz, & Snow, 2006). These standards embody general principles of English language acquisition and view the education of ELLs as a holistic endeavor, incorporating attention to sociocultural, linguistic, and cognitive development (p. 17). Academic language is viewed from three perspectives: word level, sentence level, and extended text level (pp. 18–19).

More specifically, the authors draw upon the extensive work of Jim Cummins in distinguishing between social language ("basic interpersonal communicative skills") and academic language ("cognitive/academic language proficiency") (Cummins, 2001, p. 112). In addition to differentiating between these two types of language, Cummins emphasizes that cognitive/academic language proficiency (CALP), or academic language, transfers across languages, citing various research studies that support this notion. As discussed in Chapter 1, this transfer is especially critical in understanding the different learning trajectories of students with interrupted or limited formal schooling compared with students who come to U.S. classrooms with uninterrupted schooling in their first languages. Students with minimal educational backgrounds (in comparison to their age-level peers) have not yet fully developed cognitive/academic language proficiency in their first languages. As a result, these students are lacking content knowledge and academic language skills in the first language and, therefore, cannot transfer that background knowledge and L1 academic language proficiency to the second language. Cummins and others (e.g., Freeman & Freeman, 2002) clarify that school-based learning for students with interrupted or limited formal schooling is far different from that of their counterparts who have a strong and consistent educational background. Both groups and their respective needs will be discussed throughout the remainder of this book.

Building on the notions of social and academic language, we recognize that language development is contextualized within various social and academic settings. TESOL's five English language proficiency standards (Gottlieb et al., 2006, p. 2) offer teachers specific guidance in considering the types of language associated with these contexts:

Standard 1: English language learners communicate for social, intercultural, and instructional purposes within the school setting.

Standard 2: English language learners communicate information, ideas, and concepts necessary for academic success in the area of language arts.

Standard 3: English language learners communicate information, ideas, and concepts necessary for academic success in the area of mathematics.

Standard 4: English language learners communicate information, ideas, and concepts necessary for academic success in the area of science.

Standard 5: English language learners communicate information, ideas, and concepts necessary for academic success in the area of social studies.

In defining academic language itself, we draw upon the work of Bailey (in press, as cited in Bailey, 2007). According to Bailey (2007, pp. 10–11), academic language proficiency is

knowing and being able to "use general and content-specific vocabulary, specialized or complex grammatical structures, and multifarious language functions and discourse structures—all for the purpose of acquiring new knowledge and skills, interacting about a topic, or imparting information to others." (Bailey, 2007)

We share Bailey's view that academic language proficiency includes vocabulary, grammar, language functions, and discourse structures needed for classroom learning. We also recognize that these aspects of language are best taught in the context of meaningful communication that integrates all four language domains (listening, speaking, reading, and writing). In our emphasis on contextualized, meaningful language teaching, we draw from the notion of "focus on form" versus "focus on forms" (Hinkel & Fotos, 2002). The "focus on form" approach that we advocate is not motivated by strict instruction in forms of language that may be decontextualized (i.e., the "focus on forms" approach). Rather, we support the instruction of language components within the context of teaching that focuses on communication of meaning that combines the use of listening, speaking, reading, and writing in authentic ways. Strategies for addressing these aspects of language will be addressed throughout the remainder of the book in terms of both language instruction and assessment.

Perspectives on Reading Instruction

While principles of second language acquisition drive our work, specific discussion of literacy instruction is warranted in a book that addresses the needs of ELLs with limited formal schooling. Within the context of our work, literacy is defined as reading and writing. Pre-literate students are those who are unable to read or write in any language.

We recognize that different genres impact literacy development in different ways. For instance, storytelling is a culturally bound activity; some cultures tell stories in a more linear or "topic-centered" style, whereas others construct narratives that are more episodic or "topic associated" in nature (Garcia, 2008). As a result, an ELL's understanding and production of stories may appear to be faulty when she or he incorporates culturally bound narrative styles that contrast with the more linear, three-point style of traditional Western narratives. For these students, instruction in both reading and writing development will need to include specific attention to culturally bound styles of writing, including guidance in how to construct narratives in a linear fashion (in keeping with typical U.S. school expectations).

In addition to the organizational style of stories in English, topics and vocabulary may pose a challenge for students from different backgrounds. For instance, many children's stories focus on castles, knights, and the like. Such topics may be entirely unfamiliar to students from other narrative traditions, resulting in the need for additional conceptual and vocabulary instruction. Further, certain grammatical structures common to narratives (e.g., "Once upon a time . . .") may warrant explanation.

Narratives are not the only genre that may be challenging to ELLs; other genres may also require extra attention. For instance, the direct style of communication often seen in persuasive or argumentative writing may be somewhat shocking to a student whose culture indicates that an indirect style is more suitable. Students may require assistance in understanding ways in which to appropriately construct and support an argument that are in keeping with more individualistic U.S. school expectations.

For many ELLs, nonfiction instructional text may be easier to grasp than other genres because of the many supports that often accompany text materials (e.g., headings, pictures, captions). However, ELLs, just like non-ELLs, must be taught how to interpret and take advantage of these text features.

Reading instruction, like all instruction for ELLs, must focus on providing comprehensible input for learners. That is, we advocate a meaning-based approach that is more whole-to-part than vice versa. The discrete aspects of language (e.g., pronunciation, grammar, spelling) should be taught within the context of a meaningful piece of written communication. This is not to say that language teaching takes a backseat to reading instruction; rather, language teaching is embedded in meaningful reading instruction.

Facilitating reading development for students across the five levels of proficiency requires graduated, incremental scaffolding. The specific kinds of scaffolding vary according to student background; ELLs with limited or interrupted formal schooling will need far more support than their counterparts who are on grade level in the first language. For both groups, teachers can use best practice in reading instruction for native speakers of English as a starting point, broadening these practices to focus on essential cultural and linguistic issues throughout the process. For example, ELLs may need supplemental instruction to add to their background knowledge, and they will most certainly require a wide variety of supports in terms of how to make sense of text, including special attention to vocabulary development.

For both pre-literate and first language-literate ELLs, first language knowledge and life experiences can serve as a springboard for meaningful instruction that focuses on vocabulary development and comprehension. Monolingual ESL teachers can build on the native languages of their students by respecting and welcoming the use of those languages by students in the classroom, pointing out cognates (words that are virtually the same in two languages) where possible, inviting parents into the classroom, providing multilingual multicultural books for students to take home for family literacy activities, and other relevant and innovative bridge-building activities that facilitate interlanguage connections.

Regarding specific instructional activities, Snow, Burns, and Griffin (1998) point out that "effective teachers are able to craft a special mix of instructional ingredients for every child they work with" (pp. 2–3). They list three common hindrances to early literacy development (pp. 4–5): (a) lack of understanding of the alphabetic principle (letter-sound relationships), (b) failure to transfer oral skills to reading, and (c) lack of motivation or appreciation of reading. Although Snow and colleagues advocate for teaching ELLs to read in the L1 first, they suggest that if that is not possible, ELLs should be allowed to develop some oral proficiency before formal reading instruction is introduced. An important part of this oral proficiency is the ability to hear and recognize the sounds of the new language (phonemic awareness) and, ultimately, to produce them. According to some (August and Shanahan 2006), phonemic awareness is essential to the learning of reading in English for ELLs. If students do not know the sounds of the language, how can they produce them when reading aloud? Following the guidance of Franco (2005), we recommend that students' phonemic awareness be built within the context of meaningful oral language development activities before they are expected to read.

With this second language (L2) phonemic awareness in place, students are prepared to learn and apply the alphabetic principle, mentioned earlier as a common hindrance to literacy development. Teachers of older students who are not literate in the L1 must realize the importance of these indispensible building blocks to literacy development (phonemic awareness and the alphabetic principle) and make certain to address student needs for oral and aural development as they provide reading instruction. (Interestingly, the need for initial oral proficiency lines up with the recommendations of Koda [1996] in situations where L1 literate students are learning to read in a new writing system.) Echoing Franco's (2005) guidance, we suggest that, regardless of the first language of the student, he or she not be expected to engage in independent reading activities until he or she is able to speak at the simple sentence level (Level 3), at a minimum.[1]

In literacy classrooms where ELLs are served, the importance of visual support through the use of pictures, realia, graphs, maps, and other visual aids cannot be overemphasized. Franco (2005) admonishes teachers that if activities do not focus on vocabulary and comprehension, the activities are not useful for ELLs. In addition, the use of such visual materials is not of benefit only to ELLs; many native speakers of English are

---

[1]Of course, there are instances where a student may arrive with lower speaking proficiency than his or her reading proficiency in English. Students who have been taught literacy skills in English prior to the development of speaking ability may well be able to read independently before achieving Level 3 in speaking. However, they will still need instruction in phonemic awareness if they are to incorporate all of the sounds of English into their speech and oral reading.

visual learners and will benefit from the incorporation of more visual aids into instruction.

Returning to the hindrances raised by Snow and colleagues (1998), the use of visual aids can significantly contribute to the teaching of the alphabetic principle. Language experience stories in which the teacher acts as a scribe as students describe shared experiences can be a means to bridging the oral-written language divide. (Students are at an advantage when asked to read print that was written based on their own oral language production.) Appreciation of reading and motivation to engage in the learning of reading skills can be facilitated by reading books of interest to students. Freeman and Freeman (2000) advocate for teaching thematic literature-based units that focus on themes relevant to students. This use of interesting thematic topics is a means not only of engaging students, but also of fostering vocabulary development through the natural recycling of vocabulary that occurs in thematic studies.

We also support the creation of a print-rich environment in which students regularly see reading and writing used in real-life contexts, in keeping with recommendations found in the educational literature (e.g., Peregoy & Boyle, 2008). The use of big books; word, language, and concept walls accompanied with pictures; and other displays of meaningful print can foster the process of literacy emergence. Though this strategy is often thought of as one for elementary teachers, educators at all levels will do well to make increasing amounts of meaningful print available to students as a resource.

In terms of structuring a program of reading development for ELLs who can read in their first languages and for those who cannot, we appreciate and concur with the guidance offered by Anderson (1999). He provides a list of eight strategies that apply equally well to emergent literacy instruction and to the teaching of more advanced ESL reading (p. 6):

- Activate prior knowledge
- Cultivate vocabulary
- Teach for comprehension
- Increase reading rate
- Verify reading strategies
- Evaluate progress
- Build motivation
- Select appropriate reading materials

We emphasize the importance of activating prior knowledge. This approach is echoed throughout the educational literature (e.g., Echevarria et al., 2008; Everson & Kuriya, 1998; Lenski & Ehlers-Zavala, 2004). For pre-literate students who cannot draw on L1 reading experiences, this is perhaps even more important than for L1-literate students. Cultivating vocabulary is, of course, an essential part of developing reading ability, though, in keeping with educational research, we assert that it is imperative that vocabulary be taught in meaningful, contextualized ways (e.g., Bernhardt, 1991; Goodman, 1994). In order to teach for comprehension, Anderson (1999) recommends explicit teaching of metacognitive skills, as well as content-based teaching, an approach advocated by a variety of researchers and practitioners (e.g., Chamot & O'Malley, 1994; Echevarria et al., 2008) and one that we espouse, as well. Increasing the reading rate of students requires that they be given numerous opportunities to engage in reading. We recommend the reading workshop format of classroom instruction (Hindley, 1996) as one possible means for differentiating reading instruction.

As stated previously, the use of strategies must be explicitly taught and practiced. Progress can be evaluated in a range of level-appropriate ways, to be discussed here and in Chapters 3 through 7. We acknowledge that motivation can be addressed through the engagement of students in interesting and meaningful reading activities, and we support that approach. Finally, we believe that ELLs must be engaged in authentic, meaningful activities in all facets of their education. We concur with Anderson's (1999) recommendation that the authentic use of reading materials should be emphasized over the authenticity of the materials themselves. (This echoes the sentiments of Everson & Kuriya [1998], who also assert that adapted materials have their place in beginning reading instruction.)

Supported by the guidance of various literacy researchers and our own experience, we recommend that oral language be developed before students are expected to read independently and that all pre-reading and reading/writing activities should focus on making meaning. This position will be borne out in the reading and writing strategies described for both assignments/assessments and instruction.

Having addressed a variety of general guidelines pertaining to the teaching of ELLs and the second language acquisition and literacy development processes, we now turn to an explication of the general assignment/assessment strategies outlined on the chart. Assessment is addressed before instruction in this book in keeping with the notion of "backward lesson design" (Wiggins & McTighe, 2006), wherein teachers design assessment procedures and then create instruction specifically designed to support students to succeed in demonstrating what they know and can do.[2] Each general strategy will be addressed in turn.

General Assignment /Assessment Strategies

In order to effectively assess ELLs at all proficiency levels, teachers must incorporate differentiated, authentic, and culturally and linguistically appropriate assessments of ELLs into their practice. Further, ELLs at all proficiency levels are capable of engaging in both lower-order (e.g., knowledge- and comprehension-based) and higher-order (e.g., application, analysis, synthesis/creation, and evaluation) thinking skills. Effective assessment requires, again, that teachers consistently apply their own creativity in developing and implementing ways that students can demonstrate higher-order thinking, regardless of language proficiency level. The student background factors described in Chapter 1 must also be considered in the assessment process. The interrelationship of language proficiency, relevant student factors, and essential learning based on content standards and curricula is exemplified in Figure 2.2.

Ideas for accomplishing this level-specific goal are outlined in subsequent chapters.

A number of general practices will, however, help to facilitate meaningful assessment of ELLs in each of the five proficiency levels. These are found on the chart that accompanies this book in a large row spanning the proficiency levels and are described here.

Ensure that academic assessment targets the same academic content standards for all students (non-ELLs and ELLs alike.) As stated earlier and for the sake of academic parity, teachers must ensure that all students in the classroom are learning the same content. That is, ELLs cannot focus on alternate content because of their language proficiency levels. This imperative calls for intentional differentiation of both instruction

---

[2]Although we advocate backward lesson design, particularly for teachers who are new to serving ELLs, the chart lists instructional strategies before assignment/assessment strategies because we recognize that this approach is likely to be more intuitively appealing to educators.

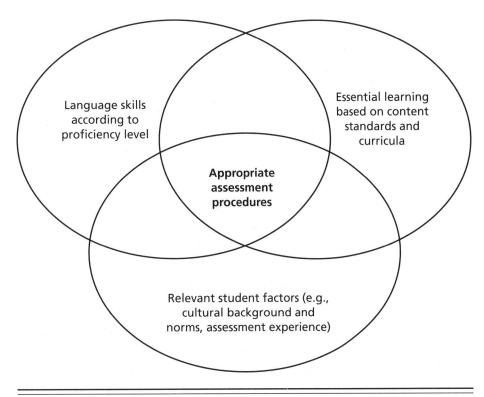

Figure 2.2 Factors that must inform appropriate ELL assessment

and assessment. For instance, if the assignment is for students to create group presentations, ELLs at lower proficiency levels must be allowed to contribute to the presentation verbally according to their linguistic abilities. While a Level 2 student might speak a few sentences, the Level 1 student might simply pronounce key words for the audience with visual accompaniment.

Consider students' language proficiency levels, and differentiate assessments/assignments accordingly. Inasmuch as students at any proficiency level can produce predictable amounts and kinds of language in English, assessment instruments must draw upon and match those specific skill levels when measuring learning. For example, rather than expecting a five-paragraph compare-contrast essay from a Level 2 student, a teacher might assign the creation of a Venn diagram or T-chart that would require the student to correctly place words and phrases accompanied by pictures. In this way, students at all language proficiency levels can exhibit higher-order thinking skills differentiated according to their individual language proficiency levels.

Ensure that directions are clear; confirm that students understand them.
Students whose school experiences may not be commensurate with U.S.
classroom practices will need explicit instruction in terms of how to
complete assignments and assessments. Teachers are urged to incorporate sensory supports (e.g., modeling, work samples) to ensure understanding. When giving directions, teachers might consider incorporating
the skills of a bilingual paraeducator to confirm that students do, indeed,
understand directions and can follow the specified protocol. Teachers
can also ascertain whether students understand directions for assignments and assessments by asking for indications of comprehension that
go beyond a simple "yes" (e.g., having students restate the directions or
demonstrate understanding nonverbally).

Differentiate standards-based scoring rubrics according to students' language proficiency levels. (Weight grading to emphasize content understanding more than linguistic perfection at lower levels of proficiency.)
Differentiated assessments born of differentiated instruction call for differentiated scoring. Further, it makes sense to support students in scaffolding their simultaneous acquisition of language and content by emphasizing content understanding over language mastery at lower levels of
language proficiency. Multiple representations of conceptual learning
(e.g., posters, dioramas, labeled charts) must be accepted and fully credited as legitimate demonstrations of content mastery (unless, of course,
the content standards require high levels of language production). Meanwhile, linguistic conventions (e.g., grammar, spelling) will be afforded appropriate weights with expectations aligned to students' individual language proficiency levels in cases where language is not part of what is
being assessed. For example, linguistic conventions might not be graded
at all for Level 1 and 2 students. (Refer to the Student Descriptors on the
chart, and see Chapter 8 for further discussion of differentiated rubrics.)

**Share differentiated rubrics with students at the time that assignments
are given.** Best instructional practice demands that teachers share
grading expectations with students in advance of the completion of an
assignment or assessment; students should clearly understand the learning targets throughout the learning and assessment cycle. Further,
knowing the expectations in advance empowers students to actively
aim for and meet achievement criteria. (For students at lower proficiency levels, teachers can present their expectations to ELLs in the

form of simplified rubrics and can support understanding by exemplifying sample assignments.) This assessment "rule of thumb" applies to non-ELLs and ELLs alike. (See Chapter 8 for further discussion of differentiated rubrics.)

Utilize the same supports used in instruction (e.g., pictures, charts, graphs) when assessing students. Good assessment is a reflection of instruction. That is, supports that are provided to students during instruction should also be available during the assessment process. For example, if pictures are used during instruction to support learning, pictures should also be included as part of the assessment process whenever possible (e.g., if a word bank is provided on an assignment or assessment, icons or clip art can be used). The use of accommodations should be mirrored in assessment and instruction; if accommodations are used in one part of the teaching-assessment cycle, they should be used consistently throughout the cycle.

Encourage students to demonstrate content knowledge, skills, and abilities, regardless of level of language proficiency, using a variety of differentiated performance-based and authentic assessments (e.g., demonstrations, dioramas, collages, journals, art projects, maps, models, posters). Teachers should feel free to use their imaginations and creativity when designing assessment tools and procedures to gauge the learning of ELLs. In fact, using innovative assessments is the only way to gain accurate insight into the knowledge, abilities, and skills of many ELLs, particularly those at the lower proficiency levels. All students, including ELLs at beginning levels of language proficiency, are capable of sophisticated thoughts and complex ideas. Teachers who know their students and their content well are best equipped to develop meaningful and imaginative assessments that reflect their students' content knowledge, skills, and abilities matched to individual language proficiency levels. For example, one family and consumer science teacher allowed students to demonstrate understanding of the components of a balanced meal based on the food pyramid by submitting a nontraditional "test." This assessment took the form of displaying a specified number of food groups on a paper plate by cutting out, affixing, and labeling magazine pictures on the plate. The resulting artifact is an excellent example of devising a creative way to support students in demonstrating content knowledge without language mastery.

Allow ELLs to exercise personal choice in assignments (when appropriate) and to apply their background knowledge in order to enhance motivation. As mentioned previously, ELLs bring tremendous funds of knowledge with them to the classroom. Allowing students to make assignment-related selections that allow them to capitalize on this knowledge can pay significant dividends in terms of student motivation and academic performance. For instance, a teacher could allow a student to do a project on her or his country of origin rather than a randomly assigned country.

If traditional paper and pencil tests must be used with ELLs, focus on essential learning when creating them; create tests that are aligned with content objectives, of reasonable length, and matched to the linguistic levels of students. While content standards and curricula must not be "watered down" for ELLs, teachers must acknowledge the incremental process of learning content in a new language. This process will likely take longer for students of low language proficiency than for their more fluent peers. Teachers must focus on the most critical aspects of each lesson during instruction and create appropriate assessments to scaffold the individual learner toward the next level of proficiency. During this process, care must be taken to ensure that all students are assessed on the same content objectives while not burdening ELLs with unreasonable linguistic demands. For example, teachers might create a new version of a paper and pencil assessment to be used for more advanced ELLs; this test could be written in simplified English and incorporate supplementary icons and pictures (Fairbairn, 2006).

Use a variety of assessment procedures to obtain an accurate picture of what students know and can do in the content areas. This strategy applies equally to ELLs and non-ELLs. Some students tend to perform better on certain test formats than on others. In addition, some formats are typically more language intensive than others (e.g., multiple-choice tests versus demonstration). By using a range of assessment procedures, teachers can obtain a broader sample of student work and, as a result, get a more accurate picture of what students know and can do. Specific strategies for assessing students at each proficiency level are provided on the chart and discussed in Chapters 3 through 7.

Focus error correction on specific, level-appropriate aspects of language. When working to assist ELLs in perfecting their language skills, educators must be careful not to overwhelm students with an inordinate number of corrections. Rather, teachers must focus their efforts on specific types of errors that are appropriate to the student's level of language proficiency. For instance, if a teacher is grading a Level 3 student's writing, he or she may focus on particularly meaningful aspects of language, such as the correct use commonly used verb tenses, rather than on less critical facets of the student's writing that are inaccurate (e.g., spelling of infrequently used words).

When grading, avoid comparing students with each other; grade students according to predetermined standards for success that are aligned with students' language proficiency levels. In today's standards-based environment, students must be graded against standards rather than against each other. Comparing ELLs to their native English-speaking peers is not supported by the data that describe ELLs' developing levels of language proficiency. Rather, teachers must compare all students' accomplishments to specified content standards and benchmarks. Given that the purpose of grading is to provide meaningful information about student achievement to students and their families or guardians, it is crucial that the grade reflect the simultaneous acquisition of content *and* language knowledge, skills, and abilities. Since the learning curve for ELLs follows a different trajectory than that for native speakers, the best information about student achievement relates specifically to each student's progress in comparison with standards (both content and English-language-proficiency standards), rather than in comparison with other students.[3,4]

Provide students with as much time as they need to complete assessments (unless the test is one that measures speed, such as a math computation test). Most tests (including many large-scale standardized achievement tests) are focused on measuring students' knowledge, skills, and abilities without factoring in time pressure. Extra time is certainly an

---

[3]When differentiated grading is used, school districts can determine whether such grades are "flagged" in order to indicate the use of differentiation. This consideration may be particularly important when high school students' grade point averages are compared for computing class rank. Districts should develop a comprehensive grade reporting policy that addresses such needs.

[4]When students ask how they are doing in comparison with "the American students" (as they sometimes do), providing an "undifferentiated" grade (using scoring schemes devised for native speakers) can offer the kind of standards-based information that students seek, informing them of where they stand in reference to the range of performance of their native English-speaking peers.

appropriate accommodation for ELLs on these tests, since it gives them a greater opportunity to process the language demands of the test. This can result in a more accurate picture of what students know and can do.

Employ appropriate language-related accommodations (e.g., a word-to-word dictionary, giving directions in the student's first language) for classroom and large-scale assessments, in accordance with students' English proficiency levels. ELLs are certainly deserving of accommodations when taking tests that have challenging language demands. However, these accommodations should be provided in alignment with students' individual linguistic needs, rather than in a "one-size-fits-all" approach. See Fairbairn (2007) for further guidance.

For large-scale standardized achievement tests, use only accommodations consistently used in the classroom and approved by the test developers. It is not appropriate to introduce new accommodations to students while large-scale standardized tests are being administered. In fact, the utilization of such accommodations can actually hinder student progress on such a test (e.g., a student who is unaccustomed to using a bilingual dictionary may spend more time trying to figure out how to use it than on the test items). Further, only certain accommodations are appropriate for these high-stakes tests; lists of such accommodations can be found in the technical manual or other guidance documents that accompany the tests. Deviating from these approved accommodations can endanger the validity of the interpretations made of students' test scores, meaning that the unapproved accommodations can undermine what is tested and result in inaccurate scores.

Explicitly prepare students with background knowledge and test-taking strategies needed for participating in classroom and large-scale standardized testing. Some students may not be familiar with important skills and strategies needed for success on traditional classroom and large-scale standardized tests. For instance, ELLs may not be familiar with how to negotiate a "bubble sheet" when answering questions. Further, they may not realize that referring to a reading passage is generally acceptable when taking a reading comprehension test. For detailed guidance in issues that may need to be addressed, refer to Fairbairn (2007).

Work creatively to include gifted ELLs in gifted and talented programming across proficiency levels. Lack of English language proficiency level should not preclude ELLs from participating in gifted and talented programming. However, the measures that may typically be used in identifying students for such programming may not reveal ELLs' giftedness because of the confounding factor of (limited) language proficiency. For this reason, teachers must innovate to create assessment procedures that can accurately reveal students' giftedness in order to entitle them for gifted and talented programming. After identification gifted ELLs must be instructed according to their individual language proficiency levels. (See Castellano & Diaz [2001] and Iowa Department of Education & The Connie Belin and Jacqueline N. Blank International Center for Gifted Education and Talent Development [2008] for excellent guidance related to working with gifted and talented ELLs.)

Ensure that appropriate assessment tools and procedures are used to identify ELLs for special education services, if indicated. Lacking language proficiency is not, in and of itself, a reason for entitlement to special education programming. Nor is a lack of academic proficiency that is due to limited formal schooling experiences indicative of a cognitive impairment. However, in order to separate issues of language from those of disability, particular care must be taken. Assessment procedures that may be appropriate for non-ELLs may seem to incorrectly identify ELLs for entitlement to special education services. This entitlement, however, is not likely to serve students well who do not have disabilities. For example, many teachers who specialize in this area often do not have adequate educational backgrounds in serving students who are still acquiring English. For excellent guidance on how to determine if ELLs need special education services, see Hamayan, Marler, Sanchez-Lopez, and Damico (2007).

General Instructional Strategies

Instructional strategies must be designed and implemented in such a way that they support student learning and later demonstrations of that learning. In planning instruction, teachers must bear in mind the specific types of evidence that will be accepted as demonstration of learning, in keeping with backward lesson design (Wiggins & McTighe, 2006). This instruction must also take into account the language proficiency levels and content knowledge, skills, and abilities of students. Four principles guide effective instruction of ELLs at all levels (Kauffman, 2007a, p. xiv):

- Increase comprehensibility
- Increase student-to-student interaction

- Increase higher-order thinking and the use of learning strategies
- Make connections to students' background knowledge

The first task of teachers during instruction is to ensure that teaching is accessible to all students in the classroom. In order to increase comprehensibility, teachers may incorporate visual support, recycle vocabulary, employ multimedia technology, and utilize a host of other teaching strategies designed to meet the needs of students still acquiring English. Interaction between and among students and the teacher is facilitated through a variety of opportunities to talk about what is being learned (e.g., think-pair-share, small group discussions). Higher-order thinking can be incorporated using graphic organizers and other instructional methods, while the use of strategies by students must be explicitly taught and practiced. Making connections to students' background knowledge is only possible by knowing one's students, as described in Chapter 1. Examples of all these principles are found for each level of language proficiency in upcoming chapters and in the general instructional strategies that follow.

Ensure that your classroom welcomes all students by representing the culture of each student, using pictures, flags, souvenirs, etc. It is essential that newcomers to your classroom and school feel a sense of belonging; this will facilitate a level of comfort that allows students to settle into the learning process. One way to accomplish this purpose is through the display and incorporation of various cultural artifacts in your room and in your teaching. For example, teachers might display international items that were purchased during travel or received as gifts from students across the globe. There might also be a special place in the classroom where students of all nationalities can exhibit cultural items relevant to the curriculum.

Learn key words and phrases in ELLs' first languages in order to build relationships with students and create a welcoming environment. Students can gain a sense of belonging in a new school when they hear their teachers using their first languages. Such a simple thing as morning greetings in children's native tongues can mean the difference between students wondering if they will ever fit in and their beginning to feel at home. Learning a few simple words in various languages enables teachers to heighten attention by giving first-language commands such as

"Listen," "Sit down," "Please," and "Thank you." Far more than validating the importance of each student's language, such comprehensive inclusion of all of the languages represented in the classroom serves as a model to all students of the value and worth of heritage languages and of respect for all cultures and languages.

Afford access to the curriculum by using realia, pictures, diagrams, models, demonstrations, graphic organizers, nonverbal communication, videos, computer-assisted instruction, etc. All instruction must be accessible to all students; rather than creating separate lessons for ELLs, teachers must assist those students in being able to understand and take part in the standards-based lessons that they create. Various instructional aids are essential to achieving this end. For example, a high school biology teacher brought in a cow's heart for a lesson on the heart and the circulatory system. This teacher was able to show students the parts of the heart and "demonstrate" the flow of blood by referring to the heart.

Apply the same academic content standards to the learning of all students (non-ELLs and ELLs alike). Since ELLs are generally accountable for learning the same content as non-ELLs, teachers must be careful to ensure that their instruction targets the same instructional goals for both sets of learners, a concept introduced in the "General Assignment/Assessment Strategies" section. Although ELLs at the lower levels of language proficiency may have more difficulty in accessing content instruction, teachers must create ways for these students to do so. For instance, rather than "excuse" ELLs from a unit on mitosis and meiosis because it seems too complex and language intensive, a teacher might require students to demonstrate the processes through the manipulation of concrete objects. This calls to mind a wonderful example focusing on this very topic in which ELLs outperformed non-ELLs in explaining cell division as a result of their practice in demonstrating the process with plastic forks and spoons, pipe cleaners, and other hands-on materials in the ESL classroom. The science teacher in this case creatively and capably exemplified the strategy of maintaining the same content standards for all students by employing this activity. The hands-on work meant that ELLs could meet the standard and it was helpful to non-ELLs, as well. Additional ideas for implementing the same content standards for all students are described throughout the remainder of the book.

Build capacity for learning in your ELLs by explicitly and continuously teaching social *and* content/academic language (including cross-curricular academic words such as *compare/contrast, analyze, synthesize*), using visual support and contextualized examples. In the current standards-based environment, ELLs no longer have the luxury of concentrating on language development before focusing on content learning; the two processes must occur simultaneously. It is possible to achieve this purpose only when teachers ensure that students are able to learn the language needed to function in school and associated with the curricular content that is the focus of instruction. For instance, teachers can explicitly teach academic language by modeling its meaning through the use of graphic organizers, as in the use of a Venn diagram to teach the words *compare* and *contrast.*

Inform your students of the daily objectives for each lesson in terms of both language and content. Students will benefit from the use of language and content objectives to keep them informed about exactly where each lesson is going. Language objectives help both teachers and students to focus on ways to use language in order to achieve content objectives. In developing those objectives and sharing them with students, teachers will be able to differentiate expectations for classroom participation according to students' language proficiency levels. We advocate that objectives be explicitly shared with students both orally and in writing (e.g., written on the board, discussed at the beginning of the lesson, and reviewed at the end of the lesson), in keeping with the *SIOP Model* (Echevarria et al., 2008). When students know the objectives, they learn to be accountable for achieving them. In addition, they may enjoy holding the teacher accountable for addressing all the objectives, as one of our colleagues shared with us.

Tailor instruction and assignments/assessments to the language proficiency levels of each student. The chart that accompanies this book outlines student descriptors at each of the five language proficiency levels for each language domain (listening, speaking, reading, and writing). These descriptors clarify what students at different levels are able to do linguistically. Understanding the characteristics of students at all levels and the actual proficiency levels of individual students in each language domain enables teachers to tailor expectations to specific student abilities (e.g., a given student may be at Level 4 in speaking, Level 4 in listening, Level 3 in reading, and Level 2 in writing). Throughout the book, practical ideas and examples for achieving this differentiation are provided. In addition, Chapter 8 includes a template that will assist you in designing differentiated assignments/assessments for students across all five levels of proficiency.

Ensure that directions are clear; confirm that students understand them. As is the case for assignments and assessments, it is imperative that students understand the directions for all instructional activities. Teachers must bear in mind that the general academic language found in directions (e.g., summarize, infer, compare) may be unfamiliar to ELLs (and some non-ELLs). Checking for understanding of necessary explanations will best avoid the classic question "Do you understand?" Students may say yes just to please the teacher or for other cultural reasons. Rather, checks for understanding will be more productive if they require students to actively demonstrate their comprehension of expectations. The few moments that are required to carefully clarify directions and check for understanding will pay worthwhile dividends in student achievement. For example, if students are to first create an outline and then write an essay based on it, teachers might ask students to explain the steps for the assignment rather than asking a yes/no question to check for understanding.

When giving oral directions, also provide written directions. ELLs (and non-ELLs) benefit when information is shared in more than one modality. Oral directions accompanied by written directions (especially those that also use pictures or icons) will be more comprehensible to students who are still mastering the language. For example, teachers should consider posting templates for assignments regularly utilized in their content areas (e.g., a sample format for a lab report).

Capitalize upon ELLs' backgrounds and prior experiences. ELLs do not enter U.S. classrooms as "blank slates;" they bring with them a wealth of knowledge, skills, and abilities. Teachers who appreciate and draw upon these funds of knowledge will foster more rapid learning of both language and content. For instance, some high school ELLs have served as social studies class panelists addressing the war in the former Yugoslavia, since they had firsthand knowledge of the realities of the situation. Further examples of these kinds of activities are discussed in subsequent chapters.

Activate ELLs' interests and prior knowledge as they relate to content. Interest is a form of intrinsic motivation (Ormrod, 2008), while prior knowledge serves as "mental Velcro" to which students can attach new knowledge. In the same way that taking advantage of these characteristics of non-ELLs facilitates learning, ELLs will be well served by teachers who intentionally capitalize on their individual interests and make connections to their prior knowledge. For example, teachers can allow students to focus assigned projects on topics that interest students (e.g., for ELLs, teachers could tailor a health assignment on forms of recreation to focus on soccer as opposed to football, since many ELLs come from countries where soccer is played rather than football).

Honor ELLs' first languages and cultures in the classroom. An important part of making students feel welcome and of priming them for learning is valuing what they bring with them to the classroom. The knowledge, skills, and abilities that ELLs possess are not liabilities; rather, they can serve as classroom resources. Honoring these types of expertise can be as simple as letting students teach each other phrases in various languages or asking ELLs to share about different climates in which they have lived. All students will benefit from such exchanges in terms of increased understanding across linguistic and cultural groups and within the curricular content. Another example of honoring ELLs' first languages is to grant them foreign language credit toward graduation for their heritage language proficiency.

When possible, use students' first languages to support learning in the content areas. While the implementation of bilingual or dual language education is not possible for speakers of all languages in all school districts, teachers are encouraged to allow ELLs to capitalize upon the language or languages that they bring with them to facilitate classroom learning. Students might use bilingual dictionaries (if they are literate in the first language), they might work with a bilingual paraeducator, or they might work with other students who share the same first language, to name just three examples. While ESL programming aims to teach English through the medium of English, this generalization does not preclude the use of a student's first language to enhance learning. Clearly, the first language is a significant asset, not a problem to be overcome.

Teach cross-linguistic features (e.g., cognates, grammatical constructions, prefixes, suffixes, and root words) to expand student language ability. Students can benefit from explicit instruction in terms of cognates (words that are nearly the same in two languages, such as *decidir* in

Spanish and *decide* in English). Students may not automatically recognize these similarities, so teachers are urged to assist students in making these connections. Comparisons of the grammar of the student's first language with English can also serve helpful (e.g., pointing out that although adjectives come after the noun in Spanish, they come before the noun in English). Teachers are also reminded that the instruction in prefixes, suffixes, and root words that builds the vocabulary skills of native speakers of English is also beneficial to ELLs.

Involve ELLs' families in school activities to support student achievement, communicating with families in the language that they understand best. Although cultural understandings of the role of parents in the schooling process vary, ELLs' parents can and should be encouraged to participate in school activities just as the participation of parents of non-ELLs is encouraged. Clear explanations regarding how activities work (e.g., What is "game night" at an elementary school?) may be useful. Further, invitations and these explanations may need to be shared in the first language of the parents. Communication can be facilitated through the use of bilingual paraeducators, translation services, community volunteers, and other means. One more thought: in some cultures, a personal (verbal) invitation is needed in order to ensure attendance at an event. Bear this fact in mind when preparing for parent-teacher conferences; these represent an excellent opportunity to make connections with parents that can facilitate other types of school involvement.

Support the development and maintenance of literacy in ELLs' first languages to enhance their acquisition of English. Although this volume focuses on the acquisition of English and content-area knowledge, we certainly advocate for the continuation and expansion of first language skills. As cited previously, research supports the notion that first language skills can transfer to the second language. Further, support of students' first languages instills in them a sense of pride in their heritage, an important part of identity development. Teachers do not have to be fluent in a student's first language to emphasize its value. For instance, they can encourage parents to continue to use the first language in the home for both speaking and reading/writing activities.

Offer access to multicultural and first language books. Family literacy activities have been increasingly emphasized in recent years. It is empowering for families to see their own traditions and practices in the wide range of multicultural books that are now available. Non-ELLs and their families can also benefit from learning about other cultures through these multicultural books. For ELLs and their parents who are not yet fluent in English, family literacy activities can also be fostered through the availability of books in various languages. See Resource 2.1 at the end of the chapter for sources of first-language materials.

Make available high-quality, age-appropriate, and visually supported lower-reading-level books that are aligned with content curriculum. Teaching ELLs who are not on grade level in terms of reading requires differentiation of materials. These materials must address standards-based curricular topics, but must also be accessible to students at lower levels of reading and language proficiency. Sources of such materials are listed in Resource 2.2.

Facilitate multiple, regular, and consistent opportunities for ELLs to interact with native speakers through cooperative learning activities and heterogeneous grouping. Many ELLs do not speak English in their home environments and wholly depend on school-based language interactions to develop their English skills. While the continued use of the first language is to be encouraged, students must be given plenty of time to practice and manipulate their newly developing language skills during the school day. ELLs need to interact with peers who have a strong command of the language during this time. It is necessary for ELLs to work not only with other ELLs; moreover, ELLs need to learn from grade-level peers who can demonstrate appropriate use of both social and academic language. Heterogeneous grouping requires that ELLs not be grouped exclusively with one another, with students receiving special education services, or with struggling students. ELLs require opportunities to work with a range of native speakers whose command of English assists in scaffolding their ELL peers to proficiency. For example, ELLs and non-ELLs might be grouped together on a research project focused on a current events topic pertinent to the ELLs' home countries. In this way, all students bring expertise to be shared in the completion of the project.

Embed the development of higher-order thinking (e.g., application, analysis, synthesis, creation, evaluation) throughout instruction. Some teachers mistakenly assume that students at lower levels of proficiency are incapable of higher-order thinking. However, language level is not necessarily indicative of cognitive development. Though teacher creativity is required in designing appropriate and accessible activities, even Level 1 students are fully capable of engaging in higher-order thinking. For example, the placement of pictures in a simple Venn diagram exemplifies a student's ability to evaluate. Graphic organizers are an excellent way to foster higher-order thinking in ELLs with lower levels of proficiency.

Make the abstract comprehensible by first demonstrating concrete applications or examples (e.g., modeling with manipulatives, experiential activities). Students new to English as the language of instruction need plenty of support in order to make sense of classroom lessons. This need is particularly significant when students are learning abstract concepts. In these situations, teachers must capitalize on more tangible examples to facilitate understanding of the abstract, especially those involving multisensory experiences. For example, in a lesson about gravity, teachers might involve students in an activity in which they ride an amusement park ride, providing a sensory experience at the outset. Additional examples of this kind of support will be provided in subsequent chapters.

Focus error correction on specific, level-appropriate aspects of language. As in assessment, error correction during instruction should target only certain, level-appropriate aspects of language. For instance, when teaching Level 4 students, a brief contextualized lesson on the correct use of dependent clauses would be more appropriate than emphasis on a list of grammatical constructions that might well be overwhelming to ELLs (and non-ELLs).

Scaffold ELLs' learning by facilitating tutoring by other students or volunteers. There are countless benefits to be gained through peer tutoring and through creating a team of volunteers to assist with classroom learning. Peer tutors learn about others and hone teamwork skills, while volunteers can expand their understandings of "the cultural other" as well. Best of all, ELL learning is fostered. Both authors have enjoyed the benefits of engaging the assistance of student and community-based volunteers in our classrooms; these individuals can be invaluable in supporting the learning of ELLs of all ages and extending overstretched budgets. Remember to provide these tutors with guidance in what topics to address with ELLs and with strategies to use during their tutoring sessions.

Create a print-rich environment using word, language, and concept walls or posters that include pictorial support. While word, language, and concept walls and posters may be initially considered to be teaching strategies suitable to the elementary setting, these all-important aids should be implemented in the secondary context as well. Many students prefer and even rely on visual learning, so the benefit of pictorially supported word, language, and concept walls and posters cannot be underestimated for the entire class, ELL or non-ELL.

While word walls may be familiar to readers, language walls are designated areas of the classroom that focus on larger chunks of language necessary in the student work. For instance, a teacher may post suggested phraseology for giving opinions (e.g., "I believe that . . ." or "It seems to me that . . ."). Concept walls are areas that introduce entire concepts (e.g., magnetism) using visuals as well as relevant words and language. In such cases, pictures, photos, and icons are all appropriate supports.

Socialize students into their new culture by explicitly guiding them in norms of behavior, speech conventions (polite ways to make requests or apologize, etc.), nonverbal communication (body language, personal space, eye contact, etc.), and other facets of the culture. In many schools, the ratio of ELLs to ESL/bilingual teachers is very high. This means that *all* teachers must not only teach language, but also serve as cultural brokers for newcomers. Anyone who has ever traveled to another culture understands the tremendous value of a kind soul willing to share insights about the "rules of the game" in the new context (e.g., how to hail a taxi, how to greet individuals of different status). As educators of students new to U.S. culture, we must embrace the role of the "kind soul" who assists newcomers in making sense of the norms and conventions of U.S. culture. These may include such simple things as how to get a turn on the playground swings or how to negotiate the cafeteria lunch line.

When utilizing the assistance of (bilingual) paraeducators, provide them with clear guidance regarding their roles and how to work effectively with students and families. Paraeducators are invaluable resources to teachers who serve ELLs and to the students themselves, often possessing bilingual abilities. However, many paraeducators may not bring with them a background in teaching. Further, these all-important staff members are not always afforded the professional development that teachers receive. Therefore, teachers must provide clear guidance to these instructional partners in terms of the characteristics of ELLs at different proficiency levels, instructional strategies appropriate for individual students, and ways to meaningfully and accurately assess ELLs at various proficiency levels. Rather than handing over a textbook and saying, "Teach her Chapter 5," teachers must provide paraeducators with specific teaching and assessment guidelines and expectations (of the kind listed on the chart and described in this volume) that are appropriate for individual students. In addition, teachers must support paraeducators, whether they are bilingual or not, in serving students from all first-language backgrounds. By sharing cultural and linguistic insights (including those gained in collaboration with others), teachers can empower paraeducators to effectively assist students from a range of cultural and linguistic backgrounds in the learning process.

Include appropriately identified ELLs in gifted and talented programming, across proficiency levels.   As mentioned earlier, limited English language proficiency does not preclude ELLs from participating in gifted and talented programming. Specialists can utilize the information presented on the chart and in this book to tailor their services to the unique needs of gifted ELLs.

Maintain English language support for ELLs who receive special education services, across proficiency levels.   In the preceding assessment section, it was pointed out that special education teachers do not often possess expertise in how to assist students in the language acquisition process. Further, there seems to be a common, though mistaken, belief that students cannot "double dip," or receive services from two programs (e.g., English language development programs and special education programs) simultaneously. In fact, correctly identified students can receive all programming to which they are entitled. Providing these services calls for collaboration across programs in some cases. Special education teachers can certainly make use of the chart and book to guide their work with ELLs, even while those students are receiving the benefit of ESL/bilingual/dual language programs.

Take steps to ensure that ELLs across proficiency levels have equal access to and participation in extracurricular activities.   When analyzing membership in each curricular or extracurricular group, it must be noted whether there is balanced representation of all students. In terms of extracurricular activities such as music lessons, (marching) band, chorus, school newspaper, after-school clubs, drama teams, and sports teams, teachers should not overlook the benefits of participation for ELLs. Such activities can provide ready-made networks of social connections based on common interest to promote interaction and simultaneously hasten language acquisition. For example, one high school band teacher agreed to provide summer trumpet lessons for a newly arrived Level I 9th grader. As a result, the student, who had never had music lessons previously, was able to participate in the marching band during all four years of his high school career, making friends, attending school events, traveling with the band, and enhancing his language development.

Subsequently, a program to collect donated musical instruments from graduating seniors was implemented so that elementary ELLs, whose families might be unable to afford the monthly rental cost for an instrument, could begin to study music at an early age with their native English-speaking peers. Fueled by the success of this effort, teachers began to interrogate the equity of other school programs.

Conclusion

This chapter has described fundamental considerations and general guidelines for effective teaching and assessment of ELLs. Chapters 3 through 7 address ELL assessment and instruction for each of the five language proficiency levels by providing level-specific student scenarios and descriptions and describing practical strategies with teacher-friendly examples for classroom implementation.

Professional Development Activities

Activity 1.1   Planning for Strategy Implementation

Make a list of the three general assignment/assessment strategies that you consider to be most important:

1. _____

2. _____

3. _____

Why are these most important?

_____

_____

_____

When will you begin to employ them? (List specific assignments/assessments.)

_____

_____

_____

Make a list of the three general instructional strategies that you view to be most important:

1. _____

2. _____

3. _____

Copyright © 2010. Caslon, Inc. All rights reserved. The first purchaser may photocopy this page for classroom and personal use.

Why are these most important?

_____

_____

_____

When will you begin to employ them? (List specific lessons.)

_____

_____

_____

Copyright © 2010. Caslon, Inc. All rights reserved. The first purchaser may photocopy this page for classroom and personal use.

Professional Development Resources

Resource 2.1 Sources of Materials in Students' First Languages

Asia for Kids
4480 Lake Forest Drive, No. 302
Cincinnati, Ohio 45242
(800) 888-9681
www.asiaforkids.com

Colorín Colorado:
   Helping Children Read . . . and Succeed!
www.colorincolorado.org

Multicultural Books and Videos
28880 Southfield Road, Suite 183
Lathrup Village, MI 48076
800-567-2220
www.multiculturalbooksandvideos.com

MyLibros.com
6446 River Ridge Road
New Port Richey, FL 34653
727-847-0246 or 941-448-1985
http://www.mylibros.com/

Pan Asian Publications (USA), Inc.
29564 Union City Boulevard
Union City, CA 94587
800-909-8088
www.panap.com

Russian Publishing House
www.russianpublishinghouse.com

SBD Spanish Book Distributor
6706 Sawmill Road
Dallas, Texas 75252-5816
1-800-609-2113
http://www.sbdbooks.com/

SpanishToys.com
P.O. Box 70250, Suite 206
San Juan, PR 00936-8250
800-436-3449
http://www.spanishtoys.com/

Resource 2.2   Sources of High-Quality, Age-Appropriate, Lower-Reading-Level Materials

Delta Systems, Inc.
(ESL phonics materials and other resources)
1400 Miller Parkway
McHenry, IL 60050-7030
1-800-323-8270
http://www.deltapublishing.com/index.cfm

Lakeshore Learning Materials
(developmental prereading and reading
  materials)
2695 East Dominguez Street
Carson, CA 90895
1-800-778-4456

Millmark Education
(content books aligned with TESOL
  Standards)
P.O. 30239
Bethesda, MD 20824
1-877-322-8020
www.millmarkeducation.com

National Geographic School Publishing
Hampton-Brown
(inZone Books—Grades 6–12
  [reading levels: grades 1–9)
P.O. Box 4002865
Des Moines, IA 50340
www.ngsp.com

Perfection Learning
(content-based leveled readers, content-
  based materials designed for ELLs)
1000 North Second Avenue
P.O. Box 500
Logan, IA 51546-0500
1-800-831-4190
www.perfectionlearning.com

Rigby Publishers
(InStep Readers—Levels A through T)
(Sails Literacy Series)
HMH Supplemental Publishers
181 Ballardvale Street
P.O. Box 7050
Wilmington, MA 01887
1-800-289-4490
www.rigby.com

Saddleback Educational Publishing
(content-based leveled readers)
Three Watson
Irvine, CA 92618-2767
1-888-735-2225
www.sdlback.com

3

Differentiation Strategies for Level 1 Students

What the best and wisest parent wants for his own child,
that must the community want for all of its children.
any other idea for our schools is narrow and unlovely;
acted upon, it destroys our democracy.

—John Dewey

The ability to recognize and meaningfully address the range of student capabilities at each level of developing English language proficiency is the key to English language learner (ELL) differentiation. In this chapter, using scenarios based on real students, we pinpoint student characteristics of Level 1 ELLs and describe in detail what Level 1 students know and can do or will soon be able to do. We then suggest appropriate and meaningful assignment/assessment and instructional strategies that these students can comprehend and engage with so that teachers can meet Level 1 students "where they are."

While the suggested strategies are designed to elicit production for Level 1 students in listening, speaking, reading, and writing, teachers are reminded to make it their goal to push students to reach ever higher targets, providing scaffolding in instruction and assessment designed to support students' advancement to the next level of both content knowledge, skills, and abilities *and* language proficiency. This purpose can be accomplished by both eliciting Level 1 language and, where possible and appropriate, providing and eliciting examples of Level 2 language production.

Considering Variation in Level 1 Students' Backgrounds

Student
Scenarios

Corina is a 7th grade student who has just arrived from Guatemala and enrolled in an urban middle school. In the classroom, her teachers note that she often keeps to herself with downcast eyes. She does not communicate verbally with classmates or the teacher, though she will sometimes respond to some commonly used classroom verbal cues that are visually supported. Teachers are concerned that when presented with a textbook, Corina is unsure of how to hold or open the book. She is unable to write her name or even hold a pencil.

Fajar is another 7th grader who has just begun to attend the same urban middle school, though he is from Indonesia. He, too, is silent in class, but teachers immediately notice that he seems ready to try to engage with print materials. Though he can only respond to basic verbal commands at this point, Fajar can write his name and can copy writing from the textbook and other print materials.

Corina and Fajar, while both Level 1 students, exemplify the difference between students with no formal education and undeveloped first-language literacy and their counterparts who arrive in U.S. classrooms with varying amounts of previous schooling and, in some cases, demonstrate grade-level achievement in their first languages. Though both Corina and Fajar fall within the same English proficiency level (Level 1), they are very different in terms of their readiness to participate in middle school learning activities. Each will require distinctly different and specific approaches to both assessment and instruction that take into consideration their disparate academic preparation.

Corina, as a student preliterate in any language, must receive instruction in early literacy development from the very beginning of her enrollment in U.S. schools, despite the fact that this kind of literacy instruction is not typically part of the middle school curriculum. As preliterate and low-literate students arrive in the upper grades, the urgency for immediate, meaningful literacy instruction dramatically intensifies. Remedial literacy instruction (designed to "shore up" earlier instruction) that may be available in some middle school contexts is not appropriate for Corina. Rather, she needs separate instruction that is grounded in best practice for initial early literacy development and is, at the same time, sensitive to the needs of culturally and linguistically diverse learners. Her mainstream teachers at the upper grade levels cannot be expected to provide this intensive developmental literacy instruction in their content classrooms; instead, school districts must create programs to meet the literacy development needs of students with limited and interrupted formal schooling.

Statistically, Corina is considered at-risk and will likely drop out if she does not receive responsive instruction.

In contrast with Corina, Fajar comes to the classroom having already developed grade-level literacy in his first language. This fact makes him fundamentally different from Corina in terms of his assessment and instructional needs. The research literature clearly reveals that literacy skills acquired in one's first language transfer to the second language (Dressler & Kamil, 2006), accelerating and supporting the process of learning to read in the second language. While Corina has little to no experience with print to draw upon in becoming an English reader and writer, even needing practice learning to hold and manipulate a pen or pencil, Fajar is prepared to transfer and apply his previously developed skills to learning English reading and writing.

Level 1 Student Descriptors

Level 1 students come to English-speaking classrooms with little to no English proficiency. Often, such students are in a state of shock, having come from situations vastly different from U.S. classrooms. As a result, many newcomer students are unclear about what to expect and how to behave in their new environment. Many times, such students attempt to integrate into their new schools by copying the conduct of native speakers of English. Further, the newcomers display predictable characteristics of the typical language acquisition and acculturation processes. These behaviors may be interpreted by some educators as indicative of inappropriate attitudes, learning difficulties, or cognitive deficits, as discussed in Chapter 1. This potential confusion requires an informed advocate who understands both the language acquisition process and the cultural factors that impact each student's integration into the classroom. Every teacher who works with an ELL must be that advocate. With a range of cultural issues addressed in Chapter 1, the linguistic characteristics of Level 1 students will be considered next.

Listening

In terms of listening, learners at Level 1 may be hearing new sounds not generally articulated or heard in their first languages. This initial stage of language learning is critical, since being able to hear and recognize new individual sounds is a precursor to being able to articulate them verbally. In addition, students will begin to understand words, phrases, and commands that are commonly used and followed by modeling (e.g., "Sit down" accompanied by a gesture toward the student's chair). Level 1 students cannot be expected to make sense of lecture or text alone; they rely on context clues in the environment in order to construct meaning from classroom-based communication.

Speaking

Teachers should not make the mistake of thinking that students who are silent are not learning. In terms of speech production, Level 1 students are often experiencing the "silent period" (Krashen, 1982), absorbing and processing new input in preparation for future language production. (Note that the length of this silent period is variable; students may be nonproducers of spoken language for days, weeks, or months.) Students may be able to respond with nonverbal communication, but oral communication is generally brief or memorized, often characterized by individual words or memorized phrases (e.g., "How are you?"). However, students at the higher end of the Level 1 continuum may also generate original chunks of language.

During this time, students' language development is largely focused on "survival English," an important aspect of basic interpersonal communication skills (BICS) (Cummins, 2001). It is essential that every teacher take responsibility for assisting students to learn formulaic language related to successful daily interactions and tasks (e.g., "Good morning" or "How are you?") by promoting interaction with peers. These informal interactions assist the ELL in becoming comfortable and in developing a repertoire of meaningful words or phrases to successfully take care of "social business," whether on the playground, in the lunchroom, in the hallway, or in other contexts. Such opportunities for sustained peer interaction should be embedded in daily instruction; engaging with peers allows ELLs to develop successful communication skills by manipulating language and modeling after native-English-speakers. Such linguistically developmental opportunities might be the only times the ELL engages with a native speaker, particularly if English is not spoken in the home.

In terms of academic language, students at Level 1 are, of course, only starting the journey toward proficiency. Recall the definition given for academic language proficiency in Chapter 2:

> knowing and being able to "use general and content-specific vocabulary, specialized or complex grammatical structures, and multifarious language functions and discourse structures—all for the purpose of acquiring new knowledge and skills, interacting about a topic, or imparting information to others" (Bailey, 2007, pp. 10–11)

Students at Level 1 are just beginning to become familiar with general vocabulary and language structures, though they may begin to become aware of some of commonly used academic language functions in the classroom (e.g., those used in classroom routines, such as requests to take out or put away classroom materials).

Reading

With regard to reading, the difference between students who can read in their first languages and those who cannot quickly emerges. Students who are pre-literate in any language cannot yet be expected to garner meaning from print; instead, they rely on context clues (e.g., pictures and other visual supports) in order to make sense of print-based materials. In contrast, students who have reading skills in their first languages may begin to transfer those skills to English. Before new English sounds and letters can be matched, however, ELLs must have a strong foundation and familiarity with the range of English sounds (phonemic awareness).

Writing

As with reading, the writing skills of Level 1 students are very limited, but with appropriate instruction, these students can begin to produce some written language. At the lower end of the Level 1 continuum, their work may take the form of drawing or copying letters, words, or longer stretches of written text. As writing ability develops, Level 1 students may (depending upon their level of speaking proficiency) also dictate words and phrases. Level 1 students can also write letters, words, and phrases across the range of Level 1 writing proficiency. However, again, the differences between preliterate students and those who can transfer writing ability from their first language must be recognized and acknowledged. Students with limited L1 literacy skills will naturally take longer to progress in the area of writing than their more L1-literate counterparts. Even copying letters may be a laborious process for these students.

A Word About Language Objectives

As teachers write language objectives for their lessons, these goals and expectations should be aligned with what students at different proficiency levels are able to do linguistically. Teachers are advised to use the student descriptors from the chart (explicated for Level 1 students in the preceding paragraphs) in crafting appropriate language objectives. The guidance for assessments/assignments, discussed next, offers further direction in terms of appropriate language objectives for Level 1 students, while the instructional strategies discussed toward the end of the chapter provide advice in how to facilitate Level 1 student achievement of both language and content objectives.

A Sample Differentiated Assignment for Level 1 Students

In Chapter 8 we provide a template for differentiating assignments for ELLs across all five proficiency levels. In order to assist teachers in thinking about differentiation for students in each of the levels as they read the book, we include a sample assignment in Chapters 3 through 7 using a portion of the template. These sample differentiated assignments include the assignment as it is designed for fully English proficient students, a differentiated assignment for students at the chapter's focal language proficiency level (Level 1 in this chapter), and a differentiated assignment for students at the next higher level of language proficiency (Level 2 in this chapter). The inclusion of these sample assignments aims to achieve three goals:

1. For teachers to see how a single assignment might be differentiated for students at each proficiency level as they read all the level-specific chapters.

2. For the sample assignments to introduce some of the level-specific assignment/assessment strategies and instructional strategies discussed in each chapter.

3. For teachers to recognize and internalize the importance of pushing students to the next higher level of language production by thinking about those expectations as they consider their work with students at a given proficiency level.

The assignment that we will use to exemplify differentiation in each of the five level-specific chapters focuses on getting students to write a clear set of instructions. Students are able to choose the task that they write instructions for and are given some scaffolding and support in order to be able to complete the assignment successfully. Further, essential learning (Wiggins & McTighe, 2006) has been identified for the assignment: clarity in communicating steps in a process, use of transition words, and logical sequencing. The essential learning is conceptualized here as the focal learning of the assignment that is tied to the standards and the curriculum.

In order to think about how to differentiate assignments for ELLs, we must consider the aspects of the assignment that can or should be differentiated. In most cases, the standards-based content or topic (from the curriculum) must remain the same at all levels of language proficiency, since all students must generally be taught to the same set of standards. Therefore, the aspects of the assignment that can be differentiated are the language-based expectations and the scaffolding and support. In order to focus on each of these three areas specifically, we offer a template that divides any assignment vertically into these three aspects:

- Language-based expectations (row 1 of the template)

- Standards-based content or topic (from the curriculum) (row 2 of the template)

- Scaffolding and support (row 3 of the template)

Table 3.1 is a sample template for the sake of illustration. Note that the template-based assignment for students at each proficiency level is read vertically by following the template column that indicates a given proficiency level.

Table 3.1 Sample template

(Language proficiency level listed here)
Language-Based Expectations:
Standards-Based Content or Topic (from the curriculum):
Scaffolding and Support:

Returning to the sample assignment used in all five level-specific chapters, recall that it focuses on having students write a set of instructions. The assignment is conceptualized for fully English proficient students as follows:

Write a set of instructions using grade-level vocabulary and sentence structures for a self-selected task **using a model assignment, a teacher demonstration of the task using a "think-aloud," a sequential graphic organizer for planning to write, a language wall with sequencing words and key sentence structures, and feedback designed to push students to full proficiency according to grade-level writing standards to guide writing.**

(Essential learning: clarity in communicating steps in a process, use of transition words, logical sequencing)

You may immediately notice that the language of the assignment is a bit stilted, but there is clear reason for this. The italicized print in the sample assignment denotes the language-based expectations for the assignment that are written in the first row of the template. (This is the aspect of the assignment that is differentiated according to students' language proficiency levels. As such, the demands of this aspect will be greater for students at higher proficiency levels.) The plain-font section of the assignment is the standards-based content or topic taken from the curriculum, which is written in the second row of the template. (This should *not* be differentiated for students at varying proficiency levels, as the goal is to maintain the same content standards for all students.) Finally, the bold-faced section represents the scaffolding and support offered to students, and this is written in the third row of the template. (Note that the scaffolding and support offered to students will likely be greater for students at lower proficiency levels.) The essential learning (Wiggins & McTighe, 2006) noted with the assignment clarifies the instructional goals of the assignment and provides guidance regarding how to differentiate expectations for students at different proficiency levels.[1]

Table 3.2 is the preceding sample assignment converted to template format, with each aspect of the assignment noted in its respective row. Using a mini-template with three columns, teachers can then differentiate the assignment for students at different proficiency levels by

* adjusting the language-based expectations based on the "student descriptors" and "assignment/assessment strategies" listed on the chart and discussed in this volume (keeping the essential learning in mind),

* maintaining the standards-based content or topic for all students, and

* providing the necessary scaffolding and support based on the "instructional strategies" listed on the chart and discussed herein.

In Table 3.3, the assignment designed for fully English proficient students is differentiated for students at Level 1 (the focal level of this chapter) and Level 2. Again, the purpose for including the Level 2 assignment is to remind teachers that they must always bear in mind the next higher level of proficiency when working with individual students in order to

---

[1]Though the essential learning of each assignment must be facilitated for students at all proficiency levels, we recognize that there are times when this aspect of the assignment may need to be adjusted because it is dependent upon students' language abilities (e.g., "Essential learning: construction of a five-paragraph essay"). In these cases, teachers must work to ensure that the eventual achievement of this essential learning is the focus of the assignment, yet they can differentiate expectations accordingly.

Table 3.2 Sample assignment

Fully English Proficient
Language-Based Expectations: Write a set of instructions using grade-level vocabulary and sentence structures
Standards-Based Content or Topic (from the curriculum): for a self-selected task
Scaffolding and Support: using • a model assignment, • teacher demonstration of the task using a "think-aloud," • a sequential graphic organizer to use in planning to write, • a language wall with sequencing words and key sentence structures, and • feedback designed to push students to full proficiency according to the grade-level writing standards to guide writing.

push students toward the kinds of language production needed at that level.

As you can see in Table 3.3, the assignment has been adjusted to make it accessible for students at Level 1.[2] Teachers might collaborate in a wide range of ways to facilitate this kind of planning and related instruction. For instance, ESL/bilingual and content/classroom teachers might work together to plan the differentiated assignment, and the ESL/bilingual teacher might pull Level 1 ELLs out of the mainstream classroom for supplementary instruction and support.

---

[2] This is, of course, only one way to differentiate this particular assignment; this goal could be achieved in many other ways, as long as teachers ensure that expectations are appropriate to students' proficiency levels and necessary scaffolding and support are in place.

Table 3.3 Sample assignment differentiated for Levels 1 and 2

Consider these expectations to be the "next step" for a Level 1 student

Standards-based assignment created for fully English Proficient

Differentiation based on the "student descriptors" and "assignment/ assessment strategies" on the chart

Differentiation based on the "instructional strategies" on the chart and in the book

Fully English Proficient	Level 1	Level 2
Language-Based Expectations: Write a set of instructions using grade-level vocabulary and sentence structures	*Language-Based Expectations:* Copy words and phrases for a set of instructions	*Language-Based Expectations:* Write a set of instructions using occasional content/academic vocabulary and simple sentences
Standards-Based Content or Topic (from the curriculum): for a self-selected task		
Scaffolding and Support: using • a model assignment, • teacher demonstration of the task using a "think-aloud," • a sequential graphic organizer for planning to write, • a language wall with sequencing words and key sentence structures, and • feedback designed to push students to full proficiency according to the grade-level writing standards to guide writing.	*Scaffolding and Support:* using • a model assignment, • teacher demonstration of the task using a "think-aloud," • a sequential graphic organizer for planning to write, • photographs of chosen processes, • a language wall with sequencing words (focus on ordinal numbers), • word and picture cards featuring pretaught vocabulary (to be used when labeling the poster), • a supplementary "think-aloud" demonstration of labeling, • pictorially supported procedure texts, • realia related to processes (e.g., materials for making a peanut butter and jelly sandwich), and • level-appropriate feedback designed to push students to the next level of proficiency in writing to guide writing.	*Scaffolding and Support:* using • a model assignment, • teacher demonstration of the task using a "think-aloud," • a sequential graphic organizer for planning to write, • a language wall with sequencing words and key sentence structures, and • feedback designed to push students to full proficiency according to the grade-level writing standards to guide writing.

Necessary Assignment/Assessment Strategies for Level 1 Students

Recognizing that large-scale standardized assessment tools and classroom-based assessment tools designed for native speakers of English are inappropriate for Level 1 ELLs, teachers must develop sensitive and useful assessment procedures that take into account the cultural and linguistic needs of these students. Teachers are wholeheartedly encouraged to "think outside the box" in creating new ways to gather information about what ELLs know and can do. Knowing what students are able to do at Level 1 (described earlier) and understanding relevant student factors discussed in Chapter 1 (e.g., cultural backgrounds and norms, assessment experience) informs the development of these more appropriate and meaningful assessment procedures. In particular, the knowledge of Level 1 students' linguistic abilities prepares teachers to craft tasks appropriate for these students that are still aligned with essential learnings in the content standards and curriculum. The resulting assessment procedures will promote more accurate measurement of the content knowledge, skills, and abilities of students whose language skills preclude their meaningful participation in assessments designed for native speakers. Readers are reminded that appropriate assessment procedures can only occur at the intersection of student language proficiency, relevant student factors, and essential learning based on content standards and curricula (Figure 2.2).

Including Level 1 students in daily instruction and assessment based on the content standards and curriculum set for all students is crucial. Such inclusion not only represents best practice and is essential to maximizing ELL access to the curriculum, but it is also critical to achieving academic parity. Bear in mind that ELLs do not have the luxury of waiting until they are fluent in English to engage in essential learning of content material. From the first day in a U.S. school, each ELL is playing "catch-up" with native English-speaking peers, having to backfill vocabulary along with content, further complicated by cultural factors. As a result, the achievement of ELLs and non-ELLs is disparate from the beginning. Teachers must, through competent instruction and assessment, empower their students to take charge of their own learning, join their native English-speaking peers in achievement, and reach their full potential.

We now turn to an explanation of assessment activities for each of the language domains (listening, speaking, pre-reading, and writing). Although the assessment and instructional strategies are presented by language domain (listening, speaking, reading, and writing), the authors do not mean to imply that language domains should not be integrated in assessment and instruction. Rather, strategies are presented by domain as a way to clearly describe differentiation considerations for each domain. Best practice for assessment and instruction of ELLs integrates the four domains of language with content in natural, authentic ways.

In General

Teachers are reminded when assessing ELLs (and non-ELLs!) that assessments and instruction must be aligned in terms of both content and format. While it is obvious that students should only be assessed on that which was taught, teachers must also bear in mind that Level 1 ELLs, due to their minimal level of language proficiency, cannot be expected to linguistically extrapolate learning in a variety of ways that have not been explicitly taught. That is, ELLs must be assessed using a format similar to the format of instruction. For example, if students are taught a concept using a graphic organizer and visual support, they should also be given the benefit of those scaffolds when they are assessed. (This approach may also be appropriate for non-ELLs.)

While some assessment strategies are tied to specific domains of language (listening, speaking, reading, and writing), others are more general in nature. These are addressed next.

Create and use assignments/assessments that allow students to demonstrate content knowledge, skills, and abilities without language mastery. As Level 1 students begin to understand and produce language, they are likely to understand much more than they are able to demonstrate using only language. Empowering these students through the use of teacher-created assessments that capitalize upon what Level 1 students *can* do is essential to their academic development and motivation. For example, rather than expecting a Level 1 student to complete a multiple-choice test focused on story comprehension, a teacher might ask the student to sequence pictures to demonstrate understanding of the plot of a specific story.

Focus on correct answers rather than errors and omissions. In an effort to encourage newcomers, teachers can increase engagement by focusing on student successes rather than shortcomings. Making a special effort to recognize and validate Level 1 students' attempts to communicate pays dividends as students increase production in a comfortable environment. For example, if students recount the steps in a process (e.g., washing one's hands), teachers should focus on the meaning without correcting pronunciation.

Allow students to complete assessment procedures under the guidance of a bilingual teacher or paraeductor.   Level 1 students may understand far more than they are able to express in English. For this reason, bilingual teachers and paraeducators can be invaluable in assessing what students know and can do in the content areas. This support can be provided individually or, perhaps, in a small-group setting. One example of bilingual support would be translating the directions into the ELL's first language. Another example would be translating parts of test questions, if language is not part of what is being assessed and graded. These supports both lead to a more accurate picture of what students know and can do in the short term and to increased student independence in the long term.

A third type of support that falls in a somewhat separate category is allowing students to process content in their first languages. This processing pays large dividends in terms of content learning. Working with a bilingual educator can transform the assessment experience into one that facilitates both learning and assessment. While some teachers, at first blush, may be concerned that turning the test into a teaching and learning situation seems to constitute "giving students the answers," we must remember the purpose of our entire enterprise: student learning. If the ELL gains understanding of a given concept only at the time of the assessment, so be it! (This result is better than no learning at all.) Such situations may call for repeated or "cyclical" assessment at a later date to ensure that learning has "stuck." This cyclical assessment is appropriate and necessary if the initial assessment was the student's first opportunity to learn the material, as could be the case with highly abstract concepts. Affording students the "opportunity to learn," even so late as during an assessment, is an inherent part of fairness, as described in the *Standards for Educational and Psychological Testing* (AERA, APA, & NCME, 1999). If test procedures are not fair, then the whole assessment process loses utility. The usefulness of the assessment is lost because, without fairness, validity becomes questionable. If test scores do not truly reflect what students know and can do, the interpretations of the student's test score are not valid and the entire assessment procedure is meaningless.

Note: Under no circumstances should a test be translated in its entirety. Doing so does not tend to result in equivalent tests (Solano-Flores & Trumbull, 2003) and is an unreasonable demand to place on bilingual paraeducators.

Weight graded components according to students' linguistic strengths. Realizing that acquiring listening and speaking typically happens before the development of reading and writing skills, teachers should consider weighting oral demonstrations of learning more heavily for students at the lower levels of language proficiency. If, however, the student has learned English in isolation, focusing on developing reading and writing without the benefit of authentic verbal interactions, as is the case in some programs abroad, teachers could consider weighting written demonstrations of learning more heavily. Such linguistically responsive assessment practice recognizes the continuum of language development while seeking to ascertain student learning in the content areas. Since teachers of ELLs already have access to language proficiency assessment data that outline students' linguistic capabilities, they already know that the reading and writing abilities of Level 1 students are underdeveloped. Teachers also know that listening and speaking usually develop before reading and writing. As a result, it makes sense at Level 1 to weight the domains of listening and speaking more heavily than those of reading and writing for grading purposes. There is no reason to punish a language learner for a predictable language development phenomenon. The demonstration of the desired content knowledge, skills, and abilities, often in oral format, should be given the greatest weight in determining an ELL's grade. Issues of language usage should, most likely, not be graded at Level 1. This point will be elucidated further in Chapter 8 where differentiated grading is discussed.

Make the assignment/assessment process comprehensible by explaining the directions orally and providing visual support (e.g., realia, icons, manipulatives, modeling and models). In order to accurately determine what Level 1 students know and can do, it is imperative that students understand the assessment task or assignment at hand. Since these students likely have very limited listening and speaking skills (though some students at Level 1 in reading and writing may exhibit higher levels of listening and speaking), it is recommended that special attention be given to the directions. While oral explanation certainly facilitates the understanding of written directions, teachers are also advised to provide visual clarification such as demonstrations or examples. Only when students understand the task can their performance be considered to be a true indication of what students know and can do in the content areas.

Listening and Speaking

When assessing Level 1 students' content knowledge, skills, and abilities using listening and speaking, teachers must remain mindful that these students may be at a preproduction stage of second language development. This level of language proficiency limits the kinds of activities in which Level 1 ELLs can engage or participate. Nevertheless, Level 1 students can demonstrate their cognitively advanced understanding in a variety of ways, assuming that hearing is not an issue. (That is, students at low levels of language proficiency are capable of higher-order thinking.) Furthermore, such assessment opportunities lend themselves to incremental and graduated scaffolding, the ideal means for facilitating the simultaneous acquisition of language and content knowledge, skills, and abilities.

Evaluate comprehension by means of student nonverbal communication (e.g., locating or selecting by pointing, mimicking, "thumbs up/thumbs down," gestures). At the very heart of learning and communicating in a new language is a student-teacher relationship that encourages and invites a student to participate, as in where a welcoming and supportive teacher can work with a comfortable newcomer to facilitate both language and content learning. One key way to achieve this goal with Level 1 students is through the use of physical response to indicate understanding. Examples include having students point to demonstrate their comprehension of various concepts in such situations as answering simple "survival" questions (e.g., "Where is your locker?" or "Which lunch do you want?"). Another way that students can use physical response to demonstrate cognitive engagement is to mimic, as in repeating steps in a modeled activity (e.g., planting a seed). A third example of physical response is to display judgment or evaluation by showing a "thumbs up" or "thumbs down" signal. Other kinds of gestures would include nodding or shaking of the head and raising the hand.

Note that intercultural awareness is essential when working with gestures; the "thumbs up" signal has different meanings in different cultures, and students use different techniques to get a teacher's attention in different countries (e.g., snapping of fingers). Teachers must ensure that students understand what is meant by gestures used in the class-room.

Ask for demonstration of understanding (e.g., pointing; drawing; matching; copying; using pictures or realia to sequence, categorize, prioritize, or evaluate). Demonstration is a second general way that students can show understanding of concepts without language mastery. Students can simply point at objects to demonstrate understanding. Another example is drawing. Though it must be understood that not all ELLs are artists, students can create simple sketches to depict content knowledge, skills, and abilities (e.g., habitats for different types of animals). Matching can also be used to ascertain student learning; for example, students can match various picture cards to show that they understand relationships (e.g., types of rock and how they are formed). Copying is a third method that students can employ in demonstrating understanding (e.g., labeling layers of the rain forest). Students can also use realia and pictures to sequence concepts (e.g., phases of the water cycle), categorize items (e.g., food groups), prioritize importance (e.g., levels of the food chain), and evaluate (e.g., effective means of controlling erosion).

Prompt the repetition of a teacher cue or a short response. Repetition represents a third technique that teachers can utilize in ascertaining student learning. For example, teachers can ask students to repeat key "survival" words (e.g., yes or no) in response to questions. Alternatively, students can be expected to produce short responses, whether individual words or memorized phrases (e.g., Teacher prompt: "What is this?" with student response: "mammal"—in a categorizing task contrasting mammals, reptiles, and fish).

Test orally using everyday language to elicit individual words and brief chunks of language. Through authentic engagement with classroom learning and social activities, Level 1 students can be expected to begin producing relevant language in context. Teachers can consider their anecdotal observations of student interactions an appropriate indicator of students' learning or they can "interview" students to ascertain their level of content understanding. Everyday language includes common, nontechnical language used in general communication. In contrast, general academic language is that which does not typically appear in a social conversation, but includes vocabulary and structures exclusive to classroom instruction, academic texts, and standardized and, often, classroom tests. Level 1 students may not be able to engage with this type of language. So, when assessing students in social studies, a teacher might ask students to describe "what the land in states is like" rather than "the terrain of states."

Allow first-language oral responses, when appropriate. Students can also respond in their first language to demonstrate listening comprehension. In order to ascertain their understanding, teachers would, of course need a working knowledge of the student's first language or would need to rely on the assistance of another school professional. For example, this strategy could be used to determine if students understand the meaning of a given word in English (e.g., the teacher says a word in English and the student responds with the word in the first language).

Pre-reading and Reading

It is important to bear in mind that the age of an ELL is an inadequate predictor of literacy development in the first language. Further, particularly in the case of the older pre-literate ELL, early literacy activities and development are essential. Teachers must ensure that the explicit development of literacy skills assumes a high priority. It should be noted that this is not remedial reading instruction; rather, this may be a student's first exposure to literacy instruction of any kind. Since the student is acquiring English while working to "catch up" to native English-speaking peers, special attention must be given to integrating meaningful content and literacy instruction. For high school students, this instruction must facilitate literacy development in order to empower students to earn graduation credit in a very timely manner. This urgency may require that new classes or programs be developed and put in place if ELLs are to be afforded the opportunity to engage with the curriculum, achieve academically, and graduate from high school.

Recall that students at Level 1 should not be expected to gain meaning from print alone. However, Level I students can engage with information read aloud, as long as it is visually supported. Pre-literate students should also be engaged in pre-reading activities such as the learning of letters, print directionality, book-handling skills, sounds (phonemic awareness), letter-sound relationships (phonics), and vocabulary. Students can demonstrate their learning using pre-reading skills through the following strategies:

Use high-quality, age-appropriate, lower-reading-level materials that provide extensive visual support, expecting comprehension to be dependent upon visuals provided. Level 1 students must not be expected to read tests in order to demonstrate their learning. Instead, if reading is required for assessment tasks or assignments, teachers should employ extensive visual support to students in order to facilitate understanding of the task. For example, a teacher might put a diagram of the water cycle on a test and ask students to match key words to the various parts of the diagram rather than expect students to match words and printed definitions.

Elicit physical response (e.g., locating or selecting by pointing, hand raising). Physical response can be used to assess both pre-reading skills and content understanding of Level 1 students. For example, students can be asked to point to specific letters of the alphabet or point to a picture of a word that represents a certain category (e.g., animal, vegetable, or mineral). Students can also be asked to raise their hands to indicate recognition or understanding (e.g., when they hear a specific sound or word).

Ask for demonstration of understanding (e.g., sequencing, drawing, matching, mimicking). Students can demonstrate and use pre-reading skills in a variety of ways. They can sequence pictures to show understanding (e.g., scenes from a story that they have seen acted out with puppets). Drawing can also be used to indicate comprehension. For instance, students could be asked to sketch an example of a cell after a visually supported science lesson. Matching could be used in a variety of academic ways, as in having students match a letter to a picture of a word that starts with the sound of that letter. Finally, mimicking is a viable assessment method for prereading skills and for using prereading skills. Students can demonstrate book-handling skills (e.g., turning pages appropriately), role-play the actions of a character, or act out their interpretations of layers found in the rain forest.

Prompt the repetition of a teacher cue (speaking or singing). Repetition can also be used to assess students' pre-reading skills development and content understanding. For instance, students can simply repeat after the teacher who utters a letter name or sound accompanied by visual support (e.g., a picture or an actual object), in order to ensure accurate pronunciation. This repetition also extends to word practice. Students can also reiterate sentences read aloud, as long as they are visually supported in order to ensure comprehensibility of the content. Finally, repetition of visually contextualized poems, rhymes, chants, and songs can be used to convey and ascertain content learning (as long as the words are made comprehensible through some type of sensory support).

Ask students to retell visually supported stories and texts presented with props and acting. Students at Level 1 are capable of understanding contextualized oral presentations of material, including read-alouds of stories and other texts. However, visual support such as props and acting is crucial to this understanding. Only when teaching has been made comprehensible can students be expected to internalize information and demonstrate understanding. Students at Level 1 in reading can, depending upon their level of spoken language proficiency, retell stories and texts to demonstrate learning. Bear in mind, however, that these students may need to make use of the visual supports in their retelling to bridge gaps in communication if their oral language skill is at the beginning level. For example, to retell a story the student could use a puppet or other realia to reenact the story.

Test orally using everyday language to elicit individual words and brief chunks of language. As stated earlier, oral testing is a far better means to assess student learning than expecting Level 1 students to produce writing on traditional paper and pencil tests. Teachers are advised to "count" their observations and student responses to oral questions as test data. According to many in the field, oral language development is a critical aspect of pre-reading development for ELLs and should be an integral component of assessment of both prereading skills and content, particularly at the early stages of language development.

For students literate in the first language, support first-language reading by providing appropriate materials. Finally, as emphasized in Chapter 1, the ability to read in the first language should not be underestimated in terms of its value and support in second-language reading acquisition. Provided that students are already literate in their first languages, they might benefit from the support of content materials in those languages, particularly if they have received first-language instruction on a topic (see Resource 2.1 at the end of the chapter for a list of sources of materials in other languages). Although test translation is not recommended, as stated previously, something as simple as a glossary of terms in the first language might assist a Level 1 student in completing an assignment or assessment task (as long as the student is literate in the L1 and knows those terms in the L1).

Even if students are not literate in the first language, they can benefit from early literacy instruction in that language. This, of course, requires having a teacher who is fluent in the student's first language and skilled in the teaching of reading. The results of such early literacy development can and should be assessed using first-language materials, bearing in mind that, as a rule of thumb, the language of a test should be the same as the language of instruction.

Writing

The pre-literate ELL, regardless of age, urgently needs explicit instruction in all aspects of literacy development in the form of a comprehensive, well-planned program exclusively for students who do not have experience with the written word. The development of writing skills generally takes pre-literate students much longer than students who already have first-language literacy in place. In fact, some informed and proactive schools identify preliterate ELLs for placement in intensive programs that focus on reading and writing skills. This type of targeted literacy development is the gateway for these students to reach academic success. The need for such specific and explicit development of foundational reading and writing cannot be overstated. This instruction must be highly contextualized and focused on meaning, rather than consisting of isolated drills and decontextualized exercises. It is incumbent upon schools that serve pre-literate students to "meet them where they are" and ensure academic parity with their native English-speaking peers. The first non-negotiable step to academic achievement in the United States is making certain that every student can read and write in English.

Students who come to U.S. schools with developed literacy skills in their first language have a far simpler task, yet still require explicit attention to reading and writing development in English. However, if these students come from language backgrounds that do not share the English alphabet (e.g., Chinese, Japanese, Arabic, Hindi), they require support similar to their pre-literate counterparts. While students literate in first languages that use writing systems unlike the English alphabet understand the concepts of reading and writing, they require specific literacy instruction at the pre-reading level related to phonemic awareness, letter formation, concepts of print, letter-sound relationships, and so on. Schools should be prepared with a concrete, research-based response plan for any student who arrives without developed L1 reading and writing skills, regardless of the student's age.

By definition, Level 1 students are at the beginning of the continuum of English writing and can be expected to produce only limited amounts of print. In fact, it is entirely appropriate to credit drawing and copying as legitimate writing skills at this early stage of writing development. Clearly, Level 1 students cannot be expected to complete grade-level writing assessments. (A possible exception would be for students in kindergarten or 1st grade where early writing development is the focus of instruction for all students.) Further, for any Level 1 student, absolute accuracy, neatness, and clarity are unreasonable expectations. (Think in terms of appropriate levels of production for a native English-speaking beginning writer.) Having received visual support in instruction, Level 1 students can represent their learning on paper through drawing, copying, dictating, labeling, and writing short phrases. Following are some appropriate writing assignment/assessment strategies for Level 1 students:

Elicit beginning writing (e.g., drawing; copying or labeling; production of letters, words, numbers, and phrases). Students can demonstrate understanding of content-area information through various early writing activities. For example, drawing is an early approximation of written communication. Students can create sketches of content learning to demonstrate their understanding (e.g., a sketch of various types of animals). Producing individual letters and numbers and combinations thereof (e.g., in a dictation assignment) is a reasonable expectation for Level 1 students. These learners can also be credited with writing when copying the written word, as in labeling the stages of the water cycle on a diagram or poster. They may also generate writing of words and phrases on their own, though many errors are likely to be present.

Use visually supported graphic organizers that students complete with pictures, words, or short phrases to check for understanding. The beauty of graphic organizers is that they add an underlying deeper dimension to content that allows students to apply knowledge, make connections, and understand interrelationships. Graphic organizers serve as an excellent springboard for teachers to employ in supporting Level 1 writers because they help students to articulate ideas and relationships that they intuitively know, but need scaffolding and modeling to express. For example, students could complete a Venn diagram using pictures and, possibly, words to compare and contrast the United States and their country of birth.

Require students to supplement early writing with visual support to enhance meaning (e.g., drawing, magazine pictures, clip art). At Level 1, students begin to communicate meaning through pictures and then add the written word. When writing ability starts to develop, these pictorial representations should not be eliminated; rather, they should be insisted upon for their ability to support students' attempts to communicate meaning. Teachers can keep a supply of old magazines in the classroom for this purpose, as well as allow students to draw or use digital images to make their early writing more comprehensible.

One particularly powerful writing assignment for Level 1 students takes the form of journaling. In one authentic incarnation of this assignment, students complete a weekly journal describing what they did on the weekend. This particular assignment has been found to be an excellent entrée into the world of writing for students at the beginning of the English language acquisition process because it is explicitly linked to student experience. Further, it helps students to internalize the fact that writing is "thought on paper," which is especially important for students who are writing for the first time. As an additional benefit, teachers get to know about their students' interests and activities through this journaling assignment. To enrich the journal, students can supplement their writing with pictures or drawings to support the clarity of their communication.

For students literate in the first language, welcome first-language writing, as appropriate. Teachers can support Level 1 students who are L1-literate by encouraging writing in their first languages. Even if the teacher is not fluent in the student's native language, this beginning practice can be useful in promoting student engagement, appropriate classroom behavior, and self-esteem. Collecting first-language writing samples can be a meaningful assessment practice in terms of understanding the extent to which the student is literate in the first language (e.g., extended writing likely represents more advanced writing skill than the painstaking creation of isolated words or letters). Further, allowing the use of the first language demonstrates an acceptance of and respect for the student's heritage. Allowing writing in the first language will, in the long run, encourage increased student production and scaffold performance to writing in English. Teachers who want to gauge student understanding by allowing responses in the student's first language must possess an understanding of that language or rely on the assistance of another school professional who does. Examples of this sort of writing assessment would include a description of the student's family or neighborhood or a daily journal about the student's activities at home.

Having considered appropriate assessment strategies for Level 1 students using the four domains of listening, speaking, reading, and writing, teachers can better create assessment procedures well suited to students who are early in the process of acquiring English. Assessing the content knowledge, skills, and abilities of students at the lower levels of proficiency is necessarily limited to activities that do not depend heavily upon language mastery. The next step in the "backward lesson design" (Wiggins & McTighe, 2006) process is for teachers to consider ways to ensure that students are fully prepared to demonstrate their learning on such teacher-created differentiated assignments and assessments. This targeted and differentiated instruction, which prepares Level 1 students to engage with Level 1 assignments and assessment, is the topic of the next section.

Necessary Instructional Strategies for Level 1 Students

In order to prepare Level 1 students to demonstrate content knowledge, skills, and abilities, teachers must take four critical action steps:

1. First, they must carefully examine any assumptions they might have about an individual student's background knowledge and language development.

2. They can provide appropriate instruction only if they become familiar with the student's background, including issues of language, culture, and experience (e.g., previous schooling), as described in Chapter 1.

3. Informed by this crucial information, teachers can then pinpoint the individual instructional level of each student, thereby providing relevant and strategic instruction that advances language development and content knowledge, skills, and abilities.

4. With such an awareness of individual student indicators, teachers can supply timely and appropriate differentiated instructional "keys" that open the door to the "essential learning" (Wiggins &

McTighe, 2006) in the curriculum and that require students to use the English language according to their proficiency levels. Simultaneous instruction of content and its associated language contributes to progress in both areas and is the responsibility of all teachers.

Because of the widely varying abilities of both ELLs and non-ELLs in any given classroom, meaningful instruction will, by necessity, look different as teachers try to meet instructional needs of individuals rather than "shoot down the middle." Ask yourself, as you think about your own teaching context, if you see a wide range of student abilities. Then consider if it makes sense to teach a child content well beyond her or his level of readiness, or if it might be preferable to teach to the student's instructional level. When teaching ELLs, teachers must bear in mind the importance of matching instruction to student needs, particularly relating instruction to the student's English language proficiency level according to the chart. Educators who teach according to student needs know that differentiating the instruction of content is not "watering down" the curriculum; it is facilitating access to it. Since each student, ELL or non-ELL, is advancing on a personal trajectory toward grade-level proficiency, the content standards must remain universal, and the "essential learning" within each standard must be the focus of teaching. In the current standards-based environment, teachers are charged with making grade-level curriculum accessible to all students, regardless of background or level of language proficiency. Unless teachers embrace this task, students can never be expected to achieve on grade level. For example, if the grade-level curriculum calls for the writing of five-paragraph essays, a Level 1 student cannot be expected to perform this task. Instead, related to this standard, the teacher must find a way to help the student apply her or his current abilities to the extent possible, according to the chart (e.g., drawing pictures or copying letters or words, as appropriate), to begin the journey toward grade-level writing proficiency. Developmentally, such differentiation affords ELLs the essential steps required to reach proficiency.

Readers are reminded that assessment strategies have been consistently presented prior to instructional strategies throughout this text. The authors suggest that teachers of ELLs first consider appropriate goals for their students (in the form of assignments and assessments) according to their individual levels of language proficiency, and then design instruction that will ensure that students are able to reach those goals. The following sections outline ways to make grade-level content instruction accessible to Level 1 students so that they will be able to meet instructional goals.

In General

Following is a general strategy that will support the simultaneous learning of language and content across the four language domains of listening, speaking, reading, and writing:

Provide sensory support for *every* lesson (e.g., real objects, pictures, hands-on materials and experiences, nonverbal communication, demonstrations, modeling, simulations). In order to support listening comprehension for ELLs at Level 1, teachers must seize the opportunity to incorporate sensory support into every lesson. Sensory support includes involving each of the five senses to the extent possible. This support scaffolds new learning by allowing students to relate new information to the familiar. Further, by providing a sensory anchor, teachers have a meaningful basis on which to build new vocabulary learning. For example, one of our favorite teacher cartoons depicts a teacher and students in a roller coaster car poised at the top of a steep hill. Just before plummeting, the teacher announces, "Today, class, we are going to learn about *gravity!*" Imagine how the students felt during the experience; for students unfamiliar with the feeling of a roller coaster descent, the precipitous experience built background. Others were able to connect new terminology to a familiar feeling. The end result of this sensory plummeting experience would be that all students could attach the new vocabulary word (gravity) to a meaningful event with accompanying sights and sensations and expand learning from there.

Listening

The following listening strategies are effective for both students with limited formal education and those with stronger educational backgrounds.

Teach basic commands by modeling actions (e.g., "Please close the door," "Open your book."). An important way to ensure that Level 1 students will engage in classroom activities, paving the way to language production, is to teach basic commands by modeling actions. Often referred to as total physical response (TPR), this technique allows students to participate in classroom activities during the earliest stage of language acquisition. For example, teachers might state and demonstrate basic classroom commands (e.g., "Please sit down" or "Take out your pencil") a few times, having newcomers mirror the teacher's actions. After several repetitions, students should be able to respond to teacher commands without teacher modeling. Having learned basic classroom phrases in English, students are on their way to building a larger repertoire of vocabulary and phrases and to participating fully in classroom activities.

Use simplified, correct language, repeating or paraphrasing as needed. Simplifying communication with Level 1 students is another key strategy for facilitating listening comprehension. However, this strategy does not need to extend to oversimplification or ungrammatical language. For instance, well-meaning teachers may be tempted to speak to Level 1 ELLs only in the present tense, thinking that doing so will improve student understanding. However, while this practice may be somewhat helpful in the short term, it is unlikely to be helpful in the long term. Such oversimplification only serves to delay the inevitable need for ELLs to attend to the unfamiliar sounds of various affixes that discretely affect word meaning. Only when students develop sensitized listening skills can they become prepared for language production and classroom participation. Further, educators should be mindful that while simple repetition for students can be helpful, sometimes complete rephrasing is necessary in order to access terminology that the student can recognize. Finally, remember that loud repetition can be offensive and is not likely to foster understanding. For example, a teacher might paraphrase "Would you like to get a drink?" to "Do you want some water?" in order to utilize language that might be more familiar to a student new to English.

Allow sufficient wait time (likely several seconds). Another critical technique for facilitating Level 1 students' listening comprehension is the use of sufficient wait time. Many teachers recognize that increasing wait time leads to improved classroom performance for all students, since it allows necessary cognitive processing to take place. Wait time is particularly useful for ELLs who, even when they might have understood instruction in English, benefit from an extra moment to process language and content in order to demonstrate understanding.

Promote higher-order thinking processes during oral instruction by simultaneously modeling the completion of graphic organizers. ELLs at all ages are able to engage in higher-order thinking (e.g., application, analysis, synthesis, evaluation, creation). However, they must be supported in doing so in English-medium classrooms, particularly when they are at the lower levels of language proficiency. Higher-order thinking can be facilitated when teachers point out important ideas and their relationships during instruction through modeling the completion of visual aids such as concept maps. This can be done on an overhead projector, Elmo, Smart Board, or other advanced technology during the presentation of information.

Employ think-alouds to model both processes and language. Another way in which educators can make the learning of new content processes and language accessible to ELLs is through think-alouds. In this strategy, teachers model a thought process using a whiteboard, an overhead projector, or other technology to show students how the process works. Thinking aloud provides students with generalizable language templates with which to articulate thoughts in English. For example, a teacher might demonstrate how to scan a text for key dates in a reading passage in this way, "thinking aloud" throughout the demonstration. Both ELLs and non-ELLs can certainly benefit when teachers model cognition in this way.

Speaking

The following strategies are effective for both students with interrupted formal education (SIFE) and those with stronger educational backgrounds.

Encourage participation in discussions by eliciting nonverbal or brief communication. Level 1 students are often at the pre-production stage of language development. However, they are absorbing input and making sense of classroom happenings as they develop familiarity with the phonemic (sound) system of English and with the meanings of various words and phrases. In order to encourage beginning oral production, teachers can pose questions in a way that allows for nonverbal communication (e.g., nodding, pointing). In addition, individual words (e.g., *yes* or *no, pencil, friend*) and memorized chunks of language (e.g., "*How are you?*") represent proficiency at Level 1 and must be recognized as full communication regardless of the student's grade level. Teachers should introduce Level 1 students to new vocabulary, but, according to the Level 1 student descriptors in the chart, should not expect students to use new terminology in full sentence form. Note that general, formulaic, and memorized language, rather than academic language, typifies Level 1 comprehension and production. Finally, remember that students should not be forced to speak.

Prompt and scaffold oral language production by modeling content and academic language and providing simple sentence examples and models (e.g., "The rabbit has fur. The _____ has scales."). Although Level 1 students are not yet producing much academic language, teachers must model this language and facilitate Level 1 students' use of general language as appropriate to academic contexts, as in the present example; while students are not expected to know the word "scales," they can engage in learning and in language production by identifying a type of animal that has scales using everyday terminology. This kind of simultaneous language and content teaching can be artfully employed as a part of regular classroom instruction rather than as a separate language lesson. That is, teachers can model and frame language in their interactions with students that supports ELLs at Level 1 while still teaching content relevant to all students.

Concentrate on students' meaning rather than on correctness of expression. Another consideration for teachers of Level 1 speakers is that the vocabulary of Level 1 speakers is so limited that it may hamper their attempts to communicate. At this stage, teachers should focus on the intent of the student's message rather than correctness in pronunciation, vocabulary, or grammar. A receptive and encouraging attitude can elicit even greater effort on the part of a tentative Level 1 language learner. One teacher showed that she understood the message when her student said, "I go shopping yesterday." This teacher also modeled correct language by responding, "Oh, you went shopping?"

Build confidence by rewarding all attempts to communicate. Further, students should be rewarded for their attempts to communicate. As in the unpressured, leisurely acquisition of language by toddlers, Level 1 ELLs of all ages respond positively to sustained encouragement of their attempts to communicate. This encouragement, however, needs to be culturally responsive and not make students uncomfortable. For example, teachers could respond to student communication without singling out the individual for correction (allowing the student to preserve "face"). The development of a culturally sensitive, respectful, and encouraging classroom environment, fostered by all members of the classroom learning community, will facilitate both language and content learning by allowing ELLs to focus on learning, rather than on issues of safety and belonging.

Pre-reading and Reading

Following is a list of instructional strategies that pertain to Level 1 reading development:

At the school or program level, for L1 preliterate students, immediately implement a high-quality, research-based, culturally and linguistically sensitive reading development program. The needs of students who are pre-literate in any language are different from those who have developed the ability to read in their first languages, as discussed in Chapter 1. Even at Level 1, these students' differential needs must be considered and addressed. Practically speaking, this requirement means that even at the pre-reading level, students who have no prior literacy experience must be afforded extra time and appropriate instruction in order to develop the necessary skills to enter the world of literacy, whereas their peers who are literate in a heritage language can transfer those skills to the learning of English. The need is particularly acute for an increasing number of older ELLs with interrupted or no previous schooling who arrive in U.S. classrooms without literacy skills in any language. These students represent a crisis in today's classrooms that can only be averted by explicit, age-appropriate, needs-based, and meaningful literacy instruction. Schools must assume this critical responsibility, particularly at the middle and high school levels, or these ELLs will never have a chance to learn how to read, let alone be afforded parity of access to the curriculum.

In one example, a responsive high school enlisted the help of a retired kindergarten/reading teacher as a volunteer who taught early reading skills to a high school–age student from Africa. Her sustained support assured that this student was able to develop the requisite skills to participate in the high school curriculum and graduate in a timely manner.

For reading-related activities, use extensive visual support (e.g., posters, pictures), since Level 1 students are typically unable to derive meaning from print alone. Teachers can make use of visual support beyond that found in reading materials to support the content learning of ELLs at Level 1. Examples include content-related posters and pictures that can serve as a springboard for discussion and vocabulary development. Teachers can explicitly connect the content in these visuals to print in text materials. They can also transfer this language to the pictures themselves in the form of labels that students can continually access when posted in the classroom. These thematic pictorial supports provide students with ready references to refer to throughout a unit of instruction, enabling the expansion of vocabulary and content understanding.

Support grade-level content curriculum with high-quality, age-appropriate, lower-reading-level books aligned with content curriculum that provide extensive visual support. Teaching all students according to the same content standards requires that Level 1 ELLs receive instruction relevant to curricular essential learning, yet adapted to their linguistic needs and abilities. Grade-level reading materials are not appropriate for these students except at kindergarten and, possibly, grade 1. As a result, alternative or supplementary content materials must generally be relied upon to address the needs of Level 1 students above grade 1. These materials must be reflective of the content area addressed in the lesson or unit and serve as a foundation upon which students can build content-area understanding despite their lack of reading ability in English.

When addressing the needs of older Level 1 students, it is not generally recommended to use elementary school materials, as these are not likely to be age-appropriate. Older students may feel insulted by materials that they consider to appear "babyish," and this feeling can detract from motivation. Instead, engaging, high-quality materials that are tied to the curriculum, are written at a lower reading level, and include colorful and realistic visual supports must be utilized. Funds for such materials can be obtained, in our experience, from parent-teacher groups, civic and church organizations, and the school board. Fundraisers are another option for creative teachers to stretch their materials budgets in order to meet a wide range of student needs. Suggested sources for such materials are found in Resource 2.2.

Teach prereading skills (e.g., phonemic awareness, concepts of print, phonics). Students at Level 1 should not be expected to read independently; they first need to gain basic listening and speaking skills (Franco, 2005). Franco asserts that this need is based on the importance of phonemic awareness, or the understanding of the sound system of English. She further emphasizes that students need to be able to aurally identify and reproduce sounds that they may not have heard or articulated previously, before being expected to orally produce those sounds while reading. During this time, typical developmental and engaging activities might include rhyming, chants, segmentation, and syllabification. (For older students, these activities may well take place outside the content classroom, supported by an ESL teacher, paraeducator, or trained volunteer.)

Alphabet recognition is another essential prereading skill (Kauffman, 2007a). This includes knowing the names of letters and their shapes. A third type of pre-reading ability relates to concepts of print, which encompass a variety of skills (Kauffman, 2007a, p. 148):

- Book-holding skills

- Understanding of print directionality

- Understanding of the one-to-one matching of spoken and written words

- Understanding the connection between illustrations and graphics and print

- Understanding of punctuation marks

These two types of pre-reading skills (alphabetic principle and concepts of print) can be developed during the development of phonemic awareness. However, only when a foundation of phonemic awareness is firmly in place should instruction move to letter-sound correspondence (phonics) and identification of the written word.[3] Note that phonics can present unique challenges for some students who read in other languages, since individual letters may produce different sounds in English (e.g., *v* can sometimes be pronounced as *y*, as in "yes," in Vietnamese).

A firm base of these pre-reading skills (phonemic awareness, alphabet principle, concepts of print, and phonics) is necessary for ELL reading development. For detailed guidance in how to teach these and other reading skills to ELLs, readers are directed to *What's Different About Teaching Reading to Students Learning English?* (Kauffman, 2007a,b).

Lay a foundation for comprehension: build background and help students to make connections to prior learning and experiences. Teachers must ensure that all students in the classroom share background knowl-

---

[3] According to France (2005), independent reading should begin when students can speak in sentence form. The authors recognize that some ELLs might read at earlier stages, particularly if they have had previous literacy instruction in the L1, which supports their English reading development.

edge, skills, and abilities needed to successfully engage in learning. If students come from a range of different backgrounds, this knowledge and these skills and abilities may need to be built within the context of classroom learning. For instance, if the topic is tornadoes, students from countries where tornadoes do not occur must be given some background knowledge about this type of storm (even in the form of simple pictures or a video clip, if the instruction will focus on basic aspects of tornadoes).

Teachers must also remember that students do not automatically connect new learning to prior learning and experiences, and must assist students in making these connections. For example, if the topic is the Civil Rights movement, connections can be made for students in other countries by quickly presenting examples of similar issues in their countries.

Read or sing visually supported stories or texts to students, using props and acting to increase comprehension and develop oral language skills necessary for reading. When presenting Level 1 students with text materials, teachers must make every effort to ensure that students understand the information represented by the printed word. Such efforts are likely to include going out of one's "comfort zone" by performing "planned charades" to facilitate student comprehension. Any prop that can foster understanding is a welcome addition when using this strategy. For example, we know of a teacher who dressed up like a bee for the science lesson on bees. This attention-getting strategy could also extend to content learning when parts of the costume could be capitalized upon for teaching about the insect's anatomy. This is the sort of thoughtful presentation that will support ELLs' understanding of materials that are read aloud to the class.

Incorporate shared, shared-to-guided, and guided reading. Knox and Amador-Watson (2000) provide excellent guidance regarding how to structure balanced literacy instruction for ELLs. They illustrate the fact that a balanced approach to teaching reading to ELLs includes read-alouds, shared reading, shared-to-guided reading, guided reading, and, of course, independent reading, with spelling and phonics instruction throughout (p. 61).

As described by Knox and Amador-Watson, in shared reading the teacher reads a (big) book to students while discussion focused on strategy use and topics related to the text takes place throughout. In shared-to-guided reading, the teacher offers the support of a shared reading lesson during guided reading. In guided reading, the teacher plays the role of a coach, assisting students with strategy use, questioning, and discussing the reading by looking at parts of the text together, before students read on their own. The goal here is the creation of independent readers. Finally, in independent reading, the child reads on his or her own. The same text can be used throughout this cycle of instruction; through the gradual release of responsibility, recycling and repetition of language, and extended practice; students can develop confidence and facility in reading.

For detailed information on using shared, shared-to-guided, and guided reading in teaching ELLs, see *Responsive Instruction for Success in English (RISE): Participant's Resource Notebook* (Knox & Amador-Watson, 2000). For further guidance on guided reading, many fine resources are available, including *Guided Reading: Good First Teaching for All Children* (Fountas & Pinnell, 1996).

Implement language experience stories. The language experience approach allows teachers to use students' own words as texts for teaching reading. Following a shared experience (e.g., baking a cake), students collaboratively dictate "stories" while the teacher acts as a scribe. Then, these nonfiction "stories" are utilized as material for teaching reading. For instance, teachers can cut apart the story, giving each student a sentence. Students then work collaboratively to sequence these sentence strips. Taken a step further, these sentences could be cut apart; then students can reconstruct the sentences themselves. This approach, which allows for recycling and repetition of students' language, is ideal for situations when literacy resource materials are scarce. It supports students in developing skills such as word recognition, fluency, and comprehension. (Note that for ELLs, it is appropriate to "convert" ungrammatical language to accurate prose when transcribing the story for students. The goal is to create model texts for classroom use.)

Promote the development of higher-order thinking skills by modeling the use of graphic organizers such as Venn diagrams, T-charts, and concept maps. Graphic organizers are an excellent scaffold for student construction of meaning from print materials as learners move toward proficiency in reading. Since Level 1 students are known to have sophisticated thoughts and ideas despite their limited language proficiency, graphic organizers provide a way to represent these ideas and serve as a scaffold for students to articulate facts and to make connections to print materials. Teachers should explore a variety of organizers, being sure to incorporate visual and pictorial support into this type of student work. For instance, a teacher could use a Venn diagram to process understanding after reading a story by modeling the comparison and contrast of two characters.

Writing

Similar to the development of reading, students who can write in their first languages will progress more readily toward writing proficiency in English than their L1 pre-literate peers. Students who are not yet able to write in their first languages will require more focused and explicit pre-writing instruction, as well as increased time for practice in order to develop their writing abilities. Such practice is essential; like learning to read, learning to write is a requirement for school success and will not occur incidentally. Rather, pre-literate students, particularly those in middle and high school, need instruction that is at the most basic level. Further, this writing instruction must be tailored to the needs of students just learning to write in a language that they barely know. This type of instruction can be supported by paraeducators and skilled, trained volunteers who can work with students individually or in groups at their specific instructional levels.

These L1 pre-literate ELLs, who comprise an increasing proportion of students in American schools, are greatly at-risk. They will continue to drop out at rates higher than their native English-speaking peers, be under represented in colleges and universities, and be unable to fully participate in their communities unless they receive the instruction that they need. Following is a list of strategies designed to assist Level 1 students, whether L1-literate or not, in developing writing skills in English.

Ask students to communicate through cutting and pasting images or drawing. In teaching early writing, draw upon students' background knowledge and experiences to validate and value what each student brings to the classroom. Invite students to depict familiar ideas and concepts by drawing or by cutting, pasting, and gluing images in order to become comfortable with the representation of information in print. This kind of activity serves as a concrete step toward more abstract (letter-based) representations in print as students increase their writing proficiency. For pre-literate students, manual dexterity and eye-hand co-ordination must also be developed. Time spent learning basic drawing, cutting, pasting, and glueing techniques will pay off in terms of greater facility with a writing instrument when learning to form letters. Living in an age of computers, cell phones, and text messaging, all students need dexterity for daily activities. Further, legible handwriting is essential for success in many school-based and job-related tasks. Purposeful teaching of sometimes overlooked manual skills traditionally learned in U.S. schools at the elementary level in art classes helps to better prepare ELLs with the requisite manual dexterity for writing, keyboarding, and the like. For example, teachers can embed such developmental activities when creating posters or cutting pictures or labels for other projects.

Prompt and scaffold written language production by modeling content and academic language and providing sentence examples and models (e.g., "The rabbit has fur. The _____ has scales"). In order for students to begin writing in English, they must be provided with clear guidance and solid examples. Often, formulaic sentences like the example given here are good starting points for written production. (Teachers should post these models for student reference in their print-rich environments.) Students can begin by completing sentence models with a single word, then with phrases, and ultimately can write sentences on their own as they develop writing proficiency. Using this sort of scaffolding, Level 1 students will more readily begin the process of learning to write in English.

Incorporate modeled, shared, and guided writing activities. We recommend the model of balanced literacy presented by Knox and Amador-Watson (2000) and others, which asserts that writing instruction should include modeled, shared, and guided writing prior to expectations of independent writing (p. 61). In this type of balanced literacy instruction, modeled writing includes the presentation of the writing process with overt attention to letter-sound relationships and writing conventions. In shared writing, the teacher acts as a scribe for language that the teacher and students collaboratively compose. In guided writing, the student writes, but with teacher support. Detailed guidance on using these strategies to teach ELLs to write is outlined in *Responsive Instruction for Success in English (RISE): Participant's Resource Notebook* (Knox & Amador-Watson, 2000).

For instance, as part of an elementary unit on basic weather patterns, a teacher could write a sentence about the weather with student input. Then, students could write their own sentences with teacher guidance, and eventually, write sentences independently.

Accept drawing, copying and labeling, and self-generated approximations of words and phrases in lieu of grade-level writing. Since teachers in any grade are likely to have Level 1 students in their classes, it is helpful to remember that the progress of a Level 1 student toward achieving a content standard can only be shown through Level 1 capabilities. By definition, these ELLs are unlikely to be able to write on grade level. For that reason, teachers must accept forms of communication that are commensurate with Level 1 proficiency (refer to the Level 1 Student Descriptors in the chart). Written communication produced by Level 1 students will need to target the content standard and take the form of drawing, copying and labeling, or original writing (often with significant errors) in accordance with the student's language proficiency level.

Concentrate on student meaning rather than on correctness of expression. As with Level 1 speaking, teachers must focus their attention on the intent of the message presented through Level 1 student writing. Errors are to be expected, given that Level 1 writers have such limited language at their command. For example, a student might write, "Go mall Friday. Shoes," when she or he means, "I went to the mall on Friday and bought some shoes." Teachers who focus on the essence of student communication rather than on incidental errors encourage students to continue their efforts toward proficiency in writing. For example, if a student laboriously copies a word, yet reverses a letter, overlook the error while focusing on the effort and the result at this early stage.

Promote the development of higher-order thinking skills by modeling the use of graphic organizers such as Venn diagrams, T-charts, and concept maps. Having received instruction utilizing visual support and allowing for drawing; cutting, pasting, and glueing images; copying and labeling; and approximating words and phrases, students can enrich their expression of understanding by applying these strategies to graphic organizers. While grade-level expectations may stipulate that students write sentences on the organizer, Level 1 students must be allowed to demonstrate understanding according to their level of language proficiency. This means that Level 1 students will, instead, fill in the organizer with images (drawn or cut and pasted) and shorter bits of language.

Instruction that Integrates Language Domains

Beginning at Level 1 and throughout the language acquisition process, teachers are advised to integrate all four language domains (listening, speaking, reading, and writing) into daily curricular activities. After school, many ELLs return to homes where English is not spoken. As a result, purposefully embedding language-rich activities that integrate all four domains into the school day, when students can manipulate, practice, and improve their language skills, is essential.

Conclusion

The assessment and instructional strategies discussed in this chapter can be selectively applied either across multiple domains or within a single language domain. While some newcomers arrive exhibiting Level 1 skills in listening, speaking, reading, and writing, students can also exhibit a range of levels across language domains. For example, the authors note that many Sudanese students have arrived in U.S. classrooms at Level 1 in reading and writing, but at Level 2 or 3 in listening and speaking. When teachers note that students' proficiency levels vary across domains, they should consult the appropriate sections of the chart and this text. They can then apply indicated strategies accordingly, targeting the student's language proficiency levels in each domain.

Another important consideration, as exemplified in the student scenarios at the beginning of the chapter, is that students can possess Level 1 skills at any age. For example, many high schools currently struggle with an increased enrollment of older students at Level 1. Educators are urged to carefully consider the urgent needs of these students regarding literacy development and to take steps to provide essential instruction that means the difference between academic engagement and success versus lack of academic achievement and likely dropping out of school.

Professional Development Activities

Activity 3.1 Student Scenarios with Application Ideas

Adapt the following assignments for Corina and Fajar, who were introduced at the beginning of the chapter, according to each student's language proficiency level and any other important factors:

- Differentiate the language-based expectations based on the student descriptors and using relevant assignment/assessment strategies on the chart and in this chapter.

  - Bear in mind the "essential learning" for each assignment (noted below each assignment template) as you differentiate the expectations, so that important skills are not overlooked.

- Design appropriate scaffolding and support using relevant instructional strategies on the chart and in this chapter.

Assignment 1

Fully English Proficient	Level 1
Language-Based Expectations: Write a five-page report	*Language-Based Expectations:*
Standards-Based Content or Topic (from the curriculum): about a country	
Scaffolding and Support: [4] using • Internet resources	*Scaffolding and Support:* using •

Essential learning: researching and summarizing information about an assigned country

Copyright © 2010. Caslon, Inc. All rights reserved. The first purchaser may photocopy this page for classroom and personal use.

---

[4]Note that the scaffolding and support that is provided for fully English proficient students is also provided for ELLs, though ELLs may often need additional scaffolding and support.

Assignment 2

Fully English Proficient	Level 1
Language-Based Expectations: Give a 3–5-minute presentation	*Language-Based Expectations:*
Standards-Based Content or Topic (from the curriculum): about a current event	
Scaffolding and Support: [4] using • based on information found in online newspapers or magazines	*Scaffolding and Support:* using •

Essential learning: summarizing a current event and sharing the information with others through speaking

Assignment 3

Fully English Proficient	Level 1
Language-Based Expectations: Read a textbook chapter and answer the chapter questions	*Language-Based Expectations:*
Standards-Based Content or Topic (from the curriculum): about a curricular topic	
Scaffolding and Support: [4] using • the textbook itself and environmental print (e.g., labeled posters in the classroom)	*Scaffolding and Support:* using •

Essential learning: comprehending and recording general information about the chapter topic

Copyright © 2010. Caslon, Inc. All rights reserved. The first purchaser may photocopy this page for classroom and personal use.

Assignment 4

Fully English Proficient	Level 1
Language-Based Expectations: Complete a textbook-based assessment that incorporates multiple-choice and short answer questions	*Language-Based Expectations:*
Standards-Based Content or Topic (from the curriculum): about a curricular topic	
Scaffolding and Support: [4] using • only the information on the test and committed to memory	*Scaffolding and Support:* using •

Essential learning: displaying information learned about a given topic

Copyright © 2010. Caslon, Inc. All rights reserved. The first purchaser may photocopy this page for classroom and personal use.

Suggested Ways to Adapt Assignments

Guidance pertaining to the language-based expectations for Corina's and Fajar's assignments is presented in the following paragraphs.

Assignment 1

Students must write a five-page report about a country using Internet resources. (Essential learning: researching and summarizing information about an assigned country)

• *For Corina:* Allow Corina to focus on her country of origin. Pair her with a strong student who is interested in helping others. Allow this "buddy" to take the lead by demonstrating online research and writing up the report. Corina's task will be construct a poster outlining the main ideas of the report with a pictorial representation for each (e.g., pictures, maps, flags downloaded from the

Internet). These must be labeled. Given the fact that Corina is still learning basic letter formation, she could cut apart the key labels for the poster from a list typed by her "buddy" and affix them to the poster. (This cutting and glueing will give Corina experience with additional school-related materials and supplies, as well as activities that may be new to her.)

- *For Fajar:* Fajar would also do well in working with a buddy. The main difference is that, because he is familiar with the English alphabet, he would more likely be able to neatly write the labels on the poster by hand. Further, he could copy short descriptions onto the poster. (These must be contextualized in the source from which he is copying—e.g., with clear pictures.)

Assignment 2

Students must give a 3–5-minute presentation about a current event based on information found in online newspapers or magazines. (Essential learning: summarizing a current event and sharing the information with others through speaking)

- *For Corina:* Bear in mind that Level 1 students are likely in the "silent period," so giving even a simplified speech in front of a classroom of students is inappropriate. Some students may be willing to do so in their first language, but their willingness would depend upon the individual student and the behavior of the audience. If Corina is willing to give a short speech in her first language (worthwhile in terms of self-esteem alone), recall that she will not be able to read about the current event. She will have to hear about it from a bilingual individual or perhaps on a Spanish-language news site on the Internet. She may be able to summarize information about a current event through creation of a poster with pictures or clip art. She could share key words with the classroom/content teacher, an ESL teacher, a paraeducator, or a trained volunteer (repetition of prompts may be warranted).

- *For Fajar:* See notes for Corina. First-language literacy does not necessarily bear on the actual giving of the presentation. However, if Fajar is willing to give the presentation in his first language, he can read about the current event in his first language. First-language materials are a must for Fajar if this is the expectation. An Internet-based news website could work for this assignment.[5]

Assignment 3

Students must read a chapter in the textbook and answer the questions at the end of the chapter using the textbook itself and environmental print. (Essential learning: comprehending and recording general information about the chapter topic)

- *For Corina and Fajar:* This assignment is not appropriate for either student. Recall that neither student is ready to gain meaning from print. Instead, they need to be able to get the information by means of demonstrations, pictures, graphs, charts, video, and the like. Only then can the students be expected to demonstrate content knowledge, skills, and abilities through the methods described in this chapter. (If the textbook is visually supported, it could certainly be an aid in helping students to learn key information about a given topic.)

Assignment 4

Students must complete a textbook-based assessment that incorporates multiple-choice and short answer questions using only the information on the test and committed to memory. (Essential learning: displaying information learned about a given topic)

- *For Corina and Fajar:* This assignment is entirely inappropriate for either student. Instead, the teacher must create a Level 1–appropriate assessment that incorporates the essential concepts of the unit by following the guidelines in this chapter.

Suggested Instructional Strategies

The following paragraphs provide guidance pertaining to scaffolding and support for the assignment.

---

[5] Teachers are advised to avoid using instant translation websites to translate documents for both students and parents. These websites may not produce accurate translations and may result in more confusion than clarification.

For all assignments, teachers must make sure to build sufficient background, support students in making connections to what they already know, pre-teach relevant vocabulary, and embed opportunities for interactions with native speakers of English. It is also helpful and necessary to provide students with models of what is expected, such as samples of successfully completed assignments, since the formats of assignments may be unfamiliar to ELLs. Such purposeful practices empower ELLs to be successful on adapted classroom assignments.

Assignment 1

Students must write a five-page report about a country using Internet resources. (Essential learning: researching and summarizing information about an assigned country)

- *For both students:* Show a sample of a completed poster outlining the key points about a country. Ensure that the "buddy" knows how to support the learning of the ELL partner. Demonstrate how to copy letters, words, and sentences, emphasizing how to know what information to copy (e.g., teacher highlights portions of a document to be copied onto a poster and clarifies [by modeling] that those are the only segments to be copied).

- *For Corina:* Demonstrate how to use scissors and glue and allow her to practice before working on the "final" poster.

Assignment 2

Students must give a 3–5-minute presentation about a current event based on information found in online newspapers or magazines. (Essential learning: summarizing a current event and sharing the information with others through speaking)

- *For both students:* Select current event topics for both students based on the availability of high-quality information pertaining to issues in each student's country of origin. Find first-language news Web sites for both students, ensuring that material is presented orally for Corina, in particular. Model the creation of a poster.

Assignment 3

Students must read a chapter in the textbook and answer the questions at the end of the chapter using the textbook itself and environmental print. (Essential learning: comprehending and recording general information about the chapter topic)

- *For both students:* Ensure that material addressed in the chapter is presented to students through demonstrations, pictures, graphs, charts, video, and the like so they have access to the same curricular information as all other students in the class. The textbook can certainly be used to achieve this end; teachers can model how to use the supporting features of the textbook (headings, bold print, pictures, etc.) to find and understand key information. (Information pertaining to the print features will be more meaningful to Fajar than Corina, but both students can benefit from this type of instruction.)

Assignment 4

Students must complete a textbook-based assessment that incorporates multiple-choice and short answer questions using only the information on the test and committed to memory. (Essential learning: displaying information learned about a given topic)

- *For both students:* Teaching must be made accessible through the use of demonstrations, pictures, graphs, charts, video, and the like. Students must also be familiarized with the ways in which they are expected to demonstrate their learning. This familiarization is especially critical for Corina who has no experience with school-based tests of learning.

Activity 3.2 Applying Your Learning to Your Own Level 1 Student

Think of a student that you know who is at Level 1. (If you are not currently serving a Level 1 student, think ahead to a time when you will serve such a student.) Based on an assignment that you routinely use, differentiate expectations for your Level 1 student.

Fully English Proficient	Level 1
Language-Based Expectations:	*Language-Based Expectations:*
Standards-Based Content or Topic (from the curriculum):	
Scaffolding and Support:[6] using	*Scaffolding and Support:* using

Essential Learning: _____

_____

Copyright © 2010. Caslon, Inc. All rights reserved. The first purchaser may photocopy this page for classroom and personal use.

_____

[6]Note that the scaffolding and support that is provided for fully English proficient students is also provided for ELLs, though ELLs may need additional support.

Professional Development Resources

Resource 3.1 Appropriate Assignment/Assessment Procedures for Level 1 Students

In General	Listening and Speaking	Pre-reading and Reading	Writing
• Create and use assignments/ assessments that allow students to demonstrate content knowledge, skills, and abilities without language mastery. • Focus on correct answers rather than errors and omissions. • Allow students to complete assessment procedures under the guidance of a bilingual teacher or paraeductor. • Weight graded components according to students' linguistic strengths. • Make the assignment/assessment process comprehensible by explaining the directions orally and providing visual support (e.g., realia, icons, manipulatives, modeling and models).	• Evaluate comprehension by means of student nonverbal communication (e.g., locating or selecting by pointing, mimicking, "thumbs up/thumbs down," gestures). • Ask for demonstration of understanding (e.g., pointing; drawing; matching; copying; using pictures or realia to sequence, categorize, prioritize, or evaluate). • Prompt the repetition of a teacher cue or a short response. • Test orally using everyday language to elicit individual words and brief chunks of language. • Allow first-language oral responses, when appropriate.	• Use high-quality, age-appropriate, lower-reading-level materials that provide extensive visual support, expecting comprehension to be dependent upon visuals provided. • Elicit physical response (e.g., locating or selecting by pointing, hand raising). • Ask for demonstration of understanding (e.g., sequencing, drawing, matching, mimicking). • Prompt the repetition of a teacher cue (speaking or singing). • Ask students to retell visually supported stories and texts presented with props and acting. • Test orally using everyday language to elicit individual words and brief chunks of language. • For students literate in the first language, support first-language reading by providing appropriate materials.	• Elicit beginning writing (e.g., drawing; copying or labeling; production of letters, words, numbers, and phrases). • Use visually supported graphic organizers that students complete with pictures, words, or short phrases to check for understanding. • Require students to supplement early writing with visual support to enhance meaning (e.g., drawing, magazine pictures, clip art). • For students literate in the first language, welcome first-language writing, as appropriate.

Copyright © 2010. Caslon, Inc. All rights reserved. The first purchaser may photocopy this page for classroom and personal use.

Resource 3.2 Appropriate Instructional Strategies for Level 1 Students

In General	Listening	Speaking	Pre-reading and Reading	Writing
• Provide sensory support for *every* lesson (e.g., real objects, pictures, hands-on materials and experiences, nonverbal communication, demonstrations, modeling, simulations).	• Teach basic commands by modeling actions (e.g., "Please close the door," "Open your book."). • Use simplified, correct language, repeating or paraphrasing as needed. • Allow sufficient wait time (likely several seconds). • Promote higher-order thinking processes during oral teaching by simultaneously modeling the completion of graphic organizers. • Employ think-alouds to model both processes and language.	• Encourage participation in discussions by eliciting nonverbal or brief communication. • Prompt and scaffold oral language production by modeling content and academic language and providing sentence examples and models (e.g., "The rabbit has fur. The ____ has scales.") • Concentrate on student meaning rather than on correctness of expression. • Build confidence by rewarding all attempts to communicate.	• At the school or program level, for L1-preliterate students, immediately implement a high-quality, research-based, culturally and linguistically sensitive reading development program. • For reading-related activities, use extensive visual support (e.g., posters, pictures), since Level 1 students are typically unable to derive meaning from print alone. • Support grade-level content curriculum with high-quality, age-appropriate, lower-reading-level books aligned with content curriculum that provide extensive visual support. • Teach prereading skills (e.g., phonemic awareness, concepts of print, phonics).	• Ask students to communicate through cutting and pasting images or drawing. • Prompt and scaffold written language production by modeling content and academic language and providing sentence examples and models (e.g., "The rabbit has fur. The ____ has scales."). • Incorporate modeled, shared, and guided writing activities. • Accept drawing, copying and labeling, and self-generated approximations of words and phrases in lieu of grade-level writing. • Concentrate on student meaning rather than on correctness of expression.

Resource 3.2 *Continued*

In General	Listening	Speaking	Pre-reading and Reading	Writing
			• Lay a foundation for comprehension: build background and help students to make connections to prior learning and experiences. • Read or sing visually supported stories or texts to students, using props and acting to increase comprehension and develop oral language skills necessary for reading. • Incorporate shared, shared-to-guided, and guided reading. • Promote the development of higher-order thinking skills by modeling the use of graphic organizers such as Venn diagrams, T-charts, and concept maps.	• Promote the development of higher-order thinking skills by modeling the use of graphic organizers such as Venn diagrams, T-charts, and concept maps.

Differentiation Strategies for Level 2 Students

*There is nothing more unequal than
the equal treatment of unequal people.*
—Thomas Jefferson

Teachers must be constantly mindful of the role that they play in moving students along the language acquisition continuum, scaffolding English language learners' (ELLs') production in listening, speaking, reading, and writing to the next higher proficiency level. In this chapter, we focus on the needs of Level 2 students by describing student characteristics and assignment/assessment and instructional strategies. However, teachers should bear in mind that the range of Level 2 production is broad. They should always be thinking in terms of what students can currently do *and* what they need to develop next. Such purposeful vigilance will support ELLs in advancing along the continuum of language acquisition to the next level, Level 3, by providing and, where possible and appropriate, eliciting examples of Level 3 language production.

Considering Variation in Level 2 Students' Backgrounds

Student
Scenarios

Bayan, who wears a headscarf, is a 10th grade student from Iraq. She is a recent Kurdish refugee and has observed violence toward her family. She did not attend formal school in Iraq. She seems sad and withdrawn; some of her teachers suspect she has post-traumatic stress disorder (PTSD). Her family arrived without basic belongings and lives well below the poverty level. In terms of language, Bayan answers formulaic questions with memorized statements and can participate in academic conversations only minimally. She often uses incomplete sentences and phrases orally to convey complete thoughts, but is only able to write with considerable effort since she is not literate in Kurdish.

Estefania is a 10th grade immigrant student from Costa Rica who has arrived with her parents, who are professionals in a large international company, and her younger brother. She is from the capitol city and enjoyed the benefits of private schooling there, where she performed on grade level. She is an outgoing, fashion-conscious student who is happy to be attending her new high school. Estefania seeks opportunities to interact with classmates in social and academic contexts. Though her language production is limited, she has begun to use some general academic words and phrases, even in her writing.

Bayan and Estefania are at opposite ends of the Level 2 spectrum of abilities because of their experiences with previous instruction. As a student with no prior schooling, Bayan's task in becoming fluent and literate in English is far more daunting than that of Estefania, who can readily transfer skills learned in Spanish to English. Bayan will need more time to develop her foundational abilities in literacy than Estefania. With these divergent needs in mind, teachers must recognize that Level 2 students do not all have the same instructional needs.

Similar to Corina, the Level 1 student discussed in Chapter 2, Bayan urgently needs basic, initial literacy instruction designed to be culturally and linguistically sensitive to her needs. As such, remedial reading classes created for native speakers will not work for Bayan. Educators must embrace the responsibility to teach foundational reading and writing skills in a meaningful, contextualized approach (as opposed to decontextualized drill-based approaches) so that students like Bayan can access content curricula. Particularly for older pre-literate and low-literate students who arrive having missed basic, developmental reading instruction at the elementary level, providing such meaning-based beginning instruction in reading and writing is the critical difference between student success and failure in U.S. schools. As with Level 1 students, classroom teachers cannot be expected to provide this extensive instruction solely within the context of their content teaching; instead, it is incumbent upon school districts to create programs to meet the particular needs of students with limited and interrupted formal schooling. These students *must* learn to read and write.

In contrast, Estefania's academic readiness is supported by her previous schooling experience and her positive attitude toward her new school. She enjoys being a teenager in America and has made several friends already. Owing to this constellation of factors, Estefania is ready to continue and expand her learning and is much less in need of separate, basic literacy instruction than her classmate Bayan.

Level 2 Student Descriptors

Level 2 students are beginning to use language in generative ways rather than relying on basic and, typically, memorized language. Students are developing the ability to use academic language and, although their errors often hinder understanding, Level 2 students are far more communicative than their Level 1 counterparts. Bearing in mind that each proficiency level represents a broad range of ability, we turn now to a description of each language domain within Level 2.

Listening

The listening ability of Level 2 students is characterized by comprehension of simple, contextualized sentences related to social and academic content. Students at Level 2 are likely still becoming familiar with new sounds in English, relying on commonly heard words, chunks, and expressions to construct meaning.

Speaking

In terms of speaking, Level 2 students can use simple sentences, though they may rely on telegraphic speech (incomplete sentences that communicate complete thoughts), to talk in social and highly contextualized academic situations. Though these students' vocabularies are expanding to include general academic language, they often make mistakes that may prevent understanding. Pronunciation may not be accurate, since Level 2 students are likely still developing phonemic (sound) awareness and the ability to produce new sounds in English. Level 2 students are, however, broadening their understanding of academic language functions (e.g., using language for definitional purposes).

Reading

The prereading abilities of Level 2 students include a growing receptive understanding of the sounds of the English alphabet. These skills must be firmly in place before students are expected to match the sounds with letters. In other words, students must develop general phonemic awareness before incorporating phonics, which focuses on the visual representations of sounds in the written word. Students who are literate in their first languages start to recognize written language more readily than their L1-pre-literate classmates. Further, Level 2 students who are literate in their first language may even appear to be reading full passages, relying on first-language phonetic learning to read aloud without comprehension ("word call"). This ability to apply sounds to letters does *not* mean that the student comprehends what she or he is "reading." Teachers may be deceived, thinking that oral fluency in reading or speed in word calling indicates reading proficiency. Again, such ability to call words does not indicate comprehension of text. Only after the student learns vocabulary, preferably thematically and contextually, is s/he able to comprehend text and actually "read."

Writing

Level 2 writers range from those who can write in phrases using common, everyday and academic language to those who can create simple sentences. Errors are common and are likely to impede meaning. The L1 pre-literate student is likely to continue writing with Level 2 characteristics for a longer period of time than a student who can write in his or her first language. The L1-literate student can transfer writing skills from the first language to English and is likely to move to Level 3 (expanded sentences) with relative ease in comparison with his or her L1 pre-literate classmate.

A Word About Language Objectives

Language objectives for Level 2 students must take into account what these students can do linguistically, based on the student descriptors on the chart that we have just elaborated. The guidance in the following section on assignment/assessment strategies can also assist teachers in conceptualizing appropriate language objectives at Level 2. The instructional strategies described in the following section outline ways in which teachers can facilitate the successful achievement of language and content objectives by Level 2 students.

A Sample Differentiated Assignment for Level 2 Students

The sample assignment used for all of the level-specific chapters in the book is differentiated in Table 4.1 for students at Levels 2 and 3. (For guidance in how to interpret the information in this template, refer to Chapter 3.) While Level 2 is the focus of this chapter, teachers must always remain aware of the expectations for students at subsequent levels in order to push students toward those levels of proficiency. For this reason, Level 3 expectations are also provided in this sample assignment. Readers are reminded that, as with all of the sample assignments in this book, this is but one way to differentiate expectations and provide scaffolding and support.

Teachers can collaborate in many ways to facilitate the simultaneous learning of content and language for Level 2 students. For example, with this particular assignment, the ESL or bilingual teacher could "push in" to the content classroom to provide support to ELLs within the mainstream setting.

Necessary Assignment/Assessment Strategies for Level 2 Students

As with Level 1 students, large-scale standardized assessment tools and classroom-based assessment tools designed for native speakers of English are inappropriate for Level 2 ELLs. With that fact in mind, educators must apply their understanding of the language abilities and cultural and experiential backgrounds of their ELLs to create appropriate avenues for students to demonstrate content knowledge without fully developed English language skills. Only in this inventive and resourceful way can teachers gain accurate understanding of what their ELLs know and can do in the content areas.

Table 4.1 Sample assignment differentiated for Levels 2 and 3

Fully English Proficient	Level 2	Level 3
Language-Based Expectations: Write a set of instructions using grade-level vocabulary and sentence structures	*Language-Based Expectations:* Write a set of instructions using occasional content and academic vocabulary and simple sentences	*Language-Based Expectations:* Write a set of instructions using some content and academic vocabulary and simple/complex sentence structures
Standards-Based Content or Topic (from the curriculum): for a self-selected task		
Scaffolding and Support: using • a model assignment, • teacher demonstration of the task using a "think-aloud," • a sequential graphic organizer for planning to write, • a language wall with sequencing words and key sentence structures, and • feedback designed to push students to full proficiency according to the grade-level writing standards to guide writing.	*Scaffolding and Support:* using • a model assignment, • teacher demonstration of the task using a "think-aloud," • a sequential graphic organizer for planning to write, • photographs of chosen processes, • a language wall with sequencing words (focus on ordinal numbers, *then*, *next*) and key sentence structures, • pretaught vocabulary, • a supplementary "think-aloud" demonstration of paragraph writing, • academic sentence frames posted in the classroom, • pictorially supported procedure texts, • realia related to processes (e.g., materials for making a peanut butter and jelly sandwich), and • level-appropriate feedback designed to push students to the next level of proficiency in writing to guide writing.	*Scaffolding and Support:* using • a model assignment, • teacher demonstration of the task using a "think-aloud," • a sequential graphic organizer for planning to write, • photographs of chosen processes, • a language wall with sequencing words and key sentence structures, • pretaught vocabulary, • a supplementary "think-aloud" demonstration of paragraph writing, • academic sentence frames posted in the classroom, • pictorially supported procedure texts, and • level-appropriate feedback designed to push students to the next level of proficiency in writing to guide writing.

In General

Create and use assignments/assessments that allow students to demonstrate content knowledge, skills, and abilities without language mastery. As students acquire language and content simultaneously, it is likely that content understanding will supersede their linguistic ability to express their understanding. As a result, in order to understand what Level 2 students know and can do in a given content area, teachers must create assessments that tap into students' knowledge, skills, and abilities without depending upon fluency in English. Such flexibility in assessment allows students to demonstrate, in a variety of ways, complex concepts and ideas that they are yet unable to articulate in English. Through developing creatively inventive assessments that separate content knowledge from language production, teachers gain more accurate insight into the learning of Level 2 ELLs. Examples of flexible assessments include posters rather than essays, short answer oral tests instead of paper and pencil multiple-choice tests, and demonstrations rather than reports.

Focus on correct answers rather than errors and omissions. In the same way that the Level 1 student responds positively to sustained encouragement, Level 2 students will derive support from continuing emphasis on their successes rather than their shortcomings. Maintaining a positive and receptive classroom environment by lowering the "affective filter" (Krashen, 1982) through the reduction of anxiety allows students to focus their concentration and energy on learning both language and content. In order to facilitate this comfort level in the classroom, error correction takes a back seat to building confidence at Level 2, as it does at Level 1. For example, when a Level 2 student says, "I go store last night," teachers demonstrate understanding of the statement and simply rephrase (e.g., "Oh, you went to the store?").

Allow students to complete assessment procedures under the guidance of a bilingual teacher or paraeductor. As emphasized previously, Level 2 students are likely to understand far more than they are able to express in English. As for Level 1 students, the linguistic abilities of bilingual teachers and paraeducators can provide a much-needed bridge for Level 2 ELLs in completing assessment procedures. This support can be provided individually or, perhaps, in a small-group setting. As discussed in the previous chapter, this support may come through the translation of the directions into the ELL's first language or translating parts of test questions, if language is not part of what is being assessed and graded. ELLs may also process content with bilingual educators as a means to both learning and demonstrating what they know and can do in the content areas. These first-language supports help students to better demonstrate what they know and can do.

Teachers are reminded, also, that tests should not be translated in their entirety. This process typically results in nonparallel tests, rendering the results very difficult to interpret. Therefore, teachers should not ask that tests be translated by school personnel or others.

Weight graded components according to students' linguistic strengths. As is the case with Level 1 students, Level 2 students typically develop listening and speaking skills before reading and writing. For this reason, Level 2 students' oral demonstrations of content understanding should be weighted more heavily than their written demonstrations. See Chapter 8 for additional guidance on scoring Level 2 students' work.

Make the assignment/assessment process comprehensible by explaining the directions orally and providing visual support (e.g., realia, icons, manipulatives, modeling and models). Teachers must ensure that students understand the expectations of each assignment or assessment task if the results of that work are to be accurate indicators of what students know and can do. Since Level 2 students' listening skills are, by definition, limited, teachers are urged to use visual support to enhance student understanding of assignments and assessments. For example, teachers could show students a model of a completed diorama when giving instructions. If students do not fully comprehend what they are to do, the resulting scores will be meaningless, rendering this strategy essential.

Listening and Speaking

Test orally using everyday and general content/academic language to elicit phrases and simple sentences. At Level 2, as students continue to develop their language skills, teachers can continue to test orally, as speaking will likely be the student's major productive domain. Such oral testing should be considered in place of the kinds of testing designed for native speakers of English. For example, if an essay test item were to state, "Synthesize your learning about volcanoes," an oral assessment could be based on discussion of a picture of a volcano. The teacher could point to the volcano, eliciting what the student knows by asking, "What is it? What is happening?"

Allow occasional first-language oral responses. As ELLs acquire English proficiency, they often draw upon their existing L1 vocabulary while developing a new L2 vocabulary repertoire. Such linguistic versatility should be perceived as an advantage for bilinguals and students who know more than two languages. Interchanging words of two languages and substituting words, when the term in one language is inaccessible, is a useful and common developmental linguistic tool that should not be perceived as a hindrance. One student was overheard saying, "I dropped my 'zapato' [Spanish for 'shoe'] on the 'suelo'" [Spanish for 'floor']." Such an expression is cause for celebration, since the student is obviously acquiring vocabulary and syntax, as well as generating a complete sentence. In this case, the student is using both languages communicatively and correctly. This example clearly shows how students can apply first-language skills to the target language, setting the stage for increased student- generated oral production advancing toward proficiency.

Further, full responses to assignments or assessment tasks in a student's first language may be accepted at times for different reasons. On occasion, a teacher may simply want to allow the student an opportunity to showcase her or his first language skills to the rest of the class. In another situation, the teacher may want to build a student's communicative confidence. At yet other times, the teacher may grade the student's content understanding based on a first-language response (if she or he is proficient in the student's first language, if there is a bilingual school staff member available to assist, or if a bilingual volunteer can lend a hand).

Pre-reading and Reading

The following strategies can be applied when assessing Level 2 ELLs' pre-reading skills and when reading is involved in the content assessment process.

Use high-quality, age-appropriate, lower-reading-level materials that provide extensive visual support, expecting comprehension of frequently encountered words and phrases, often dependent upon visuals provided. ELLs at Level 2 do not have the reading skills to read tests designed for native speakers. If reading is a required part of a testing procedure, then suitable texts must be used, and visual support to aid comprehension must be provided. If reading is not being tested, however, the language load of the test must be reduced to the extent possible. One means to this end is the use of simplified texts and plenty of visual support. See Resource 2.2 for a list of sources of such materials.

Prompt the repetition of a teacher cue (speaking or singing). This strategy can be employed to ascertain students' pre-reading skills and their content understanding. For instance, a teacher might ask a student to repeat a short sentence read aloud to check for accurate pronunciation. In the content areas, teachers might use songs or raps to teach content. If a student is able to perform the song or rap with visual support (e.g., pointing to pictures at appropriate times during the performance), this ability could be taken as evidence of content learning.

Test orally using everyday and general content/academic language to elicit phrases and simple sentences. This technique is the same as that for listening and speaking, described earlier. An example in the domain of reading would be a short question and answer session focused on reading a low-reading-level passage with visual support (e.g., an informational paragraph focused on different types of trees). In another example, the student could sequence story cards with simple captions.

For students literate in the first language, support first-language reading by providing appropriate materials. Students who can read in their first languages can capitalize upon those skills during test taking. For example, a glossary in the student's first language can help him or her negotiate written material on a content test. For students who are given the benefit of literacy instruction in the first language, progress in this endeavor can and should be tested using that language (e.g., students learning to read in Spanish should be tested in Spanish).

Writing

As with reading, L1-pre-literate students will likely take longer to develop sufficient writing skills to move from Level 2 to Level 3 than their counterparts. The arduous nature of developing literacy skills in an entirely new language must be considered when testing these students using writing. It may take L1-pre-literate students longer to produce written answers or products than their L1-literate counterparts.

Elicit writing of phrases and simple sentences. At Level 2, regardless of age or grade level, students can only be expected to produce writing as delineated in the student descriptors (phrases and simple sentences). As a result, for example, a middle school assignment to write a five-paragraph essay would need to be adapted to include only phrases and simple sentences. This product would need to be graded according to the student's ability to meet the adapted expectations, rather than rating the assignment according to the native-speaker expectations for a full five paragraphs.

Teachers can elicit phrases and simple sentences by providing sentence frames, giving students pictures or other visual prompts tailored to content needs, and modeling the writing process. For instance, an academic sentence frames to describe a food chain might be "_____ [picture of birds] eat _____ [picture of worms]." The student supplies a pretaught word or phrase from memory, likely using invented spelling. Students might also access a visually supported word or language wall.

Use visually supported graphic organizers that students complete with phrases and simple sentences to check for understanding. For assessment of Level 2 students, as for Level 1 students, graphic organizers continue to be an excellent tool to gauge student learning inasmuch as they have also been used for the instruction of that learning. It is critical that teachers remember that assessment formats must be familiar to students; during assessment is not the time to introduce new formats for students to use in showing what they know and can do. Particularly for ELLs, teachers must not make assumptions about their ability to demonstrate learning through means not explicitly taught.

Allowing students to use scaffolding during assessment will enable them to better demonstrate what they know and can do in the content areas. Though the teacher may expect fully English proficient students to write answers in complete sentences without the aid of a graphic organizer, she or he can view the graphic organizer and the differentiated linguistic expectations as a data-driven practice that allows students to demonstrate their knowledge, skills, and abilities as fully as possible. One example of this type of support is a graphic organizer with a word bank for students to use in comparing the desert and the tundra.

Require students to supplement writing with visual support to enhance meaning (e.g., drawing, magazine pictures, clip art). Since the writing of Level 2 students likely includes many errors and omissions that hinder understanding, requiring students to use visual supports in their writing is necessary to reinforce their communication in a meaningful way. For example, students can be required to write a weekly journal entry about their weekend activities. The expectations, varying with student abilities, are that students use pre-taught vocabulary to describe at least five activities in phrases and simple sentences. This written journal entry must include a relevant picture, either drawn or snipped from a magazine and glued onto the journal page. Another example is having students write a description of a picture provided by the teacher.

For students literate in the first language, allow occasional first-language writing, as appropriate. This technique parallels that for speaking, in that students can be allowed to insert words from their first language into their writing in English. As with speaking, students can gain confidence in their ability to communicate, which will fuel increased motivation and effort. This ability to use both languages in the same phrase is a valuable developmental device that should be appreciated rather than discouraged. Teachers may also allow students to write in their first languages to honor those skills, to build student confidence, and even for grading purposes if someone is available to translate the answer (e.g., a narrative about a family tradition). In addition, students who are learning to write in their first languages can also make use of those languages in testing of their progress in those programs.

Necessary Instructional Strategies for Level 2 Students

Having discussed a range of strategies that can be used to elicit demonstration of Level 2 students' learning, we now address instructional strategies that will facilitate student success on those differentiated assignments and assessments. This approach follows the model of "backward lesson design" (Wiggins & McTighe, 2006), wherein teachers determine what outcomes students must achieve and then design instruction to support that achievement.

The *critical action steps* for the instruction of Level 1 students outlined in Chapter 3 apply equally to the instruction of Level 2 students:

1. Examine your own assumptions.

2. Learn about students' backgrounds.

3. Determine students' instructional levels based on content knowledge, skills, and abilities and language proficiency.

4. Teach essential learning from the curriculum and its associated language in a differentiated manner.

These ELLs have begun the language acquisition process and, with the support of knowledgeable teachers and appropriate instruction, will steadily progress toward full English language proficiency and grade-level academic performance.

The following instructional strategies can be applied generally across language domains and to the specific domains of listening, speaking, reading, and writing.

In General

Provide sensory support for *every* lesson (e.g., real objects, pictures, hands-on materials and experiences, nonverbal communication, demonstrations, modeling, simulations). As with Level 1 students, teachers are reminded to capitalize on the five senses of their Level 2 students in order to make instruction meaningful and memorable. For example, if a family and consumer science teacher is discussing the five different tastes (sweet, salty, sour, bitter, and umami), students should be afforded the opportunity to sample foods of each category. Such experiential and sensory learning contributes to long-term learning, providing "mental Velcro" to which students can attach new vocabulary and conceptual learning.

Listening

The following strategies support Level 2 students in learning language and content through listening.

Use simplified, correct language, repeating or paraphrasing as needed. Teachers are reminded that using language understandable to the Level 2 student is essential. Taking care to speak simply but correctly, teachers can engage Level 2 students in simple exchanges about social topics such as family and personal interests, as well as general academic topics related to the curriculum. Students will also be well served by teachers who repeat and paraphrase. Such conscious reinforcement supports development of a receptive repertoire of English words and phrases.

Allow sufficient wait time (likely several seconds). Since Level 2 students continue to require extra processing time, this strategy provides them a cognitive "window" for constructing meaning from speech before the opportunity is lost. This strategy is helpful for non-ELLs, as well, who can deepen their cognitive processing of teacher input, given additional time to think (even up to 10 seconds).

Promote higher-order thinking processes during oral teaching by providing graphic organizers, modeling their completion as needed. Graphic organizers help students to make connections and can assist them in developing metacognitive skills, or "thinking about their thinking." Such explicit support of content processing makes thinking visible. As appropriate, teachers can model appropriate ways to express ideas in English by filling out the organizer with students. Graphic organizers can serve as a way to make sense of content and as a note-taking device. For example, a teacher could model the completion of an outline about the solar system.

Employ think-alouds to model both processes and language. Teachers can use this valuable strategy to assist students in understanding how to do certain things and to model appropriate language use. For instance, in a lesson on paragraph writing, the teacher could demonstrate the process of writing a good topic sentence by "thinking aloud" during the process of actually writing such a sentence in front of the class. In this way, teachers can exemplify both the cognitive process and the necessary language to complete the process.

Speaking

The following strategies are designed to facilitate Level 2 students' language and content learning in the area of speaking.

Encourage participation in discussions by eliciting phrases or simple sentences. Level 2 students typically understand far more than they are able to articulate. As a result, they will benefit greatly from encouragement and patience as they begin to produce spoken English. While

Level 2 students are often able to cognitively process at high levels, they frequently report feeling "babyish" because of their diminished ability (in comparison to that in their first languages) to communicate verbally. This level of language production is a predictable product of normal linguistic development, rather than an indicator of limited cognitive ability. Nevertheless, it can be demoralizing for Level 2 students. As a result, teachers must approach these ELLs with positive assumptions about their thinking abilities and their need to expand their speaking abilities. With that in mind, teachers should maintain high expectations for student performance, working to elicit appropriate levels of language production. This process can be facilitated by visually supporting students in responding. For example, if a teacher questions a student, asking for an example of an amphibian, that teacher might provide pictures of a variety of examples and non-examples that have been previously discussed. Another key technique for eliciting student speech is to allow Level 2 students to discuss possible answers with a "shoulder partner" or with a small group, having been matched with students at higher proficiency levels. Such heterogeneous grouping assures that ELLs are exposed to native (or native-like) examples, thus learning how to articulate content knowledge appropriately.

Prompt and scaffold oral language production by modeling content/academic language and providing sentence examples and models (e.g., "The rabbit has fur. _____ _____ _____ scales."). As Level 2 students expand their vocabularies and speech production, they need opportunities to practice and manipulate academic language to the extent possible. Teachers can, based on essential learning, hasten the process of language development by modeling academic language and embedding opportunities to use such language. Specifically, teachers must provide examples of academic language structures and vocabulary for students to draw upon. This strategy will benefit both ELLs and non-ELLs, who are also learning academic English. For instance, students can complete sentences such as the example listed in the above strategy. Such content-based language development ensures that both English language learning and content learning occur simultaneously. Teachers are also urged to provide ELLs at lower levels of language proficiency with guidance in how to ask for assistance and clarification in polite ways (e.g., "Could you please help me with _____?" or "Could you tell me what _____ means?").

Concentrate on student meaning rather than on correctness of expression. Level 2 students expend much of their attention in accessing meaningful vocabulary in English in order to formulate phrases and simple sentences, checking against what they already know and comparing their English production to their first languages. When students finally produce some speech, teachers can support and encourage increased oral production by continuing to focus on meaning rather than providing detailed corrections (e.g., when a student says, "Teacher, water?" the teacher could simply give the student a pass to get a drink). Corrections can overwhelm the Level 2 student and may result in reticence, frustration, and delayed speech production. Students will be better served if teachers focus on providing meaningful input, expanding vocabulary development, and embedding opportunities for peer interaction.

Build confidence by rewarding all attempts to communicate. Like Level 1 students, Level 2 students will benefit from a positive and receptive environment and can be discouraged or embarrassed if they are singled out for correction. Consider your own foreign language learning experiences; many teachers themselves report giving up on learning a second language as a result of feelings of inadequacy when their speech was picked apart by teachers who were overly focused on accuracy at the beginning stages of language acquisition. Instead, teachers can respond to student communication in a welcoming and inclusive fashion that honors Level 2 students' progression toward language proficiency, accepting the recognizable approximation while encouraging the student to expand and sustain communication efforts. For instance, if a student were to say, "Health homework," a study hall teacher could simply begin to provide assistance, rather than insisting on a perfectly articulated request. It should be noted that this omission of minute correction is not intended to reinforce errors. Rather, teachers must recognize that speaking errors, particularly those made systematically, are part of a learning process on the path to correctness.

Pre-reading and Reading

As in Level 1, the distinct needs of students who are literate in the first language and those who are not continue to profoundly impact students' progress toward proficiency in different ways. Teachers are reminded that students who cannot read in their first languages will require more explicit reading instruction and support than their L1-literate counterparts who can transfer previously learned reading skills to English. As stated previously, programming focused on early reading development is essential for pre-literate Level 2 students so that they can gain the requisite skills to access the curriculum. Skilled, trained reading teachers and volunteers can play a key role in providing this support, working alongside school personnel.

At the school and program levels, for L1-pre-literate students, (continue to) implement a high-quality, research-based, culturally and linguistically sensitive reading development program. As is the case for Level 1 students, Level 2 students who are pre-literate in their first languages need explicit focused instruction in how to read, regardless of age. This calls for the development of programming that is tailored to the needs of ELLs rather than enrolling such students in remedial instruction designed for native speakers of English who have had early literacy instruction in the past. This programming must be culturally and linguistically sensitive in terms of materials, ensuring that making meaning is the focus of the reading instruction (rather than isolated drill approaches). In districts with small numbers of L1-pre-literate students, a well-trained and well-supported paraeducator or volunteer may play a key role in the delivery of this instruction. As an example of appropriate programming for such students, nonfiction reading materials focused on curricular topics could be the basis for oral language development and prereading skills for Level 2 students. (For further guidance, see the "Teach pre-reading skills" section that follows.)

For reading-related activities, use extensive visual support (e.g., posters, pictures), since Level 2 students are often unable to derive meaning from print alone. Visual support is essential for the reading development of Level 2 students. Such comprehensible depictions provide contextualization that ELLs can draw upon in order to increasingly make sense of the printed word. Various kinds of visual supports (e.g., posters, pictures, diagrams, models) provide a much-needed bridge to greater reading proficiency. Texts without contextualizing visual support are likely to be incomprehensible to Level 2 ELLs, who should not be expected to gain understanding from what is likely to be perceived as uninteresting or meaningless.

Support grade-level content curriculum with high-quality, age-appropriate, lower-reading-level books aligned with content curriculum that provide extensive visual support. Engaging Level 2 ELLs in the content curriculum can be accomplished with meaningful materials. At the higher grades, grade-level materials are not suitable for Level 2 students, requiring that teachers creatively assemble a body of accessible and comprehensible resources that is tied to the content curriculum, but is better suited to the language proficiency level of the ELLs in their classes. A list of sources for such materials can be found in Resource 2.2. Teachers are encouraged to seek funds for such materials from parent-teacher groups, civic and church organizations, and the school board if classroom budgets do not support the purchase of these necessary materials.

Teach pre-reading skills (e.g., phonemic awareness, concepts of print, phonics). As discussed in Chapter 2, students who are not yet speaking at sentence level should not be expected to gain meaning from print through independent reading (Franco, 2005). As mentioned in Chapter 3, as part of the development of these prerequisite oral skills, Kauffman (2007a) clarifies that students must have the opportunity to build phonemic awareness: an understanding of the sounds of English. They must also (continue to) learn the alphabetic principle (the names of the letters and their shapes) and a range of skills falling under the label of "concepts of print" (Kauffman, 2007a, p. 148):

- book-holding skills

- understanding of print directionality

- understanding of the one-to-one matching of spoken and written words

- understanding the connection between illustrations and graphics and print

- understanding of punctuation marks

These students must also be provided with meaning-based instruction in phonics in order to prepare them for independent reading, according to Kauffman. As an example, teachers can use environmental print, such as content and language objectives, as the source of this type of pre-reading skill instruction. Interested readers are referred to *What's Different About Teaching Reading to Students Learning English?* (Kauffman, 2007a,b) for additional guidance.

Lay a foundation for comprehension: build background and help students to make connections to prior learning and experiences. In order to facilitate student success, teachers must ensure that all members of the classroom community possess the prerequisite knowledge, skills, and abilities needed to actively engage in the learning process. Given the diversity of today's classrooms, this requirement means that teachers must know their students' background profiles and account for likely variability by teaching needed background information. Teachers must also help students to make connections to their own backgrounds in terms of prior learning and experiences, since many students do not do so on their own. For instance, ELLs might think about celebrations in their countries of origin when learning about Thanksgiving in the United States, since there are similar celebrations in other countries.

Read or sing visually supported stories or texts to students, using props and acting to increase comprehension and develop oral language skills necessary for reading. Although Level 2 students are gaining ground in terms of their listening skills, teachers who read or sing stories and other texts to students will need to provide visual support to facilitate understanding. When the language presented is comprehensible, students are then able to appropriate it for their own use. Thus, this kind of presentation of written material can assist with students' comprehension and their own language production. For example, a teacher might dress "in character" when reading the Emancipation Proclamation to students. Props might include pictures relating to slavery that could be referred to during the reading of the speech. Role-playing can also contribute to enhanced comprehension.

Incorporate shared, shared-to-guided, and guided reading. Although shared, shared-to-guided, and guided reading may be perceived as elementary classroom teaching strategies, Level 2 students of all ages will benefit from such specific and targeted instruction. To reiterate the discussion in Chapter 3, in shared reading, the teacher and students read an enlarged text together, discussing various points throughout the reading. Then students read this same text on their own, repeatedly, developing increasing fluency. In guided reading, the teacher literally guides small groups of students in reading a common text that is at their instructional (rather than their frustration) level. The teacher can provide individualized instruction as students read individually and simultaneously "under their breath." Shared-to-guided reading (Knox & Amador-Watson, 2000) is designed to bridge shared and guided reading by providing extra scaffolding to students during the guided reading process. All of these strategies foster early reading development in Level 2 students. For further guidance on all three of these instructional strategies, see *Responsive Instruction for Success in English (RISE): Participant's Resource Notebook* (Knox & Amador-Watson, 2000). Detailed information about guided reading is available in *Guided Reading: Good First Teaching for All Children* (Fountas & Pinnell, 1996).

These three approaches are exemplified in a unit about arctic biomes in which the teacher starts with an appropriate passage that is read using shared reading. Students could then focus their efforts on high-quality, age-appropriate, lower-reading-level books on the same topic which could be read using shared-to-guided and guided reading techniques.

Implement language experience stories. This approach, as described in Chapter 3, allows students to create texts to be used in reading instruction with the assistance of the teacher. After a shared experience, such as a field trip to the zoo, students work together to "write" a description of the outing with the teacher acting as a scribe. Teachers must elicit the full range of Level 2 abilities, pushing students toward Level 3, and ensure that the written language is grammatically accurate. They then use these student-generated texts as reading material for instruction. Both prereading (e.g., phonics) and reading skills (e.g., fluency, comprehension) can be taught with such pieces of writing.

Promote the development of higher-order thinking skills by modeling the use of graphic organizers such as Venn diagrams, T-charts, and concept maps. Teachers can help students to make sense of texts and to make connections among ideas through the use of graphic organizers. These organizers can serve as a link to assessment activities that can make use of the same instrument, allowing students to demonstrate what they know and can do. For example, when teaching a unit on the Civil War, students can categorize "big ideas" related to the North and the South by using a T-chart (e.g., military leaders, states involved, issues).

Writing

The distinct development of L1-pre-literate and L1-literate students continues to manifest in different ways as both groups advance in the area of writing. Students who cannot write in their first languages will require more intensive instruction and more time than their L1-literate peers in order to become fluent writers in English. This important need cannot be slighted, overlooked, or neglected. School districts must take purposeful steps to make certain that plans for instruction include the crucial needs of these newcomers, since their lack of writing ability positions them for failure in school.

Prompt and scaffold written language production by modeling content/ academic language and providing sentence examples and models (e.g., "The rabbit has fur. _____ _____ _____ scales."). This strategy applies equally to both speaking and writing. Level 2 students require explicit instruction in how to frame their thoughts in English as well as repeated opportunities to practice. While Level 2 students can only produce phrases and simple sentences, they can begin to incorporate academic language into their writing, if aided by visually supported examples (e.g., word walls, concept walls, teacher modeling). Non-ELLs can also benefit from explicit instruction in how to use academic language and register rather than social language in the content areas. This can take the form of sentence examples as shown earlier. As an additional example, teachers might extend students' production of content vocabulary by posting, "The roots absorb _____," (water) along with a picture to guide students in moving beyond use of the word "drink" in such an academic sentence.

Incorporate modeled, shared, and guided writing activities. Knox and Amador-Watson (2000) and others clarify these kinds of instruction within a balanced literacy framework. When teachers employ modeled writing, they show students the process of writing, teaching writing conventions and emphasizing features such as letter-sound relationships. In shared writing activities, teachers invite students to collaborate with them in producing written text that is displayed for all to see (e.g., on an overhead projector, Elmo, Smart Board). Such close, step-by-step interaction yields templates that students can use to generate their own future writing. Guided writing allows students to work on their own writing, but with teacher support. A workshop approach to writing enables teachers to meet students "where they are" and to individualize one-on-one instruction and feedback. For instance, the writing of math sentences (as a precursor to asking students to create story problems) could be taught in this way.

Accept phrases or simple sentences in lieu of grade-level writing expectations.   Always mindful of the need to push students to the next level of proficiency, teachers are, nevertheless, encouraged to maintain a flexible attitude about Level 2 student writing. Level 2 ELLs must be afforded the time and opportunity to develop their writing, not unlike their native English-speaking peers in the early elementary grades. All ELLs must be allowed to incrementally learn to write in English. Teachers are advised to accept phrases and simple sentences from Level 2 ELLs; since student language proficiency test data clarify that this level of production represents maximum capability at this stage of linguistic development, higher demands are not reasonable. For example, if native English-speaking students are expected to write a two-page biography, Level 2 ELLs might write phrases or simple sentences to communicate meaning about their assigned person, supplemented with visual support. The length of the assignment is, by necessity, shortened. Scoring of such an assignment is discussed in Chapter 8.

Concentrate on student meaning rather than on correctness of expression.   As with speaking, teachers must focus on the content conveyed by Level 2 writing, rather than on the errors that might be present in expression. When correcting writing, select one or two areas for feedback (e.g., content concepts, verb tense, use of articles) and disregard other errors. Overwhelming students with correction of every inaccuracy is unlikely to facilitate learning. In fact, it can have the opposite effect by demoralizing a student who worked very diligently to produce the submitted product.

Promote higher-order thinking skills by modeling the use of graphic organizers such as Venn diagrams, T-charts, and concept maps.   As with other language domains, graphic organizers can serve as an excellent support for the writing development of Level 2 ELLs. Organizers completed during listening and reading activities can be used as a springboard for writing. Alternatively, ELLs can produce writing by completing a graphic organizer. Visual supports throughout these organizers are essential and will enhance concept development. For instance, a teacher could use a T-chart to allow students to categorize and label pictorial examples of living and nonliving things.

Instruction that Integrates Language Domains

The more authentic a teaching and learning activity is, the more likely it is to integrate the language domains of listening, speaking, reading, and writing. Although strategies for these domains have been presented separately, teachers are urged to integrate the language domains and the appropriate strategies for each throughout their teaching. This natural approach to language use in the classroom lends itself to logical and "real" applications. For example, students might create presentations about their home countries in which they "research," prepare a written PowerPoint presentation with visual support, and deliver a speech to the class, possibly with a "buddy" or a cooperative group in which each student has an assigned, productive role.

Conclusion

Readers are reminded that students sometimes function at different levels of proficiency in different domains. If a student exhibits Level 2 writing and Level 3 speaking, for example, the use of level-specific strategies for each language domain (Level 2 for writing and Level 3 for speaking) is called for. Teachers should feel empowered to use a wide variety of assignment/assessment instructional strategies in order to meet the range of needs in their classrooms.

In addition to demonstrating different levels of proficiency across domains, students can also demonstrate different levels of proficiency at any age. That is, Level 2 students might appear in elementary, middle, *or* high school classrooms. Teachers must choose strategies that are in keeping with their students' proficiency levels, regardless of student age.

Professional Development Activities

Activity 4.1   Student Scenarios with Application Ideas

Adapt the following assignments for Bayan and Estefania, who were introduced at the beginning of the chapter, according to each student's language proficiency level and any other important factors:

- Differentiate the language-based expectations based on the student descriptors and using relevant assignment/assessment strategies on the chart and in this chapter.
  - Bear in mind the "essential learning" for each assignment (noted below each assignment template) as you differentiate the expectations, so that important skills are not overlooked.
- Design appropriate scaffolding and support using relevant instructional strategies on the chart and in this chapter.

Assignment 1[1]

Fully English Proficient	Level 2
Language-Based Expectations: Write a letter to a public official	*Language-Based Expectations:*
Standards-Based Content or Topic (from the curriculum): voicing a concern about an issue	
Scaffolding and Support: using • examples discussed in class	*Scaffolding and Support:* using •

Essential learning: writing a letter in correct format, formally voicing a concern

Copyright © 2010. Caslon, Inc. All rights reserved. The first purchaser may photocopy this page for classroom and personal use.

---

[1] In Assignments 1, 2, and 3 in this chapter, the language-based expectations and standards-based content and topic overlap, as indicated by the essential learning noted below each mini-template. In these situations, teachers are urged to focus on the essential learning to the best of their ability while differentiating the language-based expectations for students across the language proficiency continuum.

Assignment 2

Fully English Proficient	Level 2
Language-Based Expectations: Read and give a five-minute summary and plot analysis	*Language-Based Expectations:*
Standards-Based Content or Topic (from the curriculum): of a novel about social issues	
Scaffolding and Support: using • a graphic organizer for the development of the summary and analysis	*Scaffolding and Support:* using •

Essential learning: broadening understanding of social issues, developing reading comprehension by analyzing and orally summarizing text

Assignment 3

Fully English Proficient	Level 2
Language-Based Expectations: Write a detailed lab report	*Language-Based Expectations:*
Standards-Based Content or Topic (from the curriculum): encompassing the scientific method	
Scaffolding and Support: using • based on an experiment done in class	*Scaffolding and Support:* using •

Essential learning: listing and describing the steps of the scientific method, writing a lab report with appropriate format and content

Copyright © 2010. Caslon, Inc. All rights reserved. The first purchaser may photocopy this page for classroom and personal use.

Assignment 4

Fully English Proficient	Level 2
Language-Based Expectations: Create a public service announcement	*Language-Based Expectations:*
Standards-Based Content or Topic (from the curriculum): video about global warming	
Scaffolding and Support: using • the support of a small group	*Scaffolding and Support:* using •

Essential learning: identifying causes of and solutions for global warming, implementing technological skills, such as running a video camera, using computer software to create a short video clip

Copyright © 2010. Caslon, Inc. All rights reserved. The first purchaser may photocopy this page for classroom and personal use.

Suggested Ways to Adapt Assignments

Guidance pertaining to the language-based expectations for Bayan's and Estefania's assignments is presented in the following paragraphs.

Assignment 1

Students must write a letter to a public official voicing concern about an issue. (Essential learning: writing a letter in correct format, formally voicing a concern)

• *For Bayan:* This assignment will necessitate building background, since Bayan has never written a letter before. Instead of having her write to a public official that she does not know, contextualize the assignment more by asking her to write a very simple letter to the principal about a concern on her school campus. While her placement in the same class as native speakers of English who are on grade level raises questions, the authors realize that, in reality, ELLs are often placed into grade-specific courses without regard for language proficiency levels. Teachers who utilize the differentiation strategies outlined in this book can make this approach work; without such differentiation, this placement is inappropriate and ineffective, if not against the law[2].

- *For Estefania:* Estefania likely has experience in writing letters and is familiar with the notion of lobbying for her interests. Taking time to activate these schemae will prepare her to participate in this assignment by writing a very simple letter.

- *For both:* Letters will need to follow business letter format and will be graded in accordance with Level 2 language proficiency capabilities and expectations (described in detail in Chapter 8). A letter template can be used to guide their work.

Assignment 2

Students must read a novel about social issues and give a five-minute summary and plot analysis. (Essential learning: broadening understanding of social issues, developing reading comprehension by analyzing and orally summarizing text)

- *Note:* Placement in a mainstream class that requires the reading of entire novels is questionable for Level 2 students. These students cannot be expected to participate in those kinds of assignments and should be provided with alternative programming. If such programming is not yet available, refer to the suggestions that follow for adapting this assignment.

- *For both:* Rather than having these students read complex fiction, thematic nonfiction or simple fiction texts are recommended. These books should be of basic reading level, include plenty of visual support, and represent familiar topics of interest. Students can then create a summary in the form of a poster that includes plenty of visuals labeled with phrases and simple sentences. This poster

---

[2] *Lau v. Nichols* (1974) ruled that identical education is not equal education. That is, ELLs must receive instruction targeting their linguistic needs; it is not enough to simply sit in the same classroom and "hear" the same instruction as native speakers of English.

could serve as a scaffold for the oral presentation of the book. Students might organize their summary according to the organizational text features found in the book. Oral presentations would be done in a small-group format or for the teacher, paraeducator, or trained volunteer, one-on-one.

Assignment 3

Based on an experiment done in class, students must write a detailed lab report encompassing the scientific method. (Essential learning: listing and describing the steps of the scientific method, writing a lab report with appropriate format and content)

- *For both:* Rather than writing the lab report "from scratch," these students will fill in a graphic organizer that includes visual support and lists the steps of the scientific method. They will describe what they did in the experiment at each step. Students will work with a partner with greater English proficiency in order to gain guidance throughout the writing process. (These partners must be chosen wisely and given specific guidance in how to assist an ELL.)

Assignment 4

Students must work in groups to create a public service announcement video about global warming. (Essential learning: identifying causes of and solutions for global warming, implementing technological skills, such as running a video camera, using computer software to create a short video clip)

- *For Bayan:* This project represents an opportunity for Bayan's group members to mentor her, but those group members will need explicit teacher guidance in how to do so. She can participate in the production of the video by using language to the extent that she can. For instance, she might simply state some causes of global warming while pointing to pictures on a poster (e.g., car pollution, factory pollution) followed by a peer's explanation of each issue. In terms of the technological side of the assignment, Bayan will need explicit guidance and may "shadow" other students throughout the project, trying her hand at the technology once she becomes comfortable. *Note:* She must not be left out of the technological work just because her English skills are limited and she lacks background experience with technology.

- *For Estefania:* While Estefania will also need the support of her group members, she may be more familiar with some of the technological requirements of the project than Bayan, since she attended school prior to coming to the United States and because of her higher socioeconomic status, which has afforded her access to computers, video cameras, and the like. Like Bayan, Estefania can be fully involved in production of the video, using language at the phrase and simple sentence level.

Suggested Instructional Strategies

The following paragraphs provide guidance pertaining to scaffolding and support for the assignment.

For all assignments, teachers must make sure to build sufficient background, support students in making connections to what they already know, pre-teach relevant vocabulary, and embed opportunities for interactions with native speakers of English. It is also helpful and necessary to provide students with models of what is expected, such as samples of successfully completed assignments, since the formats of assignments may be unfamiliar to ELLs. Such purposeful practices empower ELLs to be successful on adapted classroom assignments.

Assignment 1

Students must write a letter to a public official voicing concern about an issue. (Essential learning: writing a letter in correct format, formally voicing a concern)

- *For both students:* Show a sample of a completed business letter that voices a concern. "Dissect" this letter with the class, pointing out formatting issues, formulaic language, and appropriate formal business vocabulary.

- *For Bayan:* Even though Bayan is Level 2 in writing and may be unfamiliar with the genre of writing a letter to voice a concern, it is likely that her listening and speaking levels will be higher than

Level 2. It will take her longer than an L1 literate counterpart to demonstrate the proficiency needed to write her own letter. She may need to practice by filling out a template that lays out the format of a business letter and even includes some key words and structures.

- *For Estefania:* Since Estefania is familiar with the genre of business letters, has grown up surrounded by print in the home (e.g., books, newspapers, grocery lists), and can transfer her Spanish writing ability to English, this assignment is less daunting for her than for Bayan. She is accustomed to the notion of "taking care of business" through reading and writing. In addition, Estefania can readily apply her background knowledge about the importance of adhering to a prescribed format in producing her letter. Her teacher, recognizing Estefania's readiness to receive academic instruction, should consider providing various basic academic sentence examples and frames (e.g., "I am writing to express . . ." or "Thank you for your time"). Estefania may not need the letter template for more than general guidance, while Bayan's task may be to simply complete the template.

Assignment 2

Students must read a novel about social issues and give a five-minute summary and plot analysis. (Essential learning: broadening understanding of social issues, developing reading comprehension by analyzing and orally summarizing text)

- *For both:* Show an example poster and demonstrate a simple narration in order to familiarize students with teacher expectations. Post and discuss a visually supported word/concept wall, complete with representative photos, illustrations, and icons.

- *For Bayan:* Part of Bayan's instruction must emphasize pre-reading development. For her, in particular, pre-teaching vocabulary will be beneficial. She needs this vocabulary because she has less facility than Estefania in decoding and other skills that will make print more meaningful. Shared and guided reading should also be incorporated in order to assist Bayan in making meaning from the visually supported text and building fluency. The teacher could provide a graphic organizer that can be filled out with assistance for Bayan to use as a model for her poster. Finally, someone (e.g., the teacher, a paraeducator, a trained volunteer) must practice the narration with her, modeling and having her repeat phrases and sentences.

- *For Estefania:* The strategies described for Bayan will also be effective for Estefania, though she is likely to progress more quickly since she has a richer academic background than Bayan.

Assignment 3

Based on an experiment done in class, students must write a detailed lab report encompassing the scientific method. (Essential learning: listing and describing the steps of the scientific method, writing a lab report with appropriate format and content)

- *For both:* Students can be provided with key words or sentence strips with accompanying pictures and icons that describe the steps of the experiment according to the scientific method. Students will select and sequence these strips in the correct order as a prewriting activity. They will then fill out a graphic organizer that includes a word/phrase bank with accompanying pictures. (The graphic organizer may be partially completed for Bayan.)

Assignment 4

Students must work in groups to create a public service announcement video about global warming. (Essential learning: identifying causes of and solutions for global warming, implementing technological skills, such as running a video camera, using computer software to create a short video clip)

- *For both:* The group members must be explicitly taught how to welcome and effectively work with an ELL of low language proficiency. Both Bayan and Estefania will benefit from the hands-on nature of the technology and the interaction with and mentoring of their group members. They will be able to expand and practice their English by both creating the poster (based on a model) and "narrating" the poster on the public service announcement. (This narration may take the form of speaking memorized lines, supported by teacher cueing, since the students may be nervous about being taped.)

Activity 4.2 Applying Your Learning to Your Own Level 2 Student

Think of a student that you know who is at Level 2. (If you are not currently serving a Level 2 student, think ahead to a time when you will serve such a student.) Based on an assignment that you routinely use, differentiate expectations for your Level 2 student.

Fully English Proficient	Level 1
Language-Based Expectations:	*Language-Based Expectations:*
Standards-Based Content or Topic (from the curriculum):	
Scaffolding and Support:[3] using	*Scaffolding and Support:* using

Essential Learning: _____

Copyright © 2010. Caslon, Inc. All rights reserved. The first purchaser may photocopy this page for classroom and personal use.

---

[3] Note that the scaffolding and support that are provided for fully English proficient students is also provided for ELLs, though ELLs may often need different kinds of or more scaffolding and support.

Professional Development Resources

Resource 4.1   Appropriate Assignment/Assessment Procedures for Level 2 Students

In General	Listening and Speaking	Pre-reading and Reading	Writing
• Create and use assignments/ assessments that allow students to demonstrate content knowledge, skills, and abilities without language mastery. • Focus on correct answers rather than errors and omissions. • Allow students to complete assessment procedures under the guidance of a bilingual teacher or paraeductor. • Weight graded components according to students' linguistic strengths. • Make the assignment/assessment process comprehensible by explaining the directions orally and providing visual support (e.g., realia, icons, manipulatives, modeling and models).	• Test orally using everyday and general content/academic language to elicit phrases and simple sentences. • Allow occasional first-language oral responses.	• Use high-quality, age-appropriate, lower-reading-level materials that provide extensive visual support, expecting comprehension of frequently encountered words and phrases, often dependent upon visuals provided. • Prompt the repetition of a teacher cue (speaking or singing). • Test orally using everyday and general content/academic language to elicit phrases and simple sentences. • For students literate in the first language, support first-language reading by providing appropriate materials.	• Elicit writing of phrases and simple sentences. • Use visually supported graphic organizers that students complete with phrases and simple sentences to check for understanding. • Require students to supplement writing with visual support to enhance meaning (e.g., drawing, magazine pictures, clip art). • For students literate in the first language, allow occasional first-language writing, as appropriate.

Copyright © 2010. Caslon, Inc. All rights reserved. The first purchaser may photocopy this page for classroom and personal use.

Resource 4.2   Appropriate Instructional Strategies for Level 2 Students

In General	Listening	Speaking	Pre-reading and Reading	Writing
• Provide sensory support for *every* lesson (e.g., real objects, pictures, hands-on materials and experiences, nonverbal communication, demonstrations, modeling, simulations).	• Use simplified, correct language, repeating or paraphrasing, as needed. • Allow sufficient wait time (likely several seconds). • Promote higher-order thinking processes during oral teaching by providing graphic organizers, modeling their completion, as needed. • Employ think-alouds to model both processes and language.	• Encourage participation in discussions by eliciting phrases or simple sentences. • Prompt and scaffold oral language production by modeling content/academic language and providing sentence examples and models (e.g., "The rabbit has fur. ____ ____ ____ scales.") • Concentrate on student meaning rather than on correctness of expression. • Build confidence by rewarding all attempts to communicate.	• At the school and program levels, for L1-pre-literate students, (continue to) implement a high-quality, research-based, culturally and linguistically sensitive reading development program. • For reading-related activities, use extensive visual support (e.g., posters, pictures), since Level 2 students are often unable to derive meaning from print alone. • Support grade-level content curriculum with high-quality, age-appropriate, lower-reading-level books aligned with content curriculum that provide extensive visual support. • Teach pre-reading skills (e.g., phonemic awareness, concepts of print, phonics).	• Prompt and scaffold written language production by modeling content/academic language and providing sentence examples and models (e.g., "The rabbit has fur. ____ ____ ____ scales.") • Incorporate modeled, shared, and guided writing activities. • Accept phrases or simple sentences in lieu of grade-level writing expectations. • Concentrate on student meaning rather than on correctness of expression. • Promote the development of higher-order thinking skills by modeling the use of graphic organizers such as Venn diagrams, T-charts, and concept maps.

Copyright © 2010. Caslon, Inc. All rights reserved. The first purchaser may photocopy this page for classroom and personal use.

Resource 4.2 *Continued*

In General	Listening	Speaking	Pre-reading and Reading	Writing
			• Lay a foundation for comprehension: build background and help students to make connections to prior learning and experiences. • Read or sing visually supported stories or texts to students, using props and acting to increase comprehension and develop oral language skills necessary for reading. • Incorporate shared, shared-to-guided, and guided reading. • Promote the development of higher-order thinking skills by modeling the use of graphic organizers such as Venn diagrams, T-charts, and concept maps.	

Copyright © 2010. Caslon, Inc. All rights reserved. The first purchaser may photocopy this page for classroom and personal use.

5

Differentiation Strategies for Level 3 Students

If your plan is for one year, plant rice;
If your plan is for ten years, plant trees;
If your plan is for a hundred years, educate children.
—Confucius

Incisive analysis of student abilities related to language proficiency levels leads teachers of English language learners (ELLs) to create useful and innovative assignments and assessments and related instruction. This type of ELL-specific differentiation empowers students to express their understanding of content without having yet fully developed language mastery. Communicating understanding of standards-based content using increasingly proficient language is the ideal vehicle to drive both enhanced content mastery and language development. In this way, students receive instruction that offers the maximum benefit: simultaneous learning related to both grade-level content and English language development. In this chapter, we focus on the language development of Level 3 students, describing these students in detail and outlining strategies that can help teachers to keep students engaged, motivated, and on track.

While the suggested strategies are designed to elicit production for Level 3 students in listening, speaking, reading, and writing, teachers are reminded to maintain their efforts in pushing students to reach ever higher targets, providing scaffolding in instruction and assessment. Such informed practice will help students advance to the next level of language proficiency, Level 4, by providing and eliciting, where possible and appropriate, increasingly refined examples of Level 4 language production.

Considering Variation in Level 3 Students' Backgrounds

**Student
Scenarios**

Toua, a Hmong 3rd grader born in a refugee camp in Thailand, is the son of parents from Laos. His family arrived in the United States two years ago, and he initially struggled in school, partly because he had received no formal education prior to his arrival. As a result, he had no experience with reading and writing in his first language. In the past two years, Toua's parents have become gainfully employed and reestablished their network with the Hmong community. In terms of language, Toua quickly developed social language, and his teachers wonder why he struggles academically, since he appears to be fluent. His reading and writing are below grade level, but his teachers suspect he might just be lazy.

Aung, a 3rd grader from Myanmar (formerly Burma), was also born in a refugee camp. Before arriving in the United States last year, Aung attended school in the camp and was taught in English by missionaries. His parents do not speak English at all and have had difficulty locating employment. Aung frequently misses school when he is excused to translate at the clinic for his parents. Aung's language skills allow him to communicate well in social situations, and classroom instruction is meaningful to him, especially when contextualized and supported visually. Since his teachers in the camp paid particular attention to the conventions of writing, Aung perfectly forms the English alphabet and works very diligently to create accurate written products, though his work is below grade level. He also struggles to make sense of grade-level reading materials.

Toua and Aung, though both 3rd grade refugees from Southeast Asia, are quite different in terms of their biographical profiles, which dictate their instructional needs. The issue of first-language literacy is a primary informant of differentiated lesson design in that Toua needs more explicit instruction in reading and writing than Aung, who can transfer some skills learned during his previous schooling experiences. Both Toua and Aung live in homes where English is never spoken.[1] As a result, both students will require repeated and sustained efforts to embed interaction with native English-speaking peers in the classroom in both social and academic situations. Such intentional opportunities for Toua and Aung to hear and practice English in authentic learning contexts are essential to their development of English language proficiency.

---

[1] Teachers are reminded that maintaining both the first language and the related culture in the home is recommended and should not urge parents of ELLs to speak English at home.

Since Toua lives in an enclave community, he has many opportunities for cultural experiences and first-language reinforcement. However, there are few occasions for him to use English outside of school, and he does not appreciate or recognize the need to learn academic English. His outgoing personality has helped him to engage with his classmates and to develop a solid foundation of social English, but his academic language abilities lag behind. In this way, Toua typifies many Level 3 students who, having developed the language they need for social interactions, still struggle with academic tasks because they lack academic vocabulary and a command of more complex discourse commonly used in the content areas and in testing. What may appear to some teachers as laziness on Toua's part is likely to be, rather, his lack of understanding and background knowledge related to academic tasks at hand. Toua may also have a lack of motivation to participate, since he may not have a meaningful relationship with his teacher and may perceive that his teacher is frustrated with him as well. This is a watershed moment for Toua; without explicit instruction in academic language, he will stagnate at Level 3 indefinitely. He is in dire need of focused, specific, and sustained differentiated instruction that will develop his weakness in academic language and launch him toward Level 4 and eventual full English proficiency.

Aung, having received instruction in English before coming to the United States, nevertheless shares some of the characteristics of Toua's biographical profile in that both 3rd grade students live in homes where English is not spoken. As a result, teachers should expect to provide increased interaction opportunities within the school setting for language development to support both Aung and Toua. Toua's language has developed more slowly than Aung's because of Toua's lack of previous formal schooling. In addition, Toua has had fewer opportunities to develop his school-based socialization skills, a fact that might be evident in his classroom behavior. In contrast, Aung behaves quietly and cooperatively, seeming very content with the protocol of school behavior, working diligently and independently as needed. His painstaking handwriting is an example for other students. He is familiar with the format of a written page in terms of neatness, margins, headings, and the like. Because of his "jump start" on literacy in English, Aung is poised to advance on the continuum toward English proficiency. However, teachers worry that his increasing absences to translate for his parents will have a negative impact on his progress.

Level 3 Student Descriptors

Level 3 students generally possess a strong foundation of social language and continue to broaden and deepen their academic language when supported with appropriate instruction. In terms of listening, Level 3 ELLs still benefit from sensory support to construct meaning from more detailed and complex discourse. These students can speak and write using increasingly complex sentence structures, though errors sometimes inhibit communication.

Listening

In the domain of listening, Level 3 students can grasp some main ideas of increasingly complex communication, though they still rely on sensory supports in order to better comprehend details. Sentence-level communication in both social and general academic situations is typically established during level 3; at this point, students will polish and expand their listening ability by building vocabulary and knowledge of more complex grammatical constructions.

Speaking

In terms of speaking, Level 3 students can generate simple sentences and often attempt higher forms of complexity which sometimes inhibit understanding. Level 3 speakers also continue to develop vocabulary and grammatical structures in speech related to both concrete and abstract topics. Because Level 3 students have an extensive ability to communicate socially, teachers could often be fooled into thinking that they are fully proficient and therefore prematurely cease differentiation strategies based on language proficiency level. Such premature and inappropriate cessation of the provision of ELL-specific teaching and assessment strategies can result in students who, deprived of scaffolding and explicit and informed instruction, become lifelong inhabitants of Level 3, a phenomenon that is reported with increasing incidence. Therefore, teachers are urged to base instructional decisions on meaningful data from sanctioned academic English proficiency tests and classroom formative assessments designed to inform educators specifically about ELLs' proficiency levels. Any other assessments that have been developed without the needs of ELLs in mind will yield far less useful or meaningful data on which to base instruction.

Reading

In Level 3 reading, as in speaking, students continue to make sense of simple text and attempt to construe meaning from increasingly complex writing, still deriving benefit from sensory support to solidify understanding. Since, at Level 3, students use their background knowledge and experiences to make sense of increasingly complex and lengthy language and associated concepts, accessing and building student background related to experiences and knowledge is essential. While the importance of background knowledge is consistent across all levels of language proficiency, possessing academic background knowledge takes center stage as linguistic and content complexity intensifies. It continues to be critical that teachers be fully knowledgeable about their students' social and academic backgrounds, including their biographical profiles, cumulative folders, and other evidence that can illuminate individual student characteristics. This knowledge provides educators with valuable insight about what students bring to bear in terms of reading skills and helps to shape appropriate differentiated instruction.

Writing

Level 3 students can generate various types of writing with increasing complexity, since their writing development tends to mirror their speaking development. Though these Level 3 ELLs are prone to making errors that can obscure meaning, their vocabulary and sentence structures are gaining sophistication across a range of concrete and abstract topics. As when teaching reading, teachers are advised to incorporate what they know about Level 3 students' backgrounds into writing instruction, "backfilling" with appropriate instruction where necessary.

A Word About Language Objectives

The description of Level 3 students' linguistic abilities listed on the chart and described in the preceding paragraphs serves as a basis for the development of language objectives for these students. The information discussed in the following assignment/assessment strategy section also clarifies reasonable linguistic goals and expectations for students at Level 3. The instructional strategies described toward the end of the chapter can assist teachers in planning lessons that facilitate success in achieving both language and content objectives.

Since all four language domains (listening, speaking, reading, and writing) have firmly taken root in the Level 3 student, these students are uniquely positioned to maximize the results of high-quality instruction that is linguistically differentiated. Such instruction is considered after the following section devoted to assessment.

A Sample Differentiated Assignment for Level 3 Students

Table 5.1 is a sample assignment differentiated for students at Levels 3 and 4. Differentiation for Level 4 students is included in this sample assignment as a reminder to teachers that they must continually bear in mind the next higher level of language proficiency in designing their expectations for students in order to push students to ever-higher levels of achievement. (For detailed guidance regarding the interpretation of this template-based differentiated assignment, refer to Chapter 3.)

In order to facilitate the learning and achievement of ELLs, teachers can collaborate in a range of ways. For example, a teacher leader with expertise in both ESL/bilingual education *and* the content area might develop lesson plans for all teachers working with ELLs in the given content area.

Necessary Assignment/Assessment Strategies for Level 3 Students

Large-scale standardized assessment tools and classroom-based assessment tools designed for native speakers of English are likely to be inappropriate for Level 3 ELLs, yielding invalid information about both what students know and what they can do, since the scores are clouded by (under-developed) language proficiency. As a result, teachers must sup-

Table 5.1 Sample assignment differentiated for Levels 3 and 4

Fully English Proficient	Level 3	Level 4
Language-Based Expectations: Write a set of instructions using grade-level vocabulary and sentence structures	*Language-Based Expectations:* Write a set of instructions using some content and academic vocabulary and simple and complex sentence structures	*Language-Based Expectations:* Write a set of instructions using some content and academic vocabulary and complex sentence structures
Standards-Based Content or Topic (from the curriculum): for a self-selected task		
Scaffolding and Support: using • a model assignment, • teacher demonstration of the task using a "think-aloud," • a sequential graphic organizer for planning to write, • a language wall with sequencing words and key sentence structures, and • feedback designed to push students to full proficiency according to the grade-level writing standards to guide writing.	*Scaffolding and Support:* using • a model assignment, • teacher demonstration of the task using a "think-aloud," • a sequential graphic organizer for planning to write, • photographs of chosen processes, • a language wall with sequencing words and key sentence structures, • pre-taught vocabulary, • a supplementary "think-aloud" demonstration of paragraph writing, • academic sentence frames posted in the classroom, • pictorially supported procedure texts, • level-appropriate feedback designed to push students to the next level of proficiency in writing to guide writing.	*Scaffolding and Support:* using • a model assignment, • teacher demonstration of the task using a "think-aloud," • a sequential graphic organizer for planning to write, • a language wall with sequencing words and key sentence structures, and • level-appropriate feedback designed to push students to the next level of proficiency in writing to guide writing.

port ELLs by creating innovative assessments that are sensitive to the linguistic and cultural realities of Level 3 students, in order to gain accurate information about what these students know and can do in the content areas.

In General

Create and use assignments/assessments that allow students to demonstrate content knowledge, skills, and abilities without language mastery. At Level 3, students' abilities to speak and write have developed such that they can begin to participate more actively in assessments that require English language production. However, persistent errors may be present and may hinder the communication process. For this reason, assessment procedures for Level 3 students must not require language production beyond student capabilities. Instead, teachers are urged to allow students to demonstrate their learning in a variety of authentic ways that allow them to show their content knowledge without full English language mastery. Teachers can ask students to generate sensory depictions of understanding such as the creation of a PowerPoint presentation or a podcast, embedding the development of technology skills.

Consider allowing students to complete assessment procedures under the guidance of a bilingual teacher or paraeductor. Some Level 3 students continue to derive much-needed support from the assistance of a bilingual educator when completing assessments. However, at Level 3, the type of bilingual support is likely to involve more clarification than extensive explanation. As for students at Levels 1 and 2, this support can be provided individually or, perhaps, in a small-group setting. For instance, a paraeducator could clarify the terms *potential energy* and *kinetic energy* if a student were confused by that academic language so the student could demonstrate content understanding.

Consider weighting graded components according to students' linguistic strengths. Recognizing that ELLs bring a wealth of background knowledge and contributions to the classroom, teachers should emphasize the positive. In order to ensure academic success for all students, teachers must advocate for parity of access not only to the curriculum, but also to educational opportunities including advanced courses, which are often determined by grade point averages. When grading students whose language abilities are not on grade level, teachers must decide what they are really grading. We advocate that content mastery, rather than English language mastery, be the focus of Level 3 students' grades. This emphasis should be based on test data that identify language proficiency level. When a student is at Level 3, he or she must be graded in a way that takes the developing language proficiency level into account, without penalizing him or her. Further guidance will be provided in Chapter 8.

Make the assignment/assessment process comprehensible by explaining the directions orally and providing visual support (e.g., realia, icons, manipulatives, modeling and models). In order to gain an accurate estimate of what Level 3 students know and can do in the content areas, teachers must ensure that students understand how to complete the assessment procedure. Hopefully, this has been clarified during instruction, but teachers are urged to use whatever means are appropriate to ensure that all students comprehend what is being asked of them during assessment. For example, teachers could familiarize students with how to answer specific types of test items by modeling the process with a sample item (e.g., drawing a line connecting "question" and a response in a set of matching items).

Simultaneously assess content and language development (e.g., through summarizing, story retelling, questioning and responding, analyzing, evaluating). Since classroom/content teachers generally teach language through their content, they are similarly charged with assessing both language and content as appropriate. This approach of simultaneously assessing language and content is not new in U.S. classrooms; for instance, teachers routinely assess non-ELLs' vocabulary development in the content areas. At Level 3, ELLs are ready to participate in this kind of assessment, though only through differentiation. Teachers must carefully attend to the student descriptors for Level 3 ELLs when creating assessments for Level 3 students, ensuring that the linguistic demands of these assessments are in accordance with students' current abilities. For example, when assessing Level 3 students' vocabulary knowledge in science (or any other content area), teachers must remember that students at this level are not on grade level in terms of vocabulary development. However, they have moved beyond only general academic vocabulary and are capable of using more specific and precise vocabulary, as scaffolded during instruction. Such vocabulary is "fair game" for assessment, though teachers could also consider using a word bank.

Listening and Speaking

Test orally using and expecting more precise and specific content vocabulary and increasingly complex grammatical structures. (Language should reflect sentence-level frames and models used during instruction.) As with instruction, the assessment of Level 3 students also presents a golden opportunity for teachers to elicit and expect no less than Level 3 responses, as a precursor to Level 4 achievement. Although Level 3 students are not fully proficient in English, they are capable of learning and using content-specific vocabulary that reflects increasing precision and specificity. There is no "equation" for determining what comprises Level 3 vocabulary; teachers must remember that Level 3 vocabulary extends beyond general academic language, but it does not represent grade-level production. For instance, when discussing layers of the rain forest, a Level 2 student might refer to the "top" of the rain forest. A Level 3 student might talk about the "ceiling," whereas a student using grade-level vocabulary would use the term "canopy."

Reading

Use high-quality, age-appropriate, lower-reading-level materials that provide extensive visual support, expecting comprehension of increasingly complex sentence- and paragraph-level text. Level 3 students are beginning to make sense of sentence- and paragraph-level texts, but are still below grade level in terms of English reading ability. To scaffold students' reading ability, the use of visually supported lower-reading-level materials is a necessity. Whereas grade-level reading materials are not likely to be at the instructional level of Level 3 ELLs, these lower-reading-level materials can contribute to increased comprehension. Therefore, grade-level reading materials should not be used for Level 3 assessment purposes, either. In addition to finding lower reading-level materials at public libraries, school libraries, area education agencies, and other venues, these materials can be obtained from a variety of publishers; see Resource 2.2 for a list.

Test orally using and expecting more precise and specific content vocabulary and increasingly complex grammatical structures. Maintaining high expectations for ELLs, closely matched with the student descriptors on the chart, will help to ensure that ELLs continue their progress from Level 3 toward proficiency in English. Only through the consistent teaching of precise and specific content/academic vocabulary can teachers expect such vocabulary to be operationalized at the time of assessment. The same is true for the teaching and assessment of increasingly complex grammatical structures. Teachers must be explicit in their instruction and insistent on the production of both content/academic vocabulary and increasingly complex grammatical structures during assessment. Further, teachers must recognize the purpose and responsibility of their assessment: to provide ELLs the opportunity to perform to the best of their linguistic abilities, showcasing the highest extent of their content knowledge, skills, and abilities. An example of increasing grammatical complexity would be moving from two simple sentences (e.g., "Glass is hard. A diamond is harder") to a complex sentence using the comparative (e.g., "A diamond is harder than glass").

When traditional paper and pencil tests must be used, employ simplified English and visual support (e.g., clip art, graphs). By definition, Level 3 students cannot effectively demonstrate their content knowledge, skills, and abilities on tests that require full proficiency in grade-level English. Further, the range of Level 3 proficiency itself is extremely broad, with students entering Level 3 differing greatly from those at the upper reaches of Level 3. Thus the language of assessments must take intra-level variations into account, providing supports for the beginning end of the Level 3 spectrum. For instance, while advanced Level 3 students might not rely heavily on pictorial support such as clip art or icons, ELLs just entering Level 3 would likely require such support in order to make sense of the assessment instrument. Simplified English may mean changing a passive construction (e.g., "A _____ [protractor] is needed to measure the size of an angle.") to an active construction (e.g., "A tool used to measure the size of an angle is a _____ [protractor].") A picture of a protractor could also be included with this test item if vocabulary alone were being assessed. See Fairbairn (2007) for additional examples and clarification.

Writing

Elicit writing of increasingly complex sentence structures using a developing range of content/academic vocabulary. When prompting students to demonstrate their content knowledge, skills, and abilities, teachers should call for Level 3 production. However, in order to do so, it is recommended that teachers frame their prompts using language that students are certain to comprehend (comparable to the simplified English mentioned earlier). Comprehension of the assessment prompt should not be part of what is assessed; rather, teachers should be assessing the written response to the prompt. If the prompt cannot be understood, then the teacher has no opportunity to evaluate a response. Once the student understands the task at hand, she or he can produce Level 3 language in response. Teachers may need to specify the kinds of vocabulary and grammar that are expected (e.g., "Use the words discussed in class, and write in complete, detailed sentences.") or provide an academic sentence frame or two to model what is expected.

When traditional paper and pencil tests must be used, employ simplified English and visual support (e.g., clip art, graphs). This strategy applies equally to tests of reading and tests of writing. Teachers must be sure to elicit responses using understandable language and visual support where needed. For instance, students could be asked "explain" the plant growth process by sequencing and labeling pictures of a seed, a sprout, a seedling, and a plant.

Necessary Instructional Strategies for Level 3 Students

As stated in Chapters 3 and 4, teachers of ELLs must

1. examine their assumptions,

2. learn about students' backgrounds,

3. determine students' instructional levels based on content knowledge, skills, and abilities and language proficiency, and

4. teach essential learning from the curriculum and its associated language in a differentiated manner.

These critical action steps are keys to scaffolding student learning of both language and content. Such incorporation of all four critical action steps is never more important than at Level 3, where students are often relegated to the status of "lifelong Level 3s." In other words, without appropriate differentiated instruction, Level 3 students are at risk for failure to progress and for taking up "permanent residence" at Level 3.[2] Since Level 3 students have developed language abilities across all domains, the instruction and assessment strategies listed in the chart and described in the following paragraphs offer distinctly powerful potential to scaffold student abilities, but only if such strategies are appropriately applied. Without such appropriate instruction and assessment, ELLs will miss the opportunity to continue their progress toward proficiency.

In General

Provide sensory support for *every* lesson (e.g., real objects, pictures, hands-on materials and experiences, nonverbal communication, demonstrations, modeling, simulations). As stated in the previous chapter, sensory experiences provide students with "mental Velcro" to which they can attach new learning of both language and content. As grade-level content becomes more complex, this strategy continues to offer excellent support for Level 3 students. For example, starting a physics class focused on the topic of friction, the teacher could begin by asking students to rub their hands together, creating heat. He or she could then build upon this shared experience to introduce vocabulary and conceptual learning related to the topic of friction, making connections to what students already know through experience.

Explicitly teach and require students to use increasingly complex content/academic vocabulary and sentence structures. At Level 3, since students have a grasp of basic sentence structure and academic vocabulary, teachers must continue their informed developmental expectations that students will expand their abilities to generate more complex language. For example, science teachers can target language development by

---

[2] Based on our own experience and on the input of teachers around the United States, native English-speakers may also be at Level 3, particularly in reading and writing. Such students need the same type of linguistically differentiated instruction as Level 3 ELLs.

providing and eliciting more complex academic sentence frames such as *"Despite the fact that* the polar ice cap is melting, _____.*"* Teachers can use such academic sentence frames across content areas and should collaborate to ensure that such frames and content/academic vocabulary are implemented throughout the curriculum. Such intentional work to build academic language will pay dividends when students participate in large-scale standardized testing, which often uses this formal register.

Listening

Prompt and scaffold students' language development by using increasingly complex language, paraphrasing as needed. As Level 3 students develop their sophistication in terms of listening, teachers must concentrate on providing increasingly complex aural input. Students will only enhance their recognition of more complex language only if they receive such stimuli, contextualized through classroom activities. As teachers strive to help students heighten their listening skills, teachers must be conscious of the incremental nature of language development, offering a range of paraphrases that clarify and restate meaning. For example, when asking a student about her or his science experiment, the teacher might ask, "What was the outcome of the procedure? That is, what happened?" In this way, students who did not understand the first question would still be able to participate through the support afforded by the second question. Through the sustained utilization of this strategy, teachers will provide essential support that Level 3 students need to develop their listening skills.

Allow sufficient wait time (likely several seconds). As Level 3 students attempt to process and generate increasingly complex language, they continue to benefit from (and require!) additional processing time and wait time, even up to 10 seconds. Especially as ELLs articulate academic sentence frames for the first time, patience on the part of the teacher will encourage sustained effort and growth in language and content learning.

Facilitate and support higher-order thinking processes during oral teaching by providing students with graphic organizers, modeling their completion, as needed. At Level 3, graphic organizers and concept maps continue to support students in understanding interrelationships among concepts in order to facilitate higher-order thinking. Level 3 students can benefit greatly when teachers incorporate strategies that allow them to conceptualize more complex ideas, despite the fact that they are not fully proficient in English. Improving the comprehensibility and contextualization of content through the use of graphic organizers facilitates the production of increasingly complex language in English. For instance, a social studies teacher could construct and complete a concept map when discussing the interrelationships between political parties.

Employ think-alouds to model both processes and language. This strategy can be utilized in the teaching of specific processes, such as the writing of a summary. The teacher models steps in writing the summary, "thinking aloud" to describe both the cognitive processes and language that are part of the summary writing process. These think-alouds can assist ELLs and non-ELLs alike in developing both content skills and abilities and important content/academic language.

Speaking

Provide opportunities to produce extended oral discourse through activities such as reporting and presentations. Level 3 students are uniquely prepared and motivated to participate in meaningful assignments and assessments through speaking, particularly when such activities are relevant, interesting, and authentic. The activities must be differentiated, and the student must receive appropriate support in carrying out the tasks. For example, one of us engaged Level 3 students through collaboration with a local university professor. Each ELL was to create a PowerPoint presentation about how to teach English as a second language, based on personal experiences, to present to future ESL teachers at the university. This authentic task was exceptionally motivating, since the students drew on their own background knowledge as ELLs and presented their content to a real university audience. Supported by a template in developing the PowerPoint, students grew in both writing and technology skills as they honed their speaking and presentation abilities. Such integrated development across domains offers an ideal avenue for language growth. Despite the fact that the task was demanding, Level 3 students succeeded with teacher and peer support (see Vann & Fairbairn, 2003).

Prompt and scaffold extended oral language production by providing visually supported sentence-level frames and models for high-quality academic discourse (e.g., "As a result of the interaction of _____ and _____ , . . ."). When teachers are conscious of the necessity for language development, they are better prepared to insist on high-quality responses, including increasingly complex sentence structures and vocabulary, rather than accepting students' one-word answers or social register as academic responses. At Level 3, teachers must insist on such high-quality responses from all students, avoiding the trap of responding to any utterance a student might produce. Insisting upon high-quality responses will support all students as they prepare not only for more advanced education, but also for viability in the future workplace. For example, rather than posing a question such as,

What is the name of the type of animal that can live both on land and in water?

which would likely elicit a one-word answer:

Amphibian,

a teacher might ask a question that elicits the characteristics of the animal:

Who can tell me some characteristics of an amphibian?

while providing an academic sentence frame, orally and in written form for student reference, and modeling it. In this case, the academic sentence frame might be

Unlike reptiles, amphibians are characterized by the fact that they _____.

Concentrate on students' meaning to a greater extent than on correctness of expression. Teachers must support Level 3 students' language development by embedding sustained teacher and peer interactions to scaffold ELLs' speaking development. In this context, teachers should continue to concentrate on the meaning of student speech rather than on errors. Detailed corrections in speaking will not be helpful to Level 3 students; rather, teachers should target limited, pre-identified aspects of language for correction (e.g., pronunciation of high-frequency academic words such as *measure*). In this way, students will learn to monitor their production incrementally, rather than become overwhelmed by a variety of confusing error corrections. For example, teachers might insist on the use of dependent clauses in oral communication about content, having provided examples using academic sentence frames.

Reading

At the school and program levels, for L1-pre-literate students, (continue to) implement a high-quality, research-based, culturally and linguistically sensitive reading development program.   As in Levels 1 and 2, the needs of students who are pre-literate in the first language continue to impact Level 3 students' progress toward grade-level reading proficiency, particularly in terms of the lack of reading ability transfer from the first language. Such L1-pre-literate Level 3 students will benefit from focused attention on reading and more time to develop and practice their reading skills. Skilled and trained reading teachers, paraeducators, and volunteers should (continue to) support Level 3 ELLs in developing their prereading *and* reading skills, since Level 3 students are ready to gain meaning from print independently. If such students do not receive targeted reading support, they will continue to be at risk for school failure. Further, to the extent possible, reading materials should reflect the full range of diverse learners in the classroom.

Use high-quality, age-appropriate, lower-reading-level books aligned with content curriculum that provide extensive visual support.   Level 3 students cannot be expected to make sense of grade-level reading materials without significant support. The best way to support the mandate to teach all students to the same content standards is by utilizing materials that match the developing reading level of students. To compensate for the inability to understand meaning presented in grade-level texts, materials that are written at a more accessible level and that incorporate a variety of visual supports must be provided for Level 3 students. See Resource 2.2 for suggested sources.

Lay a foundation for comprehension: build background and help students to make connections to prior learning and experiences.   Teachers must ensure that students begin learning experiences on a level playing field by addressing background knowledge needed for success. Teachers can and should also guide students in making connections to their background knowledge and experiences, since many students do not automatically make such connections. (For example, some ELLs may have personal experience with the curricular topic of earthquakes. This type of background knowledge should be ascertained and brought to the fore in instruction.)

Incorporate shared, shared-to-guided, and guided reading. Since Level 3 students continue to read below grade level (with the possible exception of early elementary students), continuing or beginning to use the prescribed reading strategies discussed in Chapter 3 is essential. Teachers are reminded that, regardless of the Level 3 student's age, appropriate reading instruction is always imperative. Shared, shared-to-guided, and guided reading provide irreplaceable and essential opportunities for many ELLs to practice and develop their reading abilities. Content-area books at appropriate reading levels can be used to teach reading while simultaneously supporting learning in the subject areas. Teachers might also consider sending accessible reading materials home with students, either in the form of level-appropriate curricular texts or reproducible books. (As stated previously, interested readers can consult Knox & Amador-Watson, 2000, and Fountas & Pinnell, 1996, for further guidance on these instructional techniques.)

Facilitate and support the development of higher-order thinking using graphic organizers such as Venn diagrams, T-charts, and concept maps. Level 3 students can continue to capitalize on the integration of graphic organizers for their reading development, particularly as important scaffolding to the related domain of writing. By developing "graphic-organizer literacy" through a variety of such visual representations for conceptualizing thoughts, relationships, and connections, Level 3 ELLs can sharpen complex ways of understanding and of articulating their thinking. These tools should be used routinely to ensure that ELLs have a ready schema to draw upon for fine-tuning new learning—for example, a sequential graphic organizer (with visual support as needed) can be used to demonstrate understanding of how to complete a recipe.

Writing

At Level 3, L1-pre-literate writers, as well as readers, will likely require more time than their L1-literate peers to demonstrate progress in writing. As with the incremental development of grade-level reading skills, writing development of all learners simply is, in part, a function of practice over time. With this fact in mind, students must be afforded many opportunities to write, particularly in contextualized and meaningful situations, while receiving differentiated support.

Provide opportunities to produce extended written discourse through activities such as journaling, report writing, and preparing presentations. This strategy applies equally to speaking and writing. With sufficient scaffolding (e.g., templates, individual assistance), Level 3 students can create extended pieces of writing. Guided writing, mentioned previously, may facilitate the creation of such pieces as well as reduce errors.

Prompt and scaffold extended written language production by providing visually supported sentence-level frames and models for high-quality academic discourse (e.g., "As a result of the interaction of _____ and _____ , . . .). This strategy applies equally to both speaking and writing. As with word walls and concept walls, templates for broader discourse (e.g., language walls) should be accompanied by pictures, icons, charts, and other meaningful representations. Providing templates in the form of academic sentence frames and larger models for various forms of discourse builds a repertoire of language for Level 3 students to draw on across the curriculum. Such practical templates should be visibly posted in the classroom for ease of student reference. For example, teachers could post the format of a lab report, including the required components, supported visually. Again, the need for visual support is dependent on the student's level of language proficiency, rather than on his or her age.

Incorporate modeled, shared, and guided writing activities. As Level 3 students enhance their understanding that writing is increasingly complex thought applied to paper, modeled, shared, and guided writing offer ways to enhance Level 3 students' writing abilities. As described in Chapter 3, students observe the teacher in modeled writing and interact with a peer or with the teacher. In shared writing, they can see what competent writing with increasing complexity looks like. Having experienced an appropriate writing model, Level 3 ELLs can then apply that knowledge to their own practice in a guided writing setting (with teacher support) and, eventually, independently. These techniques could work well, for example, when students are writing narratives in a workshop environment.

Accept increasingly complex sentences in lieu of grade-level writing expectations. Teachers must set their expectations for Level 3 writing in keeping with the student descriptors on the chart. While Level 3 students can write increasingly complex sentences with a developing range of academic vocabulary, they cannot produce grade-level writing, since errors can obstruct meaning.[3] Level 3 ELLs, like their Level 2 counterparts, must be afforded sufficient time and opportunity to develop their writing, as their native English-speaking peers likely experienced in the early elementary grades. For example, if the assignment is for students to write a fairy tale, Level 3 students' writing will likely be shorter and less complex (in terms of both structure and vocabulary) than that of their grade-level peers. (Length would likely be diminished because of the increased time that it takes Level 3 students to produce writing.)

Engage students in writing activities that elicit expanded sentences using a range of complexity. In an effort to ensure that Level 3 students will use a variety of increasingly complex sentence structures, teachers must provide, model, and post suggested academic sentence frames (e.g., ways to combine simple sentences into compound sentences). In this way, students will be able and expected to write longer, more complex sentences commensurate with Level 3 capabilities. Content teachers have an ideal forum to teach this meaningful augmentation of writing ability in the context of their subject areas.

Concentrate on student meaning to a greater extent than on correctness of expression. As with speaking, teachers should focus their attention on Level 3 students' messages rather than on errors included in the written message. Error correction should be limited to pre-identified, level-appropriate aspects of language. For instance, if a student were to say, "When I finish graduating, I intend to visit Mexico," a teacher might ignore the grammatical inaccuracies in the first part of the sentence and simply continue the conversation.

Facilitate and support the development of higher-order thinking skills by using graphic organizers such as Venn diagrams, T-charts, and concept maps. Graphic organizers can be utilized in conjunction with ac-

---

[3] The authors recognize that, in the lower elementary grades, increasingly complex sentences with significant errors may fall within the range of grade-level performance. Again, guidance listed on the chart and described herein must be interpreted in terms of grade-level norms for language ability.

ademic sentence frames as a springboard for complex language production. For instance, students might complete a Venn diagram comparing two countries and conclude by writing a summary based on the intersection of the two circles. The teacher could provide an academic sentence frame such as "While India produces _____ and Thailand produces _____, both countries produce ____." Such explicit language instruction provides students with more complex ways to express content meanings that they intuitively understand, but may be unable to articulate, while providing a repertoire of templates for students to draw upon for future use. All students in the classroom will benefit from this type of academic language instruction, including those who are native speakers of English.

Instruction That Integrates Language Domains

As seen in the university-school partnership mentioned earlier, the more authentic a teaching and learning activity is, the more likely it is to integrate all four language domains (listening, speaking, reading, and writing). Teachers are urged to fully integrate instruction related to all four language domains such that all four are utilized on a regular basis.

Conclusion

Teachers are encouraged to match strategies with student proficiency levels describing each individual language domain. That is, if a student is at Level 3 in speaking but at Level 1 in writing, strategies from Level 3 should be applied to speaking, while strategies from Level 1 would be appropriate in writing. This would be the case regardless of the age of the student.

Professional Development Activities

Activity 5.1   Student Scenarios with Application Ideas

Adapt the following assignments for Toua and Aung, who were introduced at the beginning of the chapter, according to each student's language proficiency level and any other important factors:

- Differentiate the language-based expectations based on the student descriptors and using relevant assignment/assessment strategies on the chart and in this chapter.
  - Bear in mind the "essential learning" for each assignment (noted below each assignment template) as you differentiate the expectations, so that important skills are not overlooked.
- Design appropriate scaffolding and support using relevant instructional strategies on the chart and in this chapter.

Assignment 1[4]

Fully English Proficient	Level 3
Language-Based Expectations: Write a two-page report	*Language-Based Expectations:*
Standards-Based Content or Topic (from the curriculum): about a president	
Scaffolding and Support: [4] using • a graphic organizer for note-taking and • library-based resources	*Scaffolding and Support:* using •

Essential learning: note-taking, summarizing, developing familiarity with the presidents of the United States

Copyright © 2010. Caslon, Inc. All rights reserved. The first purchaser may photocopy this page for classroom and personal use.

---

[4] For this assignment (and the assignments that follow), the language-based expectations and the standards-based content and topic overlap. In instances such as this, teachers are urged to focus their differentiation on ways that allow students to build the skills that comprise the essential learning for the assignment without full language mastery.

Assignment 2

Fully English Proficient	Level 3
Language-Based Expectations: Recite aloud	*Language-Based Expectations:*
Standards-Based Content or Topic (from the curriculum): an original haiku poem	
Scaffolding and Support: using • memory only based on • teacher modeling of the writing of a haiku, • teacher modeling of poetry reading, • in-class analysis of the haiku form, and • choral reading of several haiku poems	*Scaffolding and Support:* using •

Essential learning: poetry writing skills; presentation skills including eye contact, volume, expression, and fluency of speech; memorization skills; developing familiarity with poetic forms

Copyright © 2010. Caslon, Inc. All rights reserved. The first purchaser may photocopy this page for classroom and personal use.

Assignment 3

Fully English Proficient	Level 3
Language-Based Expectations: Complete a page	*Language-Based Expectations:*

Standards-Based Content or Topic (from the curriculum): an original haiku poem	
Scaffolding and Support: using • instruction in the meaning of math phrases (e.g., "greater than," "in all") and • learning from teacher modeling of the "translation" of problems from prose to numbers using manipulatives	*Scaffolding and Support:* using •

Essential learning: converting prose to an equation

Copyright © 2010. Caslon, Inc. All rights reserved. The first purchaser may photocopy this page for classroom and personal use.

Assignment 4

Fully English Proficient	Level 3
Language-Based Expectations: Create a song, rap, or chant	*Language-Based Expectations:*
Standards-Based Content or Topic (from the curriculum): about how the moon moves to create its phases	
Scaffolding and Support: using • visually supported instruction on phases of the moon, • an example as a model, • discussion of rhythm and rhyme, and • discussion and modeling of presentation skills	*Scaffolding and Support:* using •

Essential learning: developing rhythm, rhyme, and presentation skills; explaining the moon phases

Copyright © 2010. Caslon, Inc. All rights reserved. The first purchaser may photocopy this page for classroom and personal use.

Suggested Ways to Adapt Assignments

Guidance pertaining to the language-based expectations for for Toua's and Aung's assignments is presented in the following paragraphs.

Assignment 1

Students must write a two-page report about a president. (Essential learning: note-taking, summarizing, developing familiarity with the presidents of the United States)

- *For both:* These Level 3 students can take notes from a book on the current president that is written at an appropriate reading level and includes extensive visual support. A graphic organizer that includes academic sentence frames and visual support should be provided to assist these students in taking notes. Their report will be 3/4 to 1 page in length and should reflect increasingly complex sentences and academic vocabulary. (Toua's report is likely to be shorter than Aung's, since Aung's writing in English has been accelerated by his previous writing instruction.)

Assignment 2

Students must recite an original haiku poem aloud for the class from memory. (Essential learning: poetry writing skills; presentation skills including eye contact, volume, expression, and fluency of speech; memorization skills; developing familiarity with poetic forms)

- *For both:* Toua and Aung will each present a simple original haiku poem, but their support will be individualized according to their individual needs in the various aspects of the process.

Assignment 3

Students must complete a page of math story problems. (Essential learning: converting prose to an equation)

- *For both:* These students will be expected to complete a representative sample of the page of story problems, such as the even- or odd-numbered problems.

Assignment 4

Students must create a song, rap, or chant about how the moon moves to create its phases. (Essential learning: developing rhythm, rhyme, and presentation skills; explaining the moon phases)

• *For both:* Toua and Aung will each work with a "trained" buddy to complete this assignment.

Suggested Instructional Strategies

The following paragraphs provide guidance pertaining to scaffolding and support for the assignment.

For all assignments, teachers must make sure to build sufficient background, support students in making connections to what they already know, pre-teach relevant vocabulary, and embed opportunities for interactions with native speakers of English. It is also helpful and necessary to provide students with models of what is expected, such as samples of successfully completed assignments, since the formats of assignments may be unfamiliar to ELLs. Such purposeful practices empower ELLs to be successful on adapted classroom assignments.

Assignment 1

Students must write a two-page report about a president. (Essential learning: note-taking, summarizing, developing familiarity with the presidents of the United States)

• *For both:* These students will be asked to report on the current president in order to ensure that the subject matter is as familiar as possible. The materials will be selected in accordance with their language proficiency levels, and note-taking with a graphic organizer will be modeled. Assistance will be provided through process writing to ensure that the final product is comprehensible.

Assignment 2

Students must recite an original poem aloud for the class from memory. (Essential learning: poetry writing skills; presentation skills including eye contact, volume, expression, and fluency of speech; memorization skills; developing familiarity with poetic forms)

• Having modeled the writing of a haiku, the teacher will model the reading of the poem, emphasizing eye contact, volume, expression, and fluency. The form of the haiku will be analyzed with the class and templates provided. The class will then participate in choral reading of several haikus. Tips for memorization will be provided. The teacher will work with Toua and Aung individually to assist them in writing their haikus, and they will practice presenting their poems with the ESL teacher or a paraeducator before they present to the class.

Assignment 3

Students must complete a page of math story problems. (Essential learning: converting prose to an equation)

- The teacher will explicitly teach the math phrases found in the story problems that represent math functions (e.g., "greater than," "in all"). The teacher will then model the "translation" of several problems from prose to numbers, using manipulatives, and will provide opportunities for guided practice, giving Toua and Aung the extra assistance that they need.

Assignment 4

Students must create a song, rap, or chant about how the moon moves to create its phases. (Essential learning: developing rhythm, rhyme, and presentation skills; explaining the moon phases)

- The phases of the moon will be taught with video clips and manipulatives. The teacher will model (or show a video clip of) a song, rap, or chant about another topic in science. The class will analyze the elements of rhythm and rhyme; presentation skills will be explicitly discussed and modeled. Then, in a workshop format, students will begin work on their final products as the teacher circulates throughout the room to help students as needed. (She or he will give particular attention to Toua and Aung, who might write theirs together.)

Activity 5.2 Applying Your Learning to Your Own Level 3 Student

Think of a student that you know who is at Level 3. (If you are not currently serving a Level 3 student, think ahead to a time that you will serve such a student.) Based on an assignment that you routinely use, differentiate expectations for your Level 3 student.

Fully English Proficient	Level 3
Language-Based Expectations:	*Language-Based Expectations:*
Standards-Based Content or Topic (from the curriculum):	
Scaffolding and Support:[5] using	*Scaffolding and Support:* using

Essential Learning: _____

Copyright © 2010. Caslon, Inc. All rights reserved. The first purchaser may photocopy this page for classroom and personal use.

---

[5] Note that the scaffolding and support that are provided for fully English proficient students are also provided for ELLs, though ELLs often need different kinds of or more scaffolding and support.

Professional Development Resources

Resource 5.1 Appropriate Assignment/Assessment Procedures for Level 3 Students

In General	Listening and Speaking	Reading	Writing
• Create and use assessments/assignments that allow students to demonstrate content knowledge, skills, and abilities without language mastery. • Consider allowing students to complete assessment procedures under the guidance of a bilingual teacher or paraeductor. • Consider weighting graded components according to students' linguistic strengths. • Make the assignment/assessment process comprehensible by explaining the directions orally and providing visual support (e.g., realia, icons, manipulatives, modeling and models). • Simultaneously assess content and language development (e.g., through summarizing, story retelling, questioning and responding, analyzing, evaluating).	• Test orally using and expecting more precise and specific content vocabulary and increasingly complex grammatical structures. (Language should reflect sentence-level frames and models used during instruction.)	• Use high-quality, age-appropriate, lower-reading-level materials that provide extensive visual support, expecting comprehension of increasingly complex sentence- and paragraph-level text. • Test orally using and expecting more precise and specific content vocabulary and increasingly complex grammatical structures. • When traditional paper and pencil tests must be used, employ simplified English and visual support (e.g., clip art, graphs).	• Elicit writing of increasingly complex sentence structures using a developing range of content/academic vocabulary. • When traditional paper and pencil tests must be used, employ simplified English and visual support (e.g., clip art, graphs).

Copyright © 2010. Caslon, Inc. All rights reserved. The first purchaser may photocopy this page for classroom and personal use.

Resource 5.2 Appropriate Instructional Strategies for Level 3 Students

In General	Listening	Speaking	Reading	Writing
• Provide sensory support for *every* lesson (e.g., real objects, pictures, hands-on materials and experiences, nonverbal communication, demonstrations, modeling, simulations). • Explicitly teach and require students to use increasingly complex content/academic vocabulary and sentence structures.	• Prompt and scaffold students' language development by using increasingly complex language, paraphrasing, as needed. • Allow sufficient wait time (likely several seconds). • Facilitate and support higher-order thinking processes during oral teaching by providing students with graphic organizers, modeling their completion, as needed. • Employ think-alouds to model both processes and language.	• Provide opportunities to produce extended oral discourse through activities such as reporting and presentations. • Prompt and scaffold extended oral language production by providing visually supported sentence-level frames and models for high-quality academic discourse (e.g., "As a result of the interaction of _____ and _____, . . ."). • Concentrate on students' meaning to a greater extent than on correctness of expression.	• At the school and program level, for L1-pre-literate students, (continue to) implement a high-quality, research-based, culturally and linguistically sensitive reading development program. • Use high-quality, age-appropriate, lower-reading-level books aligned with content curriculum that provide extensive visual support. • Lay a foundation for comprehension: build background and help students to make connections to prior learning and experiences. • Incorporate shared, shared-to-guided, and guided reading.	• Provide opportunities to produce extended written discourse through activities such as journaling, report writing, and preparing presentations. • Prompt and scaffold extended written language production by providing visually supported sentence-level frames and models for high-quality academic discourse (e.g., "As a result of the interaction of _____ and _____, . . ."). • Incorporate modeled, shared, and guided writing activities. • Accept increasingly complex sentences in lieu of grade-level writing expectations. • Engage students in writing activities that elicit expanded sentences using a range of complexity.

Copyright © 2010. Caslon, Inc. All rights reserved. The first purchaser may photocopy this page for classroom and personal use.

Resource 5.2 *Continued*

In General	Listening	Speaking	Reading	Writing
			• Facilitate and support the development of higher-order thinking skills by using graphic organizers such as Venn diagrams, T-charts, and concept maps.	• Concentrate on student meaning to a greater extent than on correctness of expression. • Facilitate and support the development of higher-order thinking skills by using graphic organizers such as Venn diagrams, T-charts, and concept maps.

Copyright © 2010. Caslon, Inc. All rights reserved. The first purchaser may photocopy this page for classroom and personal use.

6

Differentiation Strategies for Level 4 Students

What a child can do today with assistance,
she will be able to do by herself tomorrow.
— Lev Vygotsky

In this chapter, we address Level 4 students by describing their characteristics and offering level-appropriate assignment/assessment and instructional strategies. Teachers are reminded to be relentless in their insistence that students continue to advance and develop their facility with listening, speaking, reading, and writing in order to achieve higher levels of proficiency. Only through providing consistent targeted feedback, appropriate focused assignments and assessments, and a vision of what comprises English language proficiency, can teachers support continuous development of both content and language. Teachers must be vigilant to ensure that stalling at any stage of linguistic development does not occur. In order to avoid such potential stagnation in language development (which can be due to a lack of targeted instruction), teachers are encouraged to regularly consult all data available to them (e.g., English language proficiency assessment scores, student work, portfolios). Along with the guidance on the chart and in this book, teachers can use such student-specific information to design appropriate assignments and assessments, while maintaining responsive vigilance needed to push students to higher levels of achievement and proficiency. This will support Level 4 English language learners (ELLs) in continuing to advance along the continuum of language acquisition to the next level, Level 5, as teachers are able to elicit not only Level 4 production, but also through providing and eliciting, where deemed appropriate, increasingly refined examples of Level 5 language production.

Considering Variation in Level 4 Students' Backgrounds

Student Scenarios

Mariella, a 5th grade student, was born in El Salvador and was adopted as a 2nd grader by a native English-speaking family. She now has a sister who is also in 5th grade and a brother in 1st grade. Mariella did not learn to read or write Spanish prior to arriving in the United States because she was unable to attend school due to poverty. However, she has made quick progress in learning English because her new home environment immerses her in the English language and American culture. In addition, Mariella's sister tutors her in class work. Mariella regularly reads lower-reading-level books to her brother, though she can read some 5th grade text if it is well-supported with visuals and context clues. Her writing has been advantaged by the fact that she and her sister and their friends regularly "text" each other on their cell phones. Her entire family has been very supportive and encouraging of Mariella's English language development, as well as the retention of her first language and culture. They have demonstrated consistent patience as she has had a rocky adjustment to classroom routines, because of her lack of socialization in school. Her inappropriate behavior in 3rd grade caused her teachers to refer her for special education though she was not placed in the program.

Rafael, another 5th grade student, came to the United States from Mexico with his uncle and two young cousins, in first grade. Rafael was on grade level in his Mexican elementary school and surpassed many of his peers in reading ability in Spanish. His speedy acquisition of English caused his ESL teacher to refer him for gifted and talented programming, but he could not earn a high enough score on the standardized test to qualify. While at school, Rafael is an engaged student. He completes scaffolded and supported grade-level assignments when given class time, though not when assignments are given as homework. He happily participates in group work, getting along well with his peers both in the classroom and on the soccer field. Though his English is not perfect, his errors rarely hinder understanding. He wants to play the trumpet, but his uncle cannot afford to purchase an instrument for him.

While both Mariella and Rafael speak Spanish and have experienced the struggles of low socioeconomic status, the rest of their backgrounds are quite dissimilar. Mariella's extreme living situation in El Salvador and lack of previous schooling contributed to her adjustment issues in the United States. Such difficulties with classroom socialization, peer relationships, and academic progress, specifically in terms of literacy development, can be more readily understood when teachers apply the lens of previous L1 educational experiences. Currently, in 5th grade, with appropriate instruction targeting Mariella's specific linguistic and academic needs, as well as the additional cultural and linguistic support from home, she has made excellent progress. She is approaching fluency in English and grade-level performance in the content areas. The concerns about her behavior that led to the special education referral were deflected by an astute special education teacher. This teacher recognized that Mariella's problematic behaviors and initially low levels of academic achievement were caused by the normal language acquisition process and by the need for significant social and cultural adjustments, rather than by a cognitive or behavioral disorder.

Rafael, on the other hand, arrived in his U.S. classroom with strong academic skills already developed in Spanish. This fact positioned him to transfer those skills to English, and, as a result, his teachers saw him progress quickly in English proficiency. Unfortunately, he is unable to score high enough on the standardized test, designed for native speakers of English, that is required by his district for placement in the gifted and talented program. This mismatch of testing practice does not minimize the fact that Rafael is, indeed, a gifted student. He would be much better served if his district were to adopt identification and testing procedures that were more culturally and linguistically sensitive and then serve him through appropriate gifted and talented programming.

Another issue for consideration is the fact that Rafael does not hand in homework regularly, despite reminders from his teachers. They are confused by his behavior because he attends so well to work done in the classroom and certainly does not lack the skills needed to complete the homework. What his teachers might discover in a home visit is that Rafael's uncle does not speak English and is unable to help him with his homework. Further, the uncle does not see the need to complete the homework because Rafael is doing well in the classroom, and there is no dedicated place at home for him to do his homework; his cousins interrupt any efforts to complete it. Finally, Rafael's uncle expects him to care for his two young cousins and to assume responsibility for completing a number of chores around the house, including preparing simple meals, cleaning, and doing laundry. While his uncle supports Rafael's attendance at school, he also relies on Rafael to take care of essential home duties, as when they lived in Mexico.

In keeping with his desire to learn more, Rafael would like to play the trumpet in the 5th grade band, but his uncle is unable to afford the monthly instrument fee. Some of his teachers have decided to seek donations of used instruments from former band alumni to share with students who might not otherwise be able to have this opportunity. Rafael will be able to develop his musical ability and talents only if he is afforded parity of access to both academic and extracurricular opportunities. Such resourcefulness on the part of knowledgeable and caring teachers can make all the difference in the successful integration and retention of diverse learners in the school.

Level 4 Student Descriptors

Students performing at Level 4 are well on their way to proficiency and, like some ELLs at Level 3, could be at risk of stalling language and academic developmental unless they receive targeted, linguistically differentiated instruction paired with assessments of the same kind.

Listening

In terms of listening, Level 4 students can process increasingly complex social and academic input, expanding the ability to understand language about both abstract and concrete topics. In addition, Level 4 students can derive increased meaning from longer stretches of discourse. While the need for many of the previously supplied supports has diminished, contextualizing and clarifying supports are still needed at times.

Speaking

When speaking, Level 4 students continue to deepen their ability to express language in social and academic situations. Their language is growing in complexity and in lexical (vocabulary) precision; their occasional errors do not inhibit understanding. Level 4 students likely appear to be fully fluent in social contexts and approaching fluency in academic contexts. Though errors occur at times, they do not obstruct meaning.

Reading

Level 4 readers make sense of texts of varying complexity as they approach grade-level proficiency. While these students are particularly able to comprehend text that deals with familiar topics, unfamiliar topics require the building of background knowledge or creating connections to existing knowledge and experiences. Teachers are reminded to make explicit, persistent efforts to push these students, who might appear to be fluent, to higher levels of reading proficiency.

Writing

Level 4 writing ability mirrors Level 4 speaking ability; students are capable of producing increasingly complex communication with greater precision in vocabulary and mechanics. Students are also increasingly able to write about abstract concepts. As with speaking, errors may occur, but do not impede understanding.

A Word About Language Objectives

The student descriptors listed on the chart and explicated in the preceding paragraphs are a key to writing appropriate language objectives for Level 4 students. The guidance provided next about appropriate assignment/assessment strategies can also be used to shape language objectives for Level 4 students. The instructional strategies offered in the final section of this chapter offer direction for structuring lessons that will facilitate accomplishment of the language and content objectives for lessons created for Level 4 students.

The solid linguistic foundation across all four language domains positions Level 4 students to be able to demonstrate their learning in ways that capitalize on their language development. However, grade-level expectations are not yet appropriate.

A Sample Differentiated Assignment for Level 4 Students

Table 6.1 shows the sample assignment differentiated for students at Levels 4 and 5. Readers will note that the types of scaffolding and support are the same for students at both of these levels for this particular assignment, though this is but one way to differentiate this particular assignment. Some teachers may elect to provide different types of scaffolding and support for these two levels.

Numerous collaborative possibilities exist for teachers who wish to join forces to facilitate the learning of ELLs. For instance, teachers might meet weekly to plan assignments/assessments and associated lesson plans. Then the ESL/bilingual education teacher might pre-teach important aspects of the interrelated content and language and follow up with students after the classroom/content teacher has taught the material in order to provide further support.

Necessary Assignment/Assessment Strategies for Level 4 Students

Even at Level 4, large-scale standardized tests and classroom tests designed for native speakers tend to be problematic for ELLs. In fact, the scores from such measures must be "taken with a grain of salt," since

Table 6.1 Sample assignment differentiated for Levels 4 and 5

Fully English Proficient	Level 4	Level 5
Language-Based Expectations: Write a set of instructions using grade-level vocabulary and sentence structures	*Language-Based Expectations:* Write a set of instructions using some content/academic vocabulary and complex sentence structures	*Language-Based Expectations:* Write a set of instructions demonstrating a variety of content/academic vocabulary and complex sentence structures
Standards-Based Content or Topic (from the curriculum): for a self-selected task		
Scaffolding and Support: using • a model assignment, • teacher demonstration of the task using a "think-aloud," • a sequential graphic organizer for planning to write, • a language wall with sequencing words and key sentence structures, and • feedback designed to push students to full proficiency according to the grade-level writing standards to guide writing.	*Scaffolding and Support:* using • a model assignment, • teacher demonstration of the task using a "think-aloud," • a sequential graphic organizer for planning to write, • a language wall with sequencing words and key sentence structures, and • level-appropriate feedback designed to push students to the next level of proficiency in writing to guide writing. (Note: Level 4 students may not need more scaffolding and support than Level 5 students, though they may rely on it more.)	*Scaffolding and Support:* using • a model assignment, • teacher demonstration of the task using a "think-aloud," • a sequential graphic organizer for planning to write, • a language wall with sequencing words and key sentence structures, and • level-appropriate feedback designed to push students to the next level of proficiency in writing to guide writing.

language ability is likely to be confounded with content knowledge, skills, and abilities in those scores. That is, the results from tests designed for native speakers likely reflect both language proficiency and content knowledge for ELLs, making the scores difficult to interpret; do they represent (lacking) proficiency in language or in content or in both? When a student is hindered by lack of full English proficiency, he or she is unable, by definition, to fully comprehend unmodified, grade-level questions or produce an appropriate response linguistically, particularly when measured against a field of native English-speakers. These students, like those at Levels 1, 2, and 3, need assessment procedures that are designed to take into account their current linguistic and cultural realities. While there is a tension between these needs and the language demands of many tests, ELLs must be afforded access to a level playing field where demonstration of learning is concerned. Lacking language proficiency should not and must not relegate these students to failing marks and closed doors in terms of more advanced educational opportunities (e.g., qualifying for gifted and talented programs or Advanced Placement coursework). Using ELL-appropriate tests is a critical approach that allows students to demonstrate learning while progressing along the trajectory toward language proficiency. Further, such an approach recognizes the gifts and potential of individual students that are unable to be measured or identified by means of standardized or other testing that focuses on language mastery.

In General

Engage students in grade-level assignments/assessments with scaffolding and support. While students at Levels 1 through 3 may require tasks that take different forms from those designed for their native English-speaking peers, Level 4 students have acquired sufficient language proficiency to often be able to participate in grade-level assignments and assessments, as long as they receive needed scaffolding and support. Such scaffolding and support may include additional explanations about how to complete the task, extra time, peer or teacher tutoring, use of a bilingual dictionary or other differentiated resources, and so on. However, the fact that Level 4 students can begin to engage in grade-level assessments should not relegate them to comparison with their native English-speaking peers. Such inappropriate comparison with native-English-speakers can result in ELLs' discouragement and despair. We have both dealt with ELLs tearfully disparaging themselves and expressing worry that they would never "measure up," based on grade-level equivalents for their large-scale standardized content test performance and on their understanding of their disparate performance in comparison with grade-level peers on classroom assessments. ELLs often do not fully understand that language proficiency takes place incrementally and over time, requiring patience on the part of both the teacher and the learner. As a result, Level 4 students' attempts at grade-level assignments/assessments must be met with support and encouragement. In addition, they need careful, targeted corrections that will facilitate higher levels of proficiency, such as can be provided by differentiated scoring rubrics (discussed in Chapter 8). The need for differentiated scoring rubrics leads to the next recommendation.

Consider weighting graded components according to students' linguistic strengths. The grading of Level 4 students should highlight what these students can do linguistically, rather than reflect an expectation of grade-level production. Teachers must be very clear about what they are grading. Demystifying and clarifying the assessment process by using a very specific and accessible scoring rubric supports students in their understanding of expectations. This rubric can be made sensitive to the needs of ELLs by differentiating expectations according to language proficiency level. This process will be discussed and exemplified in Chapter 8.

Make the assessment process comprehensible by explaining the directions orally and providing visual support (e.g., realia, icons, manipulatives, models), as appropriate. While Level 4 students may comprehend the directions for many assignments and assessments, teachers are cautioned to make no assumptions. Some "routine" classroom tasks may be unfamiliar or bewildering to ELLs, some of whom arrive as newcomers at Level 4 with very different school experiences (e.g., extremely large classes where students rarely talk, reliance on rote memorization rather than group work). One newcomer, on grade level in his first language, failed an early assessment in math because of unfamiliarity with the true/false testing format. Two weeks later, the student was promoted from Algebra I to Algebra II, pointing out the importance of teaching test-taking skills to ELLs.

Simultaneously assess content and language development (e.g., through summarizing, story retelling, questioning and responding, analyzing, evaluating). The growing and increasingly refined language proficiency of Level 4 students allows them to articulate content learning in more precise ways. Further, they can address more abstract content using increasingly complex and accurate language. Thus it *can* be appropriate to assess both the language and content learning of Level 4 students. Teachers must embrace the responsibility to embed opportunities into assignments and assessments that provide the forum for students to produce pre-taught language to the greatest extent of their ability. This means going beyond questions that warrant one-word responses. Rather, teachers should construct tasks that require students to respond with increasingly complex discourse and commensurate vocabulary. For instance, when assigning an essay on *Romeo and Juliet,* a teacher might incorporate pre-taught language and sentence structures into the assignment itself, as in "Analyzing the Montagues and Capulets: predict what might have happened if the families had lived in the 21st century." This prompt itself indicates the kinds of language that the teacher expects. A teacher might further guide students by saying, "Use vocabulary taught in class and complex sentences when constructing your answer."

Listening and Speaking

Use and require increasingly academic and grammatically varied language about both concrete and abstract topics. (Language should reflect discourse-level frames and models used during instruction.) As with native English-speakers, Level 4 ELLs must be pushed to produce more advanced language. All teachers must recognize the importance of explicit language instruction for both native speakers of English and ELLs in order to rightfully expect this sort of performance on assignments and assessments. This advanced and precise academic language is not absorbed socially and, unless explicitly taught, is unlikely to be acquired. Intentional instruction of language takes into account linguistic developmental levels of both native speakers and ELLs, resulting in greater proficiency for both, which can and should be assessed. For example, a teacher could explicitly teach "period language" (e.g., "four score and seven years ago . . .") prior to expecting students to give presentations in which they take on the identities of famous historical figures.

Reading

Use a combination of grade-level texts (with scaffolding) and high-quality, age-appropriate, lower-reading-level materials that provide visual support. Level 4 students are able to process increasingly complex text, including a widening variety of genres, accompanied by related academic vocabulary development. Grade-level text, while sometimes beyond the comprehension level of Level 4 students, displays increasingly sophisticated sentence and discourse structures, grammar, mechanics, and vocabulary. Level 4 is the appropriate level at which students can often begin to derive meaning from grade-level texts, provided that scaffolding and support are given when needed. Teachers are reminded that texts used in assignments and assessments (e.g., reading passages on a social studies test) must be of the same variety as those used during instruction. Only use grade-level text if assessment is targeting grade-level reading; otherwise, the high reading level of the assignment/assessment materials may interfere with students' abilities to demonstrate what they know and can do related to content only.

Use traditional paper and pencil tests wisely, employing visual support (e.g., clip art, graphs) and linguistic scaffolding, as needed. Traditional paper and pencil tests may not be the most appropriate ways to ascertain what Level 4 ELLs know and can do in the content areas. Teachers are cautioned to remember that Level 4 students are not able to read on grade level, though informal (ungraded) assessments that are formative in nature can be used to inform teachers of Level 4 students' instructional gaps related to both language and content. Once these areas and items are targeted instructionally, they can be assessed through a variety of pre-taught means, both traditionally and nontraditionally. Teachers are urged to continue using authentic assessments with Level 4 students rather than relying on more traditional tests. Even though Level 4 students' language ability may be sufficient to deal with the individual words on a traditional tests, many constructions used in such tests (e.g., "which of the following," "all of the following *except*") may be unfamiliar to ELLs. It is incumbent upon teachers to examine their curriculum for such language and to explicitly teach this "test language," which also appears on mandated large-scale standardized tests.

Writing

Elicit writing of increasingly academic and grammatically varied language about both concrete and abstract topics. (Language should reflect discourse-level frames and models used during instruction.) At Level 4, it is possible to assess content knowledge by means of writing. Conversely, teachers can assess writing using specific content as the topic. When using writing assessment, teachers must decide what they are trying to "get at"; is it content knowledge, writing ability, or both? Any of these might be acceptable, but teachers must be clear about the goals of the assessment in order to develop appropriate assessment procedures and score student performance fairly. Ultimately, teachers must ensure that what their assessments measure matches the construct of interest (measurement goal). Figure 6.1 helps to illuminate this relationship.

Teachers should expect Level 4 students to produce writing that is fully representative of the range of Level 4 production. In content-testing situations, teachers may not wish to grade writing ability, as is often the case with students at Levels 1 through 3. However, many assignments could offer appropriate opportunities to expect and require Level 4 writing, reflecting both content knowledge and Level 4 writing ability (e.g., a social studies essay test question on the Revolutionary War). Holding students, both ELLs and non-ELLs, accountable for their writing ability in this way fosters authentic opportunities to demonstrate increased mastery of both content knowledge and the kinds of writing ability necessary for success in future endeavors.

Use traditional paper and pencil tests wisely, employing simplified English and visual support (e.g., clip art, graphs) and linguistic scaffolding, as needed. Teachers can begin to expect their instruction of increasingly complex and sophisticated language to be reflected in the writing of Level 4 students. At this level, students may be expected to produce collateral errors, but these are generally of a nature that does not hinder understanding. As with native speakers of English who inhabit a range of language proficiency levels and may write with frequent errors,

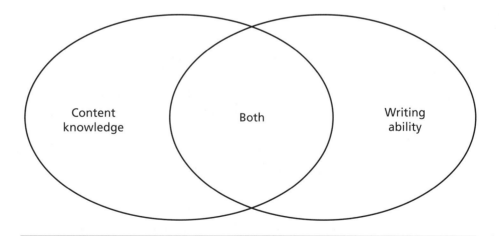

Figure 6.1 Potential construct overlap in assessing content knowledge by means of writing (and vice versa).

Level 4 ELLs can be expected to display similar characteristics across the Level 4 range. ELLs should not be held to a higher standard for achieving writing proficiency than their native English-speaking peers, nor should teachers allow any less. This is part of what we mean by "wise" use of traditional assessments (e.g., essay tests).

Another aspect of this essential wisdom is recognition that the test format itself may hinder students in demonstrating what they know and can do in the content areas. For instance, the kinds of language found on many multiple-choice tests may be a hindrance for ELLs (e.g., "All of the following *except* . . ."). Teachers are encouraged to routinely examine test questions, end-of-chapter review questions, and the like, searching for grammatical constructions that require explicit instruction. As stated elsewhere, authentic assessments may be better than traditional paper and pencil tests for the purpose of ascertaining the content knowledge, skills, and abilities of Level 4 students.

Necessary Instructional Strategies for Level 4 Students

The preceding strategies for assessing Level 4 ELLs can only be used effectively if appropriate instruction supports students in demonstrating their learning in subsequent assignments and assessments. Even with students who have achieved Level 4 proficiency, teachers are cautioned, as with students at Levels 1 through 3, to

1. examine their assumptions,

2. learn about students' backgrounds,

3. determine students' instructional levels based on content knowledge, skills, and abilities and language proficiency, and

4. continue to teach essential learning from the curriculum and its associated language in a differentiated manner.

As with Level 3, Level 4 students approaching proficiency are at high risk for stalling their progress and never reaching full English proficiency. Teachers must consistently rely on various measures (e.g., formative assessments, informal classroom observation, annual ELL assessments) to inform them of instructional gaps and needs. Routinely consulting and applying such information enables teachers to incrementally "ratchet up" and fine-tune their instruction related to both content and language. Having analyzed such assessment data regularly, teachers can explicitly and intentionally "front-load" students with necessary linguistic knowledge that, unless explicitly taught, is not likely to be casually absorbed. Such front-loading prepares students to demonstrate their knowledge, skills, and abilities in ever-improving linguistic fashion, as they increase mastery of both content and language proficiency. With such pinpointed expectations consistently maintained across various forms of assessment, students will continue progress on their trajectory toward proficiency, supported by differentiated instruction.

Readers are reminded that assessment strategies have been consistently presented prior to instructional strategies throughout this text. The authors suggest that teachers of ELLs first consider appropriate goals for their students according to their individual levels of language proficiency, and then design instruction that will ensure that students are able to reach those goals.

In General

Provide sensory support for *every* lesson (e.g., real objects, pictures, hands-on materials and experiences, nonverbal communication, demonstrations, modeling, simulations). While teachers might suspect that Level 4 students no longer need sensory supports in order to make meaning from teaching presented in English, teachers are reminded to examine their assumptions. Although some Level 4 students might be ready to exhibit more learning independence, other Level 4 students are likely to have various cultural and linguistic needs that cause them to rely on sensory support in every lesson. As a result, teachers are encouraged to familiarize themselves with students' biographical profiles in order to make appropriate educational decisions and maximize their instructional impact. Further, since the learning preferences of a majority of students are visual and kinesthetic, rather than auditory, such sensory experiences benefit both ELLs and non-ELLs on that front, as well. For example, when learning about place value, students may benefit from an activity in which different students represent different place values by lining up to represent a number (e.g., to represent 4,395.27, six students would be assigned the six digits in the number and asked to stand in order and explain their individual place values).

Explicitly teach and require students to use content/academic and grammatically varied language about concrete and abstract topics, with diminishing errors. In order for students to make progress toward language proficiency within the content areas, teachers must explicitly teach this type of language. This teaching is meaningful for both ELLs and non-ELLs inasmuch as "all students are 'AESL' (Academic English as a Second Language)" (Kinsella, 2007, slide 11). Neither native speakers of English nor ELLs are likely to "pick up" such academic language unless teachers integrate its modeling and practice into daily classroom activities. Although Level 4 ELLs are likely to continue to make some errors in their language production, teachers are urged to require academic language from these students and to provide targeted error correction as appropriate. For instance, rather than allowing students to answer questions related to a short story in simple words or phrases, teachers might require students to use complete, complex sentences with pre-taught vocabulary.

Provide scaffolding and support needed for students to engage in grade-level assignments/assessments. Although Level 4 students are not yet fully proficient in English, they are likely able to engage in many grade-level assignments, unlike their counterparts at Levels 1, 2, and 3, who still require differentiated assignments.[1] Teachers must provide scaffolding and support needed to facilitate success on grade-level assignments. Such support can take the form of additional explanations regarding expectations, supplementary materials for use in completing assignments, coaching in the completion of assignments, and so on.

Listening

Scaffold language development by modeling and prompting increasingly academic and grammatically varied language about both concrete and abstract topics. In order to set the stage for the full development of the receptive abilities of Level 4 students, teachers are reminded to examine their own classroom language production. Educators must ask themselves if the language that they themselves produce during instruction is indicative of full English proficiency, complete with complex sen-

---

[1] Level 4 students may, in some instances, need grade-level assignments and assessments to be differentiated. However, when they are able to participate in these assignments and assessments, extensive scaffolding and support are likely necessary to their success.

tence structures and sophisticated vocabulary, making it demonstrative of the discourse of academia (e.g., "When hypothesizing about the outcome of this experiment . . ."). Assuming that teachers are using high-level discourse and promoting an environment that encourages ELLs to "go out on a limb" to try something new, teachers should bear in mind that unless such opportunities occur during the course of the school day, many ELLs (and non-ELLs) will have no English language enrichment. For instance, even high school teachers could employ the "marble jar" technique in their classrooms, awarding classes a marble each time a high-level vocabulary word or sentence structure is used. (Once the jar for each class is full, the class has earned some sort of reward.)

Promote higher-order thinking processes during oral teaching by providing students with graphic organizers. When used in conjunction with both live and audiotaped lectures, presentations, and stories, as well as movies, podcasts, video clips, and the like, graphic organizers facilitate and support attending to details through listening. Providing such organizers enables students to record information they consider important and, depending on the format of the organizer, to better understand relationships among ideas and concepts. Once students develop note-taking skills using graphic organizers, they are better prepared to gain meaning from auditory input when such support is unavailable.

Speaking

Provide opportunities to produce extended oral discourse, increasingly inclusive of abstract thought. Level 4 students are linguistically prepared to engage in increasingly imaginative and complex activities across domains. Opportunities for speaking might include debate on a current event, guest speaking at a local civic or church group, speaking as a member of a panel at a local conference, or other authentic community-based activities. Such activities, while setting high expectations for students in terms of oral production, develop language across domains. Researching, editing, rewriting, rehearsing, videotaping, refining presentation skills, and so on all contribute to the students' abilities to produce extended academic discourse with increasing ease and credibility. Further, these authentic types of skills develop multiple language domains in ways that are rewarding to students and can increase their motivation and self-esteem.

Scaffold extended oral language production by providing visually supported discourse-level frames and models for high-quality academic discourse (e.g., "In accordance with our hypothesis, the results of our experiment demonstrate ____. This means that ____."). At Level 3, teachers have provided sentence-level scaffolding for the production of academic language. To advance speaking abilities at Level 4, teachers must now provide discourse-level scaffolding to expand the production of academic language. Discourse-level language includes expanded and well-organized paragraphs of varying length and complexity. Insisting on the refined organizational form of increasing amounts of oral academic language must be intentional and embedded in instruction. For example, classroom instruction could include speech featuring complex processes, persuasion, opinions, and the like, which students would, in turn, be expected to produce. During such instruction, teachers must address features of expanded academic discourse such as how to include more detail, cite data, transition between ideas, and ensure cohesiveness. Targeted discourse features can be visually posted in the form of a language wall for ease of student reference.

An often overlooked aspect of discourse development relates to questioning techniques. The development of precise questioning abilities is key in helping students to articulate what it is that they really want to know. Without this skill, students inquire without precision, accuracy, or appropriate register and may be left wondering, without the means to access essential knowledge. Or students might ask a question simply, such as "How do we get hail?" Such a simple and basic question should not be considered as representative of the language production capabilities of a Level 4 student. Teachers must seize this teachable linguistic moment to scaffold the student's questioning techniques up to a more appropriate academic register level that will serve the student well in advanced education or in the world of work. For example,

What are the factors that contribute to hail formation?

What meteorological conditions lead to the formation of large hail?

What is the difference between gropple and hail?

Both teaching students how to present orally and how to generate the types of questions that elicit more complex responses are integral components of instruction as ELLs refine their complementary skills of listening and speaking.

Insist on increasingly correct and precise language. Level 4 students are in great need of focused and pinpointed language instruction and correction by teachers. Teachers will be remiss if they simply let errors "go" when they are able to grasp a student's overall meaning, even if the utterance is stated incorrectly or just too simply (e.g., when a student states, "The author says," she or he might be prompted to use the word "asserts" rather than "says"). The oral production of Level 4 students is likely far from perfect and relies on teacher input in setting high standards for increasing precision and correctness. While teachers need not "pounce" on every error, they must continue to provide alternate structures, academic vocabulary, and models for students to adopt as they advance toward proficiency, furthering the likelihood of their success in higher education and in the professional world. It should be noted that non-ELLs, as well as ELLs, will benefit from this type of explicit insistence on the continued refinement of language.

Reading

The cultural and linguistic issues that might have precluded the rapid acquisition of reading skills for L1-pre-literate students at Levels 1–3 may have dissipated by the time that students achieve Level 4. However, teachers are reminded to continue making individually based decisions according to students' biographical profiles and linguistic needs. Also, since Level 4 students are, by definition, likely reading below grade level, it is incumbent upon school districts to ensure that appropriate reading instruction is in place, regardless of the student's age, bearing in mind that simply receiving the "same" instruction as native speakers of English is not equitable—or enough.

Use a combination of grade-level texts (with scaffolding) and high-quality, age-appropriate, lower-reading-level books aligned with content curriculum that provide visual support. Level 4 students can begin to independently read grade-level text, though they likely require support because their reading ability is not on grade level. Examples of such support include teacher explanation, pre-teaching of vocabulary, glossaries, advance organizers and outlines, and other topical resources (e.g., first-person accounts, magazine and newspaper articles, Internet research). Lower-reading-level materials can also serve as needed supplements to grade-level texts.

Provide students with graphic organizers to enhance higher-order thinking.
In addition to providing graphic organizers for students at Level 4, teachers can ask the students themselves to create organizers that are helpful in making sense of written text. Teachers might provide a critical question or prompt that would focus students' reading on higher-order thought processes (e.g., "Analyze the reasons for the Civil War from a Northern perspective"). Students would then create an organizer that would help them, as individuals, to accomplish the assigned task. By Level 4, most students have been exposed to a variety of organizers, and asking them to create their own is another way in which teachers can push student thinking to the next level.

Writing

The issues that slowed writing development of L1-pre-literate students at Levels 1–3 have likely diminished by Level 4. Though achieving Level 4 in writing likely takes longer for L1-preliterate students than for their L1-literate peers, at Level 4, the rate of development may become more consistent for the two groups of students. However, Level 4 is a very broad designation, and student performance can fall anywhere within that wide range of development. As a result, teachers are reminded of the importance of tailoring instruction to the specific needs of individual students.

Provide opportunities to produce extended written discourse, increasingly inclusive of abstract thought. At Level 4, students are often able to participate in grade-level written assignments/assessments, as long as needed scaffolding is provided. Teachers are urged to ensure that such assignments are meaningful and relevant and that they elicit extended writing reflective of abstract thought. Examples include essays in which students evaluate solutions to a given problem (e.g., pollution), persuade others to take a stand on an issue (e.g., the merits of vegetarianism), or outline the implications of a current event or issue (e.g., health care, nuclear armament).

While this strategy is equally applicable to both speaking and writing, teachers must remember that academic writing, rather than "stream of consciousness" production, is more formal in style than speaking or texting, and must follow certain conventions. This academic style must be explicitly taught, modeled, and expected of students.

Scaffold extended written language production by providing visually supported discourse-level frames and models for high-quality academic discourse (e.g., "In accordance with our hypothesis, the results of our experiment demonstrate ____. This means that ____."). For writing, as for speaking, posted templates (frames) are helpful for guiding students in language production. Such templates can offer more complex structures for organization and for expansion from sentence- to discourse-level language. For instance, teachers can assist students in analyzing high-quality writing from a variety of sources and authors in order to better understand discourse features. Then, teachers might post a frame for constructing similar writing (e.g., an argumentative essay) that provides guidance for articulating detailed reasoning, transitioning from idea to idea, enhancing cohesion, and so on.

Insist on increasingly correct and precise language. As with speaking, Level 4 presents golden opportunities for teachers to scaffold students' written language production to a higher level. Furthermore, teachers must insist on students' sustained efforts to achieve proficiency through the production of correct and precise language. Without this much-needed "push" from teachers, students are at risk of permanently residing at Level 4. For instance, if a student were to write, "The liquid in the jar began to boil after one minute," the teacher might prompt the student to use the word "beaker" instead of "jar."

Provide students with graphic organizers to enhance higher-order thinking. As with reading, Level 4 students can use graphic organizers provided by the teacher and can generate their own graphic organizers to assist in the development of their written products. These graphic organizers can serve as springboards for students to respond to complex prompts eliciting higher-order thinking and advanced discourse. For example, students might be provided with a variety of graphic organizers (e.g., outlines, concept maps) to use to help them organize their thoughts as they work to write a research paper.

Instruction That Integrates Language Domains

The integration of language domains within a single activity, assignment, or assessment becomes more straightforward as students gain proficiency across domains. As a result, the most efficient way to develop language proficiency is to attach instruction and assessment to authentic representations of the curriculum, accomplishing simultaneous instruction and assessment of both content and language.

Conclusion

In previous chapters, we have noted that ELLs can exhibit different proficiency levels in various domains (e.g., Level 4 in speaking while Level 3 in writing) and that ELLs of any age can be at any proficiency level (e.g., a 15-year-old student in 9th grade who is L1-pre-literate and Level 1). In this chapter, we have pointed out that ELLs can exhibit various exceptionalities, such as an area of giftedness or a disability. Such students are in need of all services to which they are entitled in full measure; teachers who serve these students and their families must do so in culturally and linguistically sensitive ways.

Professional Development Activities

Activity 6.1   Student Scenarios with Application Ideas

Adapt the following assignments for Mariella and Rafael, who were introduced at the beginning of the chapter, according to each student's language proficiency level and any other important factors:

* Differentiate the language-based expectations based on the student descriptors and using relevant assignment/assessment strategies on the chart and in this chapter.

  – Bear in mind the "essential learning" for each assignment (noted below each assignment template) as you differentiate the expectations, so that important skills are not overlooked.

* Design appropriate scaffolding and support using relevant instructional strategies on the chart and in this chapter.

As you work to differentiate these assignments, recall that Level 4 students may not require different types of support and scaffolding than more linguistically advanced students, but that they may rely on it more.

Assignment 1[2]

Fully English Proficient	Level 4
Language-Based Expectations: Write a letter to a relative	*Language-Based Expectations:*
Standards-Based Content or Topic (from the curriculum): in the voice of a person living at the time of the Revolutionary War	
Scaffolding and Support: using • understanding gained from in-class role plays and • teacher modeling	*Scaffolding and Support:* using •

Essential learning: writing letters, perspective-taking, articulating viewpoints of different groups at the time of the Revolutionary War

Copyright © 2010. Caslon, Inc. All rights reserved. The first purchaser may photocopy this page for classroom and personal use.

---

[2]In all four assignments presented in this chapter, the language-based expectations and standards-based content or topic overlap because part of the essential learning focuses

Assignment 2

Fully English Proficient	Level 4
Language-Based Expectations: Give a group presentation	*Language-Based Expectations:*

Standards-Based Content or Topic (from the curriculum): about the merits of recycling	
Scaffolding and Support: using • information gained from an in-class video and independent research, • a graphic organizer to guide organization of the presentation, • a video of a sample presentation from last year, and • peer and teacher feedback during rehearsal	*Scaffolding and Support:* using •

Essential learning: developing presentation skills and research skills, the importance of conservation, types of natural resources

Copyright © 2010. Caslon, Inc. All rights reserved. The first purchaser may photocopy this page for classroom and personal use.

on a language-based skill. In situations such as these, teachers must work carefully to differentiate assignments in such a way that *all* students have the opportunity to attend to the essential learning, regardless of English language proficiency level.

Assignment 3

Fully English Proficient	Level 4
Language-Based Expectations: Collect data through interviews, construct a bar or line graph, and present findings	*Language-Based Expectations:*

Standards-Based Content or Topic (from the curriculum):
about the consumer preferences of those interviewed

| *Scaffolding and Support:*

using

• modeling of the development of interview questions,

• modeling of the construction of simple graphs,

• explicit instruction in how to present information to a group, and

• a videotape of a practice presentation to use in perfecting presentation skills | *Scaffolding and Support:*

using

• |

Essential learning: appropriate data collection methods, constructing graphs, presentation skills

Copyright © 2010. Caslon, Inc. All rights reserved. The first purchaser may photocopy this page for classroom and personal use.

Assignment 4

Fully English Proficient	Level 4
Language-Based Expectations: Write a summary and make a display	*Language-Based Expectations:*
Standards-Based Content or Topic (from the curriculum): about doubling or halving a recipe	
Scaffolding and Support: using • a sample assignment provided by the teacher, • modeling of doubling and halving, • a "think-aloud" demonstration of summarizing, and • support from the family and consumer science teacher	*Scaffolding and Support:* using •

Essential learning: adding and subtracting fractions, basic cooking skills, summary writing, presentation skills

Copyright © 2010. Caslon, Inc. All rights reserved. The first purchaser may photocopy this page for classroom and personal use.

Suggested Ways to Adapt Assignments

Based on language-based expectations, Mariella and Rafael's assignments may not need to be adapted for Level 4 students, per se, but teachers need to focus and pinpoint areas for instruction that may require significant scaffolding. In particular, as both students stretch from sentence-level to discourse-level speaking and writing production, teachers should concentrate on ways to advance needed skills, outlined in the next section.

Suggested Instructional Strategies

The following paragraphs provide guidance pertaining to scaffolding and support for the assignment.

For all assignments, teachers must make sure to build sufficient background, support students in making connections to what they already know, pre-teach relevant vocabulary, and embed opportunities for interactions with native speakers of English. It is also helpful and necessary to provide students with models of what is expected, such as samples of successfully completed assignments, since the formats of assignments may be unfamiliar to ELLs. Such purposeful practices empower ELLs to be successful with adapted classroom assignments.

Assignment 1

Students must write a letter to a relative in the voice of a person living at the time of the Revolutionary War. (Essential learning: writing letters, perspective-taking, viewpoints of different groups at the time of the Revolutionary War)

- *For both:* Instruction will be designed using sensory support in order to ensure that teaching is comprehensible to students. In this class, students will reprise roles of famous Revolutionary figures with costumes and role-play before they receive this assignment. (Both students may require supplementary instruction regarding U.S. history in order to fully make sense of and participate in this assignment.) Letter writing will be modeled with a template posted on the wall. Students will then write their letters in a workshop format so the teacher can give assistance where needed.

- *For Mariella:* Mariella, in particular, may need supplementary instruction in letter formatting, since she may not have benefited from earlier instruction on letter writing because of her developing language proficiency.

Assignment 2

Students must give group presentations about the merits of recycling. (Essential learning: presentation skills, research skills, the importance of conservation, types of natural resources)

- *For both:* The class will watch a video about recycling of various natural resources, taking notes on a provided graphic organizer. They will discuss the information in the video and brainstorm a list of sources of additional information. In groups, students will access print and online materials to create their oral presentations according to a provided graphic organizer. (Mariella and Rafael may both need additional guidance in how to access print and online materials.) The teacher will show a video of a group presentation from last year, and the class will discuss the strong and weak points of that presentation. Each group will then rehearse their presentation in front of another group and obtain peer feedback. The teacher will also provide feedback during this rehearsal workshop.

Assignment 3

Students must collect data through interviews, construct a bar or line graph, and present their findings about consumer preferences. (Essential learning: appropriate data collection methods, constructing graphs, presentation skills)

- The class is divided into four groups. Each group must interview a total of 10 people from a certain age group (elementary students, middle school students, high school students, adults) about their preferences as consumers. (The practice of this kind of data collection may be less familiar to Mariella and Rafael than to their peers, and instruction should be provided accordingly.) Students must brainstorm questions, and this process will be modeled for the class by the teacher, as will the construction of sample graphs to display similar data. Students will videotape themselves presenting in order to refine their presentation skills prior to the graded presentation where they will be rated by their peers according to a shared rubric.

Assignment 4

Students must double or halve a recipe, make the recipe, write a summary about the process, and create a display about the process and results. (Essential learning: adding and subtracting fractions, basic cooking skills, summary writing, presentation skills)

- The teacher will begin by showing students a final product in the form of a display board and a batch of jam. The display board components will serve as a template for student work and will be analyzed by the class. The teacher will then model the process of doubling the recipe through adding fractions and will write a summary of the process of making the jam through a "think-aloud" using the overhead projector or document camera. After tasting the jam, students will go to work on their own recipes in a workshop format. The family and consumer science teacher will also lend a hand in the cooking of the recipes.

Think of a student that you know who is at Level 4. (If you are not currently serving a Level 4 student, think ahead to a time when you will serve such a student.) Based on an assignment that you routinely use, differentiate expectations for your Level 4 student.

Fully English Proficient	Level 4
Language-Based Expectations:	*Language-Based Expectations:*
Standards-Based Content or Topic (from the curriculum):	
Scaffolding and Support:[3] using	*Scaffolding and Support:* using

Essential Learning: _____

Copyright © 2010. Caslon, Inc. All rights reserved. The first purchaser may photocopy this page for classroom and personal use.

---

[3] Note that the scaffolding and support that are provided for fully English proficient students are also provided for ELLs, though ELLs may often need different kinds of or more scaffolding and support.

Professional Development Resources

Resource 6.1 Appropriate Assignment/Assessment Procedures for Level 4 Students

In General	Listening and Speaking	Reading	Writing
• Engage students in grade-level assessments/assignments with scaffolding and support. • Consider weighting graded components according to students' linguistic strengths. • Make the assessment process comprehensible by explaining the directions orally and providing visual support (e.g., realia, icons, manipulatives, models), as appropriate. • Simultaneously assess content and language development (e.g., through summarizing, story retelling, questioning and responding, analyzing, evaluating).	• Use and require increasingly academic and grammatically varied language about both concrete and abstract topics. (Language should reflect discourse-level frames and models used during instruction.)	• Use a combination of grade-level texts (with scaffolding) and high-quality, age-appropriate, lower-reading-level materials that provide visual support. • Use traditional paper and pencil tests wisely, employing visual support (e.g., clip art, graphs) and linguistic scaffolding, as needed.	• Elicit writing of increasingly academic and grammatically varied language about both concrete and abstract topics. (Language should reflect discourse-level frames and models used during instruction.) • Use traditional paper and pencil tests wisely, employing visual support (e.g., clip art, graphs) and linguistic scaffolding, as needed.

Copyright © 2010. Caslon, Inc. All rights reserved. The first purchaser may photocopy this page for classroom and personal use.

Resource 6.2 Appropriate Instructional Strategies for Level 4 Students

In General	Listening	Speaking	Reading	Writing
• Provide sensory support for *every* lesson (e.g., real objects, pictures, hands-on materials and experiences, nonverbal communication, demonstrations, modeling, simulations). • Explicitly teach and require students to use content/academic and grammatically varied language about concrete and abstract topics, with diminishing errors. • Provide scaffolding and support needed for students to engage in grade-level assignments/assessments.	• Scaffold language development by modeling and prompting increasingly academic and grammatically varied language about both concrete and abstract topics. • Promote higher-order thinking processes during oral teaching by providing students with graphic organizers.	• Provide opportunities to produce extended oral discourse, increasingly inclusive of abstract thought. • Scaffold extended oral language production by providing visually supported discourse-level frames and models for high-quality academic discourse (e.g., "In accordance with our hypothesis, the results of our experiment demonstrate ____. This means that ____."). • Insist on increasingly correct and precise language.	• Use a combination of grade-level texts (with scaffolding) and high-quality, age-appropriate, lower-reading-level books aligned with content curriculum that provide visual support. • Provide students with graphic organizers to enhance higher-order thinking.	• Provide opportunities to produce extended written discourse, increasingly inclusive of abstract thought. • Scaffold extended written language production by providing visually supported discourse-level frames and models for high-quality academic discourse (e.g., "In accordance with our hypothesis, the results of our experiment demonstrate ____. This means that ____."). • Insist on increasingly correct and precise language. • Provide students with graphic organizers to enhance higher-order thinking.

Copyright © 2010. Caslon, Inc. All rights reserved. The first purchaser may photocopy this page for classroom and personal use.

7

Differentiation Strategies for Level 5 Students

Let us think of education as the means of developing our greatest abilities,
because in each of us there is a private hope
and dream which, fulfilled, can be translated into benefit
for everyone and greater strength for our nation.

—John F. Kennedy

Teachers who are solidly prepared with an understanding of both the tenets of language acquisition and of content knowledge are best equipped to implement appropriate assignment/assessment and instructional strategies that support the holistic needs of English language learners (ELLs). Such teachers are uniquely qualified to scaffold students along the language acquisition continuum toward both language proficiency and mastery of content knowledge, skills, and abilities. In this chapter, we discuss Level 5 ELLs who perform close to the range of their native English-speaking peers by describing their characteristics and providing assignment/assessment and instructional strategies appropriate to this level. Teachers are reminded that at Level 5, phasing out their efforts to scaffold language development is premature.

As is the case with native speakers, Level 5 ELLs will continue to benefit from sustained, pinpointed instruction to polish and perfect their English language proficiency across domains. In fact, such continued attention to the linguistically developmental needs of ELLs is critical for maximizing postsecondary options, whether in continued education or in the world of work.

Considering Variation in Level 5 Students' Backgrounds

Student Scenarios

Minh, a Vietnamese boy who recently arrived as a 9th grader through immigrating with his family, was an excellent student in Vietnam. In fact, he was the top student in math and in English at his school in Ho Chi Minh City. However, since Minh's instruction in English focused on reading and writing, he had few opportunities to interact and develop his listening and speaking abilities. His family now lives together with his uncle in the United States. Minh is very motivated to study and hopes to attend a state university to major in electrical engineering. At his new high school, Minh has stunned his math teachers with his ability to complete computations that are far beyond his grade level. In writing, Minh produces extended discourse, although he seems to struggle with listening and speaking. His English placement test indicates that he is Level 1 in speaking, Level 2 in listening, and Level 5 in reading and writing.

Pabitra, a 9th grade girl from Nepal, arrived in the United States in 8th grade with her parents and brother. They had lived in a refugee camp all her life. While her native language is Nepali, the language of instruction by missionaries in the refugee camp school was English. Her English placement test revealed that she is Level 5 in listening, speaking, and reading and Level 4 in writing. However, she has consistently struggled with math since she arrived. Through an interpreter, her parents confirm that Pabitra was unsuccessful in math in the camp school and has always had difficulty wherever mathematical concepts are needed. Her math and ESL teachers suspect that she should be entitled to special education services because of her mathematics difficulties. However, the school principal believes that English language learners should not be placed in special education programs until they have either exited the ESL program or have been in U.S. schools for three years.

Minh's academic skills are highly developed in his first language. He also possesses very strong English skills, but in only two domains: reading and writing, which reflect the methodology utilized during his English language instruction. Minh's second language has developed without the usual benefit of oral/aural language development as a foundation. While Minh is advantaged by having the complex skills of reading and writing already in place, he will require specific and extensive instruction to develop his listening and speaking skills. Another advantage is that he has arrived with his entire family, for whom education is a top priority. As in Vietnam, his parents have high expectations for his academic achievement in the United States. Yet another advantage is that Minh is intrinsically motivated to do well in high school because of his clear professional career goals. However, he is frustrated because he is languishing in a math class that is far beneath his mathematical skill level, because his high school has an unwritten policy that ELLs cannot participate in advanced courses, such as Advanced Placement (AP) Calculus.

Minh is at an educational crossroads. He is in dire need of a teacher advocate to carefully study his biographical profile, note his strengths, and assist in designing a program of meaningful and challenging instruction. His course work must, as various federal mandates require, afford him equal access to the curriculum. Based on his language proficiency levels and level of mathematical prowess, it is very likely that Minh could be very successful in the AP Calculus class with appropriate scaffolding and support.

Pabitra, in contrast, has strong language proficiency across all domains; her slightly lower proficiency in writing is not unusual in terms of ELL language development, since reading and writing typically follow the development of listening and speaking. The main concern with her current educational programming is her lack of math skills coupled with her inability to understand mathematical concepts. Her ESL and math teachers have recognized a potential disability, corroborated by input from Pabitra's parents, regarding her longstanding math struggles. The principal's position that ELLs cannot be entitled to special education services until after a waiting period is misinformed, at best. Parental and teacher input about students' skills and abilities should be given great consideration, since they know the student best. If bona fide disabilities exist, services must not be delayed. The administrator in this case should become more familiar with current ESL and special education legislation to ensure that all students receive the educational programming that they need as soon as possible. Though care must be taken in order to accurately identify disabilities in students who are still acquiring English, clear guidance on the subject is available (see *Special Education Considerations for English Language Learners*, Hamayan et al., 2007).

Level 5 Student Descriptors

Level 5 students are approaching full English language proficiency. As they do so, they exhibit linguistic behaviors that are nearly within the range of grade-level performance of English-language-proficient students.

Listening

In the area of listening, Level 5 students can attend to most grade-level language across contexts. Students are able to comprehend language that is complex and represents both social and academic discourse. Their vocabulary is advanced and is nearly on par with that of their native English-speaking grade-level peers.

Speaking

Level 5 students' speech demonstrates high levels of complexity and vocabulary attainment. They are able to communicate using both social and academic discourse and are nearing the level of speech production of fully English proficient students in their grade.

Reading

In terms of reading, Level 5 students can read text that covers a wide range of grade-level-appropriate topics and genres. Their writing is characterized by linguistic complexity and lexical precision that is nearly commensurate with that of their grade-level contemporaries.

Writing

The writing of Level 5 students displays a variety of content/academic vocabulary, a range of linguistic complexity, and representations of social and academic discourse. While student writing is not perfect at this level, it is similar to the writing of fully proficient writers at the student's given grade level.

A Word About Language Objectives

The information on the chart and in this chapter can be utilized to create appropriate language objectives for Level 5 students. Specifically, the student descriptors outline what students at this level know and can do in terms of language, while the assignment/assessment strategies offer guidance in terms of the kinds of things that students should be able to do in each of the four language domains. Once language objectives are written based on the student descriptors and assignment/assessment strategies, the instructional strategies can be tapped in order to develop lesson plans that facilitate the achievement of both language and content objectives.

At Level 5, students are able to participate in grade-level assignments and assessments with minimal support.

A Sample Differentiated Assignment for Level 5 Students

The expectations for Level 5 students may be virtually the same as those for fully English proficient students; the differentiation may come at the time of grading these students' work (see Chapter 8 for further discussion). In Table 7.1, the sample assignment is differentiated for Level 5 students. Note that the language-based expectations are only slightly different for Level 5 students than for fully English proficient students and that the scaffolding and support are the same for both. However, Level 5 students may depend upon certain types of scaffolding and support (which is language-related) more than fully English proficient students.

In order to facilitate the success of Level 5 students in achieving the objectives of classroom assignments, teachers can collaborate in a multiplicity of ways. For instance, the ESL/bilingual education teacher and the classroom/content teacher could co-teach so that students could benefit from their respective areas of expertise.

Necessary Assignment/Assessment Strategies for Level 5 Students

In terms of language ability, Level 5 students can successfully participate in traditional tests, including large-scale standardized tests, though language accommodations may be warranted. However, teachers are advised to be aware that any assessment designed for native speakers of English may not be entirely appropriate for ELLs because of potential inherent cultural biases (e.g., references to unfamiliar topics such as knights and castles in elementary reading). As a result, these kinds of assessments should be carefully screened before they are used for ELLs. If tests deemed to be inappropriate must be used, results must be interpreted accordingly.

Table 7.1 Sample assignment differentiated for Level 5

Fully English Proficient	Level 5
Language-Based Expectations: Write a set of instructions using grade-level vocabulary and sentence structures	*Language-Based Expectations:* Write a set of instructions demonstrating a variety of content/academic vocabulary and complex sentence structures
Standards-Based Content or Topic (from the curriculum): for a self-selected task	
Scaffolding and Support: using • a model assignment, • teacher demonstration of the task using a "think-aloud," • a sequential graphic organizer for planning to write, • a language wall with sequencing words and key sentence structures, and • feedback designed to help students refine proficiency according to the grade-level writing standards to guide writing.	*Scaffolding and Support:* using • a model assignment, • teacher demonstration of the task using a "think-aloud," • a sequential graphic organizer for planning to write, • a language wall with sequencing words and key sentence structures, and • level-appropriate feedback designed to push students to the next level of proficiency in writing to guide writing.

In General

Engage students in grade-level assignments/assessments with minimal scaffolding and support.   Level 5 students may need some scaffolding or support, though it should be minimal, since these students are approaching fluency in English. Such assistance may take the form of additional explanations about how to complete the task, allowing additional time, and so on. However, these students may also be able to complete grade-level tasks without support. Even as their ability develops, their lack of full English language proficiency may still be reflected in occasional errors.

Simultaneously assess content and language development through grade-level assignments/assessments.   Although students are approaching the range of full English proficiency at Level 5, teachers are reminded to maintain high expectations for students' continued development of linguistic complexity, precise vocabulary, and conventions of discourse. Native speakers of English who have not fully developed their academic language skills may also exhibit Level 5–like skills. As a result, teachers should target both linguistic and content development in their assessments to address the differentiated needs of both ELLs and non-ELLs. This requirement does not mean that all content teachers must assess English language arts curriculum, but, rather, that teachers should expect grade-level performance in students' language production within their content areas.

Listening and Speaking

Use and require extended discourse including precise and grammatically varied language across all grade-level-appropriate topics and contexts. Level 5 ELLs continue to benefit from explicit instruction in the use of correct grade-level English. Teachers across all content areas must embed this English language instruction in order to facilitate full language proficiency for these students. Without targeted instruction combined with increasingly higher goals, Level 5 students are destined to progress no further. Even if a district elects to stop providing Level 5 students with English language development services, teachers should consider what they would want for their own children as they work to ensure that *all* students, whether receiving language development support or not, are fully competent in terms of English skills. "Good enough" is simply *not* good enough in the globally competitive workplace. For example, teachers might explicitly tell students that they must use a wide variety of connectors when writing a persuasive essay (e.g., rather than relying on language such as *also* and *in addition,* students might be expected to use *moreover* and *furthermore*).

Reading

Use grade-level texts, providing scaffolding as needed. At Level 5, ELLs are generally able to rely on stand-alone grade-level texts, though some scaffolding may be required (as may also be the case for native speakers of English). Thus, if teachers elect to use grade-level texts in their assignments and assessments, they must ensure that students can make sense of those texts. This purpose can be accomplished by providing assistance to students within the assignment/assessment (e.g., a glossary or word bank accompanying a reading selection within a test). The exception to this "rule" of support would be if the assessment is testing grade-level reading ability; in that case, such supports are not warranted.

Writing

Use and require extended discourse including precise and grammatically varied language across all grade-level-appropriate topics and contexts. As discussed in the previous chapter, teachers must decide exactly what, in terms of either language or content, they are assessing when expecting students to write in response to an assignment or assessment task. If they are, indeed, assessing grade-level production of language within the content area, teachers should expect students to produce language that is representative of Level 5 writing. They can then score this writing using a differentiated rubric, discussed in Chapter 8. If the mastery of language is secondary to concept attainment or content, teachers can devise ways of assessing that are not language dependent, allowing students to demonstrate their knowledge, skills, and abilities without language mastery.

Note: If the assessment targets both language and content, it is necessary to have explicitly taught both. An example of this situation would be in the writing of a poem in language arts; a teacher may require that students structure their writing using a certain meter and rhyme scheme, as well as exacting descriptive vocabulary.

Necessary Instructional Strategies for Level 5 Students

At Level 5, the critical action step of greatest significance is to determine students' instructional level based on their language proficiency levels, content knowledge, skills, and abilities. Next, teachers must target those instructional levels in terms of both content and language development. This focused instruction will contribute to the ongoing improvement of ELLs' grasp of content and their language proficiency. Without these intentional focused actions, ELLs are less likely to reach their full academic potential.

In General

Explicitly teach and require students to use precise and grammatically varied language across all grade-level-appropriate topics and contexts, expecting and allowing minimal errors. In order for students to make increasingly fine-grained improvements toward language proficiency within the content areas, teachers must continue to explicitly teach and model high-level language during their instruction. Particularly at Level 5, where the language proficiency levels of ELLs and non-ELLs can often intersect, continuing and sustaining instructional efforts that aim for high expectations can make a pivotal difference for both groups of students. Referencing the chart to target students' instructional needs affords teachers an authentic way to zero in on instructional gaps related to the curriculum and on overlooked discrete points of language development. This individualized and differentiated instruction is beneficial for both ELLs and non-ELLs. Without it, these students are unlikely to achieve the full English language proficiency that will allow them to gain entrance to the world of advantage. For instance, Level 5 ELLs should produce language with grammar and mechanics that is nearly on grade level (e.g., minimal errors that do not inhibit understanding could be overlooked as appropriate in a given grade level).

Engage students in the same tasks assigned to grade-level peers, diminishing scaffolding and support. The necessity to provide scaffolding and support in assignments and assessments for Level 5 students is likely to be minimal as they approach English language proficiency. Able to engage in most grade-level assignments or assessments with few errors, Level 5 students can, at times, seem fully proficient. Teachers are reminded that these students, by definition and in keeping with the results of their English language proficiency assessments, are not fully English proficient. As a result, they will continue to benefit from careful attention from teachers to interpret assessment and assignment results in order to inform instruction. Scaffolding for these students, while minimal, should be tailored to their individual needs.

Listening

Scaffold language development by modeling and prompting precise and grammatically varied language across all grade-level-appropriate topics and contexts, expecting and allowing minimal errors. Teachers must themselves generate speech worthy of emulation. In so doing, they model ways for Level 5 ELLs (and non-ELLs) to articulate concepts and ideas in formal register, using complex constructions, and with precise vocabulary. When such utterances become the norm in the classroom, students are bound to incorporate them into their own speech. For example, one teacher, when admonishing her ELLs, used the command "Modulate, people!" rather than "Be quiet!" As a result, students were later heard to exhort the class with the same terminology. The authentic use of high-level language then becomes a permanent part of student repertoires.

Speaking

Provide opportunities to produce extended discourse using precise and grammatically varied language across all grade-level-appropriate topics and contexts. Level 5 students need multiple opportunities to use the advanced language that teachers model. Such opportunities may include classroom discussions, debates, role-play, and persuasive speeches within the content areas. Teachers are encouraged to remind students to use the discourse-level frames and models that were the focus of teaching for Level 4 students. Teachers must then expect such high-level production of Level 5 students.

Emphasize the use of increasingly complex and precise language. At Level 5, teachers must continue assisting students in refining their language production within and across the content areas. Teachers should create an environment conducive and receptive to error correction, since errors at Level 5 are minimal. As a result, teachers can take opportunities to polish students' spoken language (e.g., clarifying the use of the first conditional: "I wish that I *were* . . ." rather than "I wish that I *was* . . .").

Reading

Use grade-level texts, providing scaffolding as needed. Though Level 5 ELLs are not at grade level in terms of reading proficiency, they are able to access grade-level texts to a great extent, particularly when scaffolding is provided. As with Level 4 students, this scaffolding may take the form of teacher explanation, pre-teaching of vocabulary, glossaries, advance organizers and outlines, and other topical resources (e.g., first-person accounts, magazine and newspaper articles, internet research). At Level 5, these supports should be gradually withdrawn, as appropriate.

Another way to enhance reading ability is through frequent DEAR (drop everything and read) times, during which *all* students and staff in the K–12 setting can be expected to spend time reading materials of their choice. These reading materials could include books and other materials in students' first languages, bilingual books, chapter books, novels, comic books, graphic novels, newspapers, and magazines. One school even involved the principal and custodians in this regularly scheduled schoolwide activity for a common 20-minute period. The ultimate goal in this sort of initiative is to encourage students to engage with text based on personal interest, as well as to increase their reading proficiency. Teachers must use a wide lens to determine acceptable reading materials. If students choose to read comic books or anime-style publications, we must celebrate that they are reading, in any language, and care less about the genre.

Writing

Provide opportunities to produce extended written discourse using precise and grammatically varied language across all grade-level-appropriate topics, contexts, and genres. As with speaking skills, students will not improve their writing skills unless provided opportunities to practice and perfect them. In addition to providing such opportunities, teachers must continue to elucidate their expectations through sharing samples of successful student work, presenting authentic historical examples, and modeling and supporting the writing process. The fact that students are at Level 5 does not take into consideration their familiarity (or lack of familiarity) with the various topics, contexts, and genres of writing at a given grade level. As a result, teachers must always remain mindful of the need to build and activate background knowledge and experiences that will contribute to enhanced writing. In the same way, students must be schooled in the formal style and register of written text (e.g., using third person for academic writing), in contrast with the more casual style and register of spoken language. Attentive feedback regarding levels of formality can elevate students to become more empowered to access professional and higher educational opportunities.

Emphasize the use of increasingly complex and precise language. Level 5 students are capable of expressing meaning through writing, but it is incumbent upon teachers to assist students in refining their writing to reflect more nuanced and precise language. At times, the ability to express ideas in grammatically complex ways is an integral part of communicating such shades of meaning. Consider the following examples:

Teachers must help students to be clearer.

    versus

It is incumbent upon teachers to assist students in refining their writing to reflect more nuanced and precise language.

While both sentences are talking about the same topic, the second sentence reflects the kind of powerful language that is necessary for success in the world of advantage. At first glance, it is clear which sentence is written with more authority. The second includes a variety of grammatical complexity, a much higher register, a "frozen" phrase ("it is incumbent upon"), and sophisticated vocabulary. These must all be explicitly taught.

As with Level 1–4 students, Level 5 students are likely continue to operate at a vocabulary deficit when compared to fully English proficient peers. As demonstrated by the preceding example, targeted vocabulary instruction continues to be not only appropriate, but also essential for explicitly developing and expanding student vocabularies. A number of excellent resources focusing on this all-important aspect of language development are listed in the "For Further Reading" section.

Instruction That Integrates Language Domains

Grade-level classroom activities designed for native speakers of English likely require the integrated use of listening, speaking, reading, and writing. In employing these kinds of activities with Level 5 students, teachers are reminded to be vigilant in attending to issues of language development. Since these students are able to perform, albeit below grade level, they often fall between the cracks by not receiving the critical instruction that would lift them to the next level of proficiency. Particularly at Level 5, teachers must not reduce their efforts or expectations with regard to continuing language development; teachers must not settle for "good enough."

Conclusion

In this chapter, we have emphasized that ELLs can demonstrate different levels of proficiency across the domains of language (e.g., Minh is Level 5 in reading and writing and Level 1 in speaking). Further, ELLs, like their non-ELL peers, can potentially benefit from gifted and talented programming and special education services, if appropriate. Care needs to be taken so that there is neither over—nor underrepresentation of ELLs in either of these programs.

Professional Development Activities

Activity 7.1 Student Scenarios with Application Ideas

Adapt the following assignments for Minh and Pabitra, who were introduced at the beginning of the chapter, according to each student's language proficiency level and any other important factors:

- Differentiate the language-based expectations based on the student descriptors and using relevant assignment/assessment strategies on the chart and in this chapter.

  — Bear in mind the "essential learning" for each assignment (noted below each assignment template) as you differentiate the expectations, so that important skills are not overlooked.

- Design appropriate scaffolding and support using relevant instructional strategies on the chart and in this chapter.

Assignment 1[1,2]

Fully English Proficient	Level 5
Language-Based Expectations: Write a research paper	*Language-Based Expectations:*
Standards-Based Content or Topic (from the curriculum): on a global issue as experienced in a country other than the United States	
Scaffolding and Support: using • a lecture on global issues, • a sample paper as a model, and • library and internet resources	*Scaffolding and Support:* using •

Essential learning: research paper writing, development of world citizenship awareness, recognition of global issues

Copyright © 2010. Caslon, Inc. All rights reserved. The first purchaser may photocopy this page for classroom and personal use.

---

[1] Assignments 1, 3, and 4 include language-related skills as part of their "essential learning." Thus teachers must ensure that they focus on these areas in particular for Level 5 ELLs, rather than accept whatever students produce as sufficient. That is, teachers must push Level 5 students toward full English proficiency in classroom assignments wherever possible.

[2] In some cases assignments/assessments for Level 5 students may be exactly the same as those for fully English proficient students; differentiation may appear only in the scoring of student work. (See chapter 8 for guidance on differentiated scoring.)

Assignment 2

	Fully English Proficient	Level 5
	Language-Based Expectations: Create a map that includes notes about indigenous plant and animal life, and chart a food chain	*Language-Based Expectations:*
Standards-Based Content or Topic (from the curriculum): corresponding to a local park		
	Scaffolding and Support: using • an advance organizer that outlines the unit and identifies new vocabulary needed for the assignment, • sample assignments, and • teacher modeling of map-making and food chain construction	*Scaffolding and Support:* using •

Essential learning: map-making, chart-making skills, characteristics of local plants and animals and their ecosystems

Copyright © 2010. Caslon, Inc. All rights reserved. The first purchaser may photocopy this page for classroom and personal use.

Assignment 3

Fully English Proficient	Level 5
Language-Based Expectations: Act out a scene (from a modern vantage point)	*Language-Based Expectations:*

Standards-Based Content or Topic (from the curriculum):
from Romeo and Juliet

| *Scaffolding and Support:*

• explicit instruction in how to interpret Elizabethan English in order to understand the plot | *Scaffolding and Support:*

using

• |

Essential learning: universal themes in literature, theater acting skills, basic comprehension of Elizabethan English, "translation" of Elizabethan English to modern-day English

Copyright © 2010. Caslon, Inc. All rights reserved. The first purchaser may photocopy this page for classroom and personal use.

Assignment 4

Fully English Proficient	Level 5
Language-Based Expectations: Create a poster that outlines the development and plans to adhere to	*Language-Based Expectations:*
Standards-Based Content or Topic (from the curriculum): a fact-based one-month budget for life after high school	
Scaffolding and Support: using • a lecture on budgeting, • a model assignment, and • resources related to cost of living (e.g, apartment ads, grocery fliers)	*Scaffolding and Support:* using •

Essential learning: living within one's means, how to budget, research skills related to costs, goal-setting and planning life skills

Copyright © 2010. Caslon, Inc. All rights reserved. The first purchaser may photocopy this page for classroom and personal use.

Suggested Ways to Adapt Assignments

Guidance pertaining to the language-based expectations for Minh's and Pabitra's assignments is presented in the following paragraphs.

Assignment 1

Students must write a research paper on a global issue as experienced in a country other than the United States. (Essential learning: research paper writing, development of world citizenship awareness, recognition of global issues)

- *For both:* This assignment does not need to be adjusted for either student, as they can focus on their own sending countries and can (hopefully) address a familiar topic.

Assignment 2

Students must map an area of a local park, note plant and animal life indigenous to the area, and chart a corresponding food chain. (Essential learning: map-making, chart-making skills, characteristics of local plants and animals and their ecosystems)

- *For both:* Neither of these newcomers is likely to be familiar with the names of indigenous plants, and some animal names may also be unfamiliar. In addition, map-making might be a new skill for both students. For these reasons, these students might work with a more proficient partner to complete the assignment. Such pairing would also work to promote interaction, thereby developing Minh's speaking and listening abilities, which, at Level 1 and Level 2, respectively, require considerable focused attention and sustained opportunities for development. (Note that Minh's partner will need explicit guidance in how to work with a student with advanced reading and writing skills and beginning listening and speaking skills.)

Assignment 3

Students must work in groups to act out a scene from *Romeo and Juliet* from a modern vantage point. (Essential learning: universal themes in literature, the plot of the play as an example of tragedy, theater acting skills, basic comprehension of Elizabethan English, "translation" of Elizabethan English to modern-day English)

- *For Minh:* At Level 1 in speaking and Level 2 in listening, Minh is not well equipped for success on this assignment without intentional differentiation based on the skills he has developed and can reasonably be expected to perform. Teachers must ask pertinent questions, such as

  – Will the student be able to aurally understand Elizabethan English when he is unable to fully process everyday, modern English through listening?

    – *Recommendation:* At such a discrepant level of proficiency in listening and speaking, Minh will likely not be able to make sense of Elizabethan English.

  – As a Level 1 speaker, will the student be able to produce the extended discourse required?

    – *Recommendation:* At Level 1, Minh will likely be unable to produce extended speech at all, most particularly if the difficulty in speaking is compounded by requiring him to use less comprehensible Elizabethan English.

  – How useful will this assignment be in terms of developing the student's weaker language domains (listening and speaking) and in terms of enhancing his content knowledge, skills, and abilities?

    – *Recommendation:* This particular assignment seems to be "more trouble than it's worth" in terms of helping Minh to expand his listening and speaking skills using Elizabethan English. Instead, teachers should focus on the content standard using a modern-day English version that Minh can comprehend.

  – What additional kinds of activities focusing on developing listening and speaking could be integrated to make this assignment beneficial and productive for Minh?

    – *Recommendation:* Since Minh has tried reading the Elizabethan text and has likely made little sense of it, teachers should consider providing a version in modern-day English for him to use. He could benefit from hearing a tape or CD of this modern-day version to read along and practice at home to develop fluency.

    – *Recommendation:* With a partner, Minh could read the modern-day version aloud after having listened to the tape or CD at home. He could retell the story, according to his ability (likely using visual supports such as pictures) to a partner, a peer tutor, a paraeducator, and so on. He would then be better prepared to take a (small) role in the class assignment.

- *For Pabitra:* Given that Pabitra is Level 5 in listening, speaking, and reading and Level 4 in writing, she is fairly well equipped to cope with this assignment. However, teachers must bear in mind that reading Shakespeare is often very difficult for native speakers of English. In addition, ELLs in particular may be lacking in critical background knowledge and schema. Further, making sense of Elizabethan English could be construed as a less than useful endeavor for a student who is still developing English language proficiency. Before implementing this assignment, teachers must again ask pertinent questions, such as

    — Will the student be able to aurally understand Elizabethan English?

      — *Recommendation:* Common sense would indicate that Pabitra would be less able to process Elizabethan English than her native English proficient peers, rendering the language load of the assignment extremely challenging.

    — How useful is this assignment in terms of developing the student's weaker language domains and in terms of enhancing the student's content knowledge, skills, and abilities?

      — *Recommendation:* This assignment may be at the frustration level for Pabitra, particularly in the area of reading. Her weakest domain, writing, will not necessarily be improved by completing the assignment. Her content knowledge, skills, and abilities may be improved, but she may likely have to rely on others for key parts of the assignment (e.g., "translating" the Elizabethan language to modern-day English).

    — What part of the assignment will develop Pabitra's weakest domain (writing)?

      — *Recommendation:* This assignment could be differentiated for Pabitra to incorporate more writing, based on formative assessment data that clarify the gaps in her writing skills. The teacher could inform Pabitra of specific types of errors that the two are trying to extinguish, so that Pabitra will understand the targeted nature of the corrections and pay particular attention to self-correction and using increasingly complex structures and vocabulary.

Assignment 4

Students must create a fact-based one-month budget for themselves for life after high school. They must display this work on a poster that describes how they created the budget and what steps they will take to ensure that they are able to follow the budget. (Essential learning: living within one's means, how to budget, research skills related to costs, goal-setting and planning life skills)

- *For Minh:* This assignment should be feasible for Minh, but he would benefit from having to give an oral presentation about what he creates. This may be done for the teacher or in his ESL class, rather than in front of the entire class.

- *For Pabitra:* Given Pabitra's seeming disability with math concepts, teachers might consider consulting with special education teachers about ways in which to make this assignment more achievable for her.

Suggested Instructional Strategies

The following paragraphs provide guidance pertaining to scaffolding and support for the assignment.

For all assignments, teachers must make sure to build sufficient background, support students in making connections to what they already know, pre-teach relevant vocabulary, and embed opportunities for interactions with native speakers of English. It is also helpful and necessary to provide students with models of what is expected, such as samples of successfully completed assignments, since the formats of assignments may be unfamiliar to ELLs. Such purposeful practices empower ELLs to be successful on adapted classroom assignments as they develop their schema of what coursework looks like in U.S. schools.

Assignment 1

Students must write a research paper on a global issue as experienced in a country other than the United States. (Essential learning: research paper writing, development of world citizenship awareness, recognition of global issues)

- *For Minh:* Since Minh's listening ability is far below his reading and writing ability, he should be provided with supplementary reading materials to "make up for" the fact that he likely cannot understand lecture on the topic at hand. He will also need support to understand the format required for the paper, the seriousness of plagiarism, and how to avoid it. (This support would ideally come from a bilingual staff member who could clearly explain relevant expectations and ramifications.) Perhaps Minh could be required to listen to a podcast, a television show, or a webinar on a global issue or to take notes and prepare an oral presentation in addition to his research paper.

- *For Pabitra:* This assignment perfectly focused on her weakest domain and therefore provides an excellent avenue for targeting corrections in her writing that will propel her to the next level of writing proficiency. She will also likely need assistance in understanding the format and conventions required for the research paper and in becoming informed about the seriousness of plagiarism and given guidance in how to avoid it.

- *For both:* Both students will benefit from a visually supported lecture on global issues and guidance in how to best utilize library and internet resources.

Assignment 2

Students must map an area of a local park, note plant and animal life indigenous to the area, and chart a corresponding food chain. (Essential learning: map-making, chart-making skills, characteristics of local plants and animals)

- *For both:* The teacher will provide an advance organizer that outlines the unit and identifies new vocabulary needed for the assignment. Sample assignments will be shown, and map-making and food chain construction must be modeled.

- *For Minh:* Using his advanced reading and writing skills, Minh can prepare himself to engage in instruction based on the advance organizer. Minh may also need assistance with general mapping skills, based on his educational background experiences.

Assignment 3

Students must work in groups to act out a scene from *Romeo and Juliet* from a modern vantage point. (Essential learning: universal themes in literature, acting skills, basic comprehension of Elizabethan English, "translation" of Elizabethan English to modern-day English)

- *For Minh:* After dispensing Minh from learning Elizabethan English (since learning basic English is a prerequisite to learning Elizabethan English), teachers have cleared the way for focusing on comprehension of the plot of the play. With this differentiation for his listening and speaking levels, Minh can now participate in the role-play activity, though in a limited way. Based on his educational background, role play may be an unfamiliar activity, so instruction in basic acting techniques may be warranted.

- *For Pabitra:* Pabitra is likely to benefit from instruction in basic acting techniques, as well. Further, she will need explicit guidance in how to make sense of Elizabethan English and in how to "translate" it to modern-day English (as will the entire class, though Pabitra may need more support in this area).

Assignment 4

Students must create a fact-based one-month budget for themselves for life after high school. They must display this work on a poster that describes how they created the budget and what steps they will take to ensure that they are able to follow the budget. (Essential learning: living within one's means, how to budget, research skills related to costs, goal-setting and planning)

- *For Minh:* To develop his Level 2 listening skills, teachers should provide him with advance organizers to outline what is going to be addressed in the lecture leading up to the assignment. Graphic organizers should then be provided to scaffold note-taking. He must be provided with academic sentence frames and examples to scaffold his presentation and with explicit teaching in phonemic awareness and pronunciation.

- *For Pabitra:* Pabitra's need for tutoring in math activities extends to this particular assignment. Someone (a paraeducator, a bilingual staff member, a more proficient peer, a volunteer, etc.) must assist her in developing the budget as a way of ensuring that the math is done correctly. For example the task might be broken down for her so that numbers could be added incrementally instead of all at once. Since Pabitra is Level 5 in listening and speaking, her need for advance organizers and graphic organizers is no greater than that of native speakers of English. That being said, if all students would benefit from such supports, Pabitra would also most certainly derive benefit as well.

- *For both:* The teacher can provide a visually supported lecture on budgeting, a model assignment, and guidance in where to find and how to use resources related to cost of living (e.g., apartment ads, grocery fliers).

Activity 7.2   Applying Your Learning to Your Own Level 5 Student

Think of a student that you know who is at Level 5. (If you are not currently serving a Level 5 student, think ahead to a time when you will serve such a student.) Based on an assignment that you routinely use, differentiate expectations for your Level 5 student.

Assignment 1

Fully English Proficient	Level 5
Language-Based Expectations:	*Language-Based Expectations:*
Standards-Based Content or Topic (from the curriculum):	
Scaffolding and Support: [3] using	*Scaffolding and Support:* using

Essential Learning: _____

_____

Copyright © 2010. Caslon, Inc. All rights reserved. The first purchaser may photocopy this page for classroom and personal use.

_____

[3] Note that the scaffolding and support that are provided for fully English proficient students are also provided for ELLs, though ELLs often need different kinds of or more scaffolding and support. Alternatively, Level 5 students may be expected to complete the same assignment as fully English proficient students with the same scaffolding and support but scoring of their work may be differentiated.

Professional Development Resources

Resource 7.1 Appropriate Assignment/Assessment Procedures for Level 5 Students

In General	Listening and Speaking	Reading	Writing
• Engage students in grade-level assessments/assignments with minimal scaffolding and support. • Simultaneously assess content and language development through grade-level assessments/ assignments.	• Use and require extended discourse including precise and grammatically varied language across all grade-level-appropriate topics and contexts.	• Use grade-level texts, providing scaffolding as needed.	• Use and require extended discourse including precise and grammatically varied language across all grade-level-appropriate topics and contexts.

Copyright © 2010. Caslon, Inc. All rights reserved. The first purchaser may photocopy this page for classroom and personal use.

Resource 7.2 Appropriate Instructional Strategies for Level 5 Students

In General	Listening	Speaking	Reading	Writing
• Explicitly teach and require students to use precise and grammatically varied language across all grade-level-appropriate topics and contexts, expecting and allowing minimal errors. • Engage students in the same tasks assigned to grade-level peers, diminishing scaffolding and support.	• Scaffold language development by modeling and prompting precise and grammatically varied language across all grade-level-appropriate topics and contexts, expecting and allowing minimal errors.	• Provide opportunities to produce extended discourse using precise and grammatically varied language across all grade-level-appropriate topics and contexts. • Emphasize the use of increasingly complex and precise language.	• For reading-related activities, use grade-level texts, providing scaffolding as needed.	• Provide opportunities to produce extended written discourse using precise and grammatically varied language across all grade-level-appropriate topics, contexts, and genres. • Emphasize the use of increasingly complex and precise language.

Copyright © 2010. Caslon, Inc. All rights reserved. The first purchaser may photocopy this page for classroom and personal use.

8

Bringing It All Together in Elementary, Middle, and High School Classrooms

We can, whenever and wherever we choose,
successfully teach all children . . .
we already know more than we need to know
in order to do that.

—Ron Edwards

In practice, teachers do not generally find themselves neatly assigned to classrooms with students all functioning at uniform levels of English proficiency. Rather, English language learners (ELLs) in a given classroom may be operating at different levels of proficiency, and, as discussed in previous chapters, individual students may even vary in proficiency across domains (e.g., the student in a previous scenario who functioned at level 5 in reading and writing, yet at level 2 in listening and level 1 in speaking). This chapter examines how teachers can differentiate for the range of ELLs they find in their classes.

To accomplish this purpose, we describe three hypothetical classrooms of heterogeneous students, one elementary, one middle, and one high school. Each classroom includes five English language learners from a variety of cultural and linguistic backgrounds who are functioning at a range of proficiency levels across domains. To provide a wide range of student scenarios for teacher reference, we have incorporated a number of situations that can present significant challenges to teachers. The scenarios in this chapter should not be interpreted to be representative of the proportion of challenging cases related to serving ELLs, as that proportion here is unnaturally, yet intentionally, high. However, these particular (and often, challenging) scenarios have been deliberately selected to provide teachers a broader range of reference when searching for guidance as they face similar situations.

Teachers are reminded that, in general, special education for ELLs is appropriate for a similar percentage of students as in the native English-speaking population. While some districts report disproportionality in the numbers of ELLs receiving special education services, we recommend that identification for such programming be carefully scrutinized and potential placements carefully weighed. Similarly, other district programs that require an identification process, such as those for gifted and talented students, should make use of appropriate identification processes for ELLs (other than language-dependent standardized assessments) in order to include a representative number of ELLs for participation in those programs, as well. In addition, once ELLs are identified for special programming, the principles and strategies enumerated in this book and listed on the chart should be applied to serve them, as appropriate, in such programs.

The chapter begins with a general discussion of how teachers at any grade level can differentiate assignments, assessment, and instruction, using the tandem guidance of the chart and this volume, for students functioning across all five proficiency levels. We also include specific guidance regarding teacher collaboration. The majority of the chapter then provides concrete examples of differentiation for ELLs in practice at the elementary, middle, and high school levels. In each example, we look closely at student scenarios, answer frequently asked questions about issues raised by these scenarios, and show teachers how to differentiate instruction and assessment for the ELLs in these classes using the template for differentiating assessment and instruction. The chapter concludes with recommendations for grading differentiated assignments.

Thinking About All Five Levels Simultaneously

Classroom Scenarios

Mrs. Davis serves five ELLs in her 3rd grade classroom: Hanna from China, Hiroshi from Japan, Minji from Korea, Myriam from Haiti, and Oudry from Congo. These students range from nearly proficient in English (Hiroshi) to truly beginning in the development of English language proficiency (Oudry). Mrs. Davis wonders how to teach writing, in particular, to such a diverse group of students.

In his 7th grade classroom, **Mr. Clark** is working to meet the needs of five very diverse ELLs: Martha from Sudan, Irina from Russia, Jesús from Mexico, Claudia from California, and Karol from Poland. While Karol is virtually proficient in English, Irina and Jesús are closer to the beginning of their journey toward English language proficiency. Mr. Clark is stumped about how to facilitate the effective participation of all of these students in an upcoming unit on giving speeches.

Ms. Moore has welcomed five ELLs into the sixth-period section of her 10th grade Cultural Issues class: Mercy from Liberia, Kumar from Nepal, Manivone from Laos, Yasir from Afghanistan, and Victor from El Salvador. While Victor is nearly fluent in English, Kumar and Yasir both score Level 1 in all four language domains. Ms. Moore is wondering how to prepare all five of these students for their group presentation to the school board, a service learning project selected for their group through a random drawing.

Differentiation is essential if students with diverse backgrounds and skills are to be successful academically. In the case of ELLs, the obvious impetus for differentiation is (lack of) English language proficiency. However, related literacy issues, differences in cultural norms and expectations (including those related to school-based learning), and differing sets of background knowledge pertinent to content learning all validate the need for differentiation according to individual needs. All these factors, but particularly students' language proficiency levels, require differentiation that is tailored to specific needs (rather than a "one-size-fits-all" approach for all ELLs). If diverse learners do not receive instruction that closes gaps in their knowledge, skills, and abilities, they will not meet standards for which teachers are held accountable. Further, such underserved students will fall short of reaching their full potential. The chart offers teachers a ready reference to use in planning meaningful and engaging instruction that can enable students at all levels of proficiency to appropriately meet both mandated and personal learning goals.

Teachers should routinely prepare their language and content objectives, lesson plans, and assignments/assessments by referencing the guidance in the previous chapters and in the chart in order to address the range of linguistic capabilities of students in their classrooms and to effectively engage each student in every lesson. Such effective planning can be accomplished using any lesson planning template that teachers prefer, in which they can build incremental scaffolding targeting student needs. The information on the chart and in this volume can then inform planned tasks and expectations, clearly set out in accordance with the language proficiency levels described in TESOL's *PreK–12 English Language Proficiency Standards* (Gottlieb et al., 2006). Further, this process will allow teachers to address the same content standards implemented for native speakers of English. Through enacting the principle of learning language through content and, therefore, teaching both simultaneously, teachers can meet district and state expectations for addressing content standards, as well as respect the learning needs of students at various levels of English language proficiency.

Supporting Collaboration Through Reciprocal Mentoring

Teachers of culturally and linguistically diverse students can effectively expand their knowledge and expertise by reaching out to colleagues for support and collaboration, as discussed in Chapter 1. To this end, it is essential that classroom/content teachers and ESL/bilingual teachers understand one another's roles. Classroom/content teachers must focus on teaching standards-based content in a way that is comprehensible, meaningful, and engaging for all students. Guidance on the chart and in this book clarifies key ways in which to accomplish this goal. However, it is not meant to replace the expertise of the ESL/bilingual teacher. That individual is to teach ELLs the English that they need in order to be successful both inside and outside of school and for assisting classroom/ content teachers in knowing how to best serve ELLs. However, given the large student-teacher ratios that are increasingly common in U.S. schools and the large range of needs that each ELL brings to bear (including issues related to busing, scheduling, parent communication, etc.), ESL/ bilingual teachers cannot be held solely responsible for teaching all the language that ELLs need to learn. Instead, these two groups of teachers must collaborate to determine how to best meet student needs. This cooperation may take many forms, including co-teaching, collaboration on lesson planning, intensive language instruction on certain content topics by ESL teachers, and so on. Different contexts likely call for different forms of shared responsibility. However, the chart can serve as a point of "grounding" for both classroom/content and ESL teachers, providing a common understanding, common language, and common starting point in their work to serve ELLs well.

Together, teams of educators (including not only content and ESL/ bilingual teachers, but also "specials" teachers, gifted/talented teachers, special education teachers, paraeducators, and administrators) can work collaboratively to fill in gaps about shared student needs, content and background knowledge, and useful strategies to more effectively meet the needs of students. Such reciprocal mentoring (Jones-Vo et al., 2007) empowers educators from different areas of expertise to assume equal instructional roles that, when combined, effectively meet the instructional needs of the range of students in today's classrooms. To support this highly beneficial collaboration, we provide a template for communication among educators about specific students in Resource 8.1 at the end of the chapter. This ELL Differentiation Communiqué can be used to share content and language objectives and appropriate strategies, supported by the chart, among content teachers, ESL teachers, paraeducators, and others. For example, a science teacher could fill in the content objectives for the week, including targeted vocabulary and differentiated assignment expectations, and then hand the ELL Differentiation Communiqué to the ESL teacher. The ESL teacher could then, if needed, help to refine the content teacher's plans for differentiated expectations. She or he could also suggest strategies or co-teach using appropriate strategies, accessible materials, and other cultural and linguistic insights. The Communiqué acts as a "living document" between educators to support the instruction and assessment of each ELL according to the chart.

By collaborating and recognizing that language proficiency levels are not static, teachers are better equipped to support language learners and propel them to the next proficiency level by targeting their current developmental stages and characteristics, and setting even higher expectations. This repetitive and cyclical process spirals upward in a way that fosters language proficiency development, as well as attainment of content knowledge, skills, and abilities.

Differentiating Lessons for Students at All Five Levels

To meet the need for comprehensive lesson planning that takes into account all the different language levels of students in a given classroom, we offer a template for the development of differentiated assignments/ assessments across all five levels of language proficiency. This tool allows educators to

- consider and differentiate the language-based expectations of assignments and assessments,

- ensure that students of all proficiency levels are attending to the same content standards,

- guarantee that adequate scaffolding and support are provided, and

- maintain awareness of "next steps" for students at all five levels of language proficiency by bearing in mind the expectations at subsequent levels of language proficiency.

This Differentiated Assignment/Assessment Template (Resource 8.2) will assist teachers in creating assignments and assessments that are consistent in terms of content (avoiding the "watering down" of standards) and are also attainable for students at differing proficiency levels. These differentiated assignments and assessments are made accessible for students by matching language demands to the leveled student descriptors and assignment/assessment strategies on the chart and by providing supports and scaffolding drawn from the instructional strategies on the chart.

Recall that the template is comprised of three rows: language-based expectations, standards-based content or topic, and scaffolding and support. As described in detail in Chapter 3, in the template, assignments for students at each of the individual proficiency levels are read in columnar fashion. That is, one reads the description of an assignment/assessment for students at a particular language proficiency level by following the column with that level heading (e.g., Level 1, Level 2) down the template.

When using the template for differentiating across all five proficiency levels, teachers must begin by outlining the assignment for fully English proficient students[1]. Then they can tailor the assignment for students at different proficiency levels by referring to the student descriptors and the assignment/assessment and instructional strategies listed on the chart and discussed throughout the book. Using these resources, teachers can differentiate the assignment for Levels 5, 4, 3, 2, and 1. It is recommended that teachers differentiate assignment expectations working from Level 5 down to Level 1 because, for many teachers, it seems to be easier to work in this step-wise fashion, rather than jumping from the expectations for fully English proficient students immediately to Level 1. Likely, the scaffolding and support section of the

---

[1] In the Differentiated Assignment/Assessment Template for all five levels of proficiency, the column for fully English proficient students appears on the right. This placement denotes the progression of language development form Level 1 to fully English proficient, and assists teachers in seeing the trends across levels in terms of language-based expectations and levels or kinds of scaffolding and support.

Differentiated Assignment/Assessment Template will "grow" for students at lower proficiency levels, while the language-based expectations are diminished in accordance with the student descriptors and related assignment/assessment strategies. The language-based expectations can be thought to represent language objectives for students at each proficiency level (though not necessarily all the language objectives associated with a specific lesson), while the scaffolding and support section will clarify how to design lesson plans in order to support students at each of the five different proficiency levels.

In the spirit of backward lesson design (Wiggins & McTighe, 2006), teachers should use the template to design assignments/assessments *prior to* designing their lesson plans. The use of backward lesson design enables teachers, by first considering the goals of instruction, to adjust their teaching so that students will ultimately be able to produce desired standards-based products and performances. Further, key instructional strategies are incorporated into the Differentiated Assignment/Assessment Template in the scaffolding and support section. Thus the design of assignments/assessments with the template facilitates simultaneous lesson planning.

An Elementary School Example

When explicitly considering lesson design to meet the needs of a variety of ELLs functioning at various proficiency levels across all four domains in the classroom (listening, speaking, reading, and writing), teachers are reminded to integrate meaningful instruction, productive interaction, and appropriate assessment strategies based on students' language proficiency levels; their content knowledge, skills, and abilities; and, importantly, knowledge gained from individual student background profiles.

Elementary Student Scenarios

As mentioned in the classroom scenario, our hypothetical 3rd grade class includes the following five ELLs. As indicated by assessment data, their individual levels of proficiency in listening, speaking, reading, and writing are noted using L, S, R, and W for each respective language domain.

> **Hanna** was adopted just this year by her American family from an orphanage in China where she experienced several challenges, including hearing impairment, lack of interaction with others, and confinement to a wheel chair. She is not literate in Chinese. Hanna now lives with her adoptive parents and two English-speaking siblings and has begun 3rd grade. Her parents have embarked on a series of surgeries to support her future ability to walk. They have hired a tutor to work with her English development, and they have very high expectations for her achievement. **L=2, S=2, R=1, W=1**

There are several unknown factors that may affect the English language development of Hanna, particularly the unknown orphanage conditions that she has experienced, which could help or hinder her language acquisition. Some children from certain orphanages can fail to receive the stimulation and interaction they need, some have physical or mental disabilities at birth, and others manifest the effects of fetal alcohol syndrome. With international adoption, health records can be unclear or ambiguous. As a result, teachers must be strong advocates for children when sorting out issues of language acquisition versus disability. Teachers must recognize that neither lack of exposure to education nor differences in language and culture are intrinsic indicators for special education. Further, teachers must be cognizant that students who qualify for both special education and ESL services, as twice-exceptional students, are entitled to both streams of service. In that case, reciprocal mentoring (Jones-Vo et al., 2007) can be a useful strategy for bringing the expertise of both fields to bear for the benefit of students.

> **Hiroshi** is a second-generation language learner born in the United States to parents originally from Japan. They immigrated to take research positions with American companies. He spent his early years benefiting from his parents' bilingualism. They speak and read both Japanese and English to him and encourage his growing bilingualism. Hiroshi sometimes struggles with pronunciation, but his enthusiasm for speaking is not dampened. **L=proficient, S=5, R=4, W=4**

Hiroshi appears like many of his native English-speaking classmates in terms of language development, but could nevertheless benefit from sustained, targeted instruction and assessment. Some native speakers of English could also benefit from targeted instruction across the domains of language as a means to enhanced English proficiency as they likely would not score proficient on the annual large-scale English language proficiency test. In particular, comparisons have been made between the linguistic challenges of ELLs compared with native speakers of English from low socioeconomic status. The need for both groups of students to develop vocabulary and learn academic language is paramount; using the chart and this book to focus instruction on the development of a specific language domain for any student would be useful for increasing his or her English language proficiency. Finally, even though, as a second-generation ELL, Hiroshi seems proficient in many ways, it is premature to abandon instruction to scaffold his weaker areas until he reaches full proficiency in all four domains of language.

> **Minji** has been living with her mother and her aunt, a graduate student, in a small apartment for two years. Korean is spoken exclusively in the home because her mother has not been able to study English. As a result, Minji's English language development depends mostly on her school exposure and experiences. However, her spoken and written Korean language is excellent, since her mother and her aunt work with her to maintain their language and culture. L=4, S=3, R=3, W=2

Minji's family models the importance of taking advantage of educational opportunities for her, even to the extent of leaving her father behind in Korea to achieve long-term goals for the betterment of the family. Minji's scores reflect strong listening skills, yet girls in her culture are often expected to be soft-spoken. This cultural norm could explain Minji's lower speaking score, as she tends not to initiate interactions and is a quiet student in class. The fact that her Korean writing is developed and maintained is a strong support for her continuing English literacy development.

> **Myriam** was adopted through a church organization one year ago. An under resourced student who was living on the streets of Haiti at one time, Myriam was suffering from malnutrition and attachment issues. She was also pre-literate in her native language of Haitian Creole. One year later, Myriam is learning about her American culture and adjusting to her new family and school (after some initial significant behavior issues). She has gained two years growth in reading in one year, thanks to intensive instruction by a volunteer retired reading teacher. L=3, S=3, R=3, W=2

Thank goodness for school volunteers! Teachers are reminded that the potential involvement provided by civic groups, church organizations, businesses, and the like offers a vast network of possibilities in terms of support for educational programs. In this case, a retired reading teacher intervened to make all the difference for a culturally and linguistically diverse student by regularly providing targeted literacy instruction for this struggling learner. Further, by understanding that Myriam's behavior at school was a result of her childhood experience of living without supervision, and after trying various interventions to ascertain that her learning was, in fact, progressing, teachers were better able to sort out the fact that Myriam was not a candidate for special education. Rather, Myriam is simply an ELL with limited formal schooling. This background calls for powerful instruction with emphasis on building her literacy skills so that she will be positioned for and have a chance at achieving school success.

> **Oudry** is a child from the Democratic Republic of Congo who has recently arrived in the United States with his mother after the crisis in which millions lost their lives. Prior to arriving in his 3rd grade classroom, he lived in an overcrowded refugee camp without adequate food, water, shelter, or clothing. He was not afforded any schooling opportunities in the refugee camp and is not literate in his tribal native language. On the playground, Oudry's behavior has become violent, causing teachers, on one occasion, to call the police. After it was explained to the mother (in English, since there are no interpreters in the school district) that the student should not come to school the following day, the student, nevertheless, appeared. **L=1, S=1, R=1, W=1**

Due to the fact that Oudry is the first student representing the Democratic Republic of Congo in this district, the teachers should proactively assume the role of cultural brokers by researching and informing others about the cultural and linguistic factors related to the new student and his family. This goal can be accomplished by collaborating with community organizations and agencies to gain insights and then sharing this information by means of electronic messages, staff in-service meetings, or informal consulting. In this way, the district can be informed of the background information related to newcomers: their culture, religion, name pronunciation, and other relevant characteristics.

In this case, knowing that the student is pre-literate in his first language, has experienced untold trauma, and has had to struggle for his very existence, teachers could have anticipated that he might exhibit behavior discrepant from his peers. Further, such behavior could very well be aggressive or offensive. Expecting such a student to follow traditional U.S. school guidelines from his first day of enrollment is unrealistic because such students will likely have no schema to apply to their new school setting. Teachers should realize that some survival behaviors that might be considered to be aggressive in U.S. schools are what enabled this student to prevail when others died. Learning new behaviors and appropriate socialization will assume a high priority for such students.

Teacher Questions, Concerns, and Responses

These students' 3rd grade teacher has a number of questions regarding the students themselves and how to best address their linguistic and academic needs.

Since Hanna and Myriam are living in English-speaking homes, will they need any ESL services? Although the benefit of an English-speaking home environment is certainly significant, these students are still eligible for English language development programming, based on their English language proficiency scores. They should be given the same services as ELLs at the same proficiency levels who come from homes where English is not spoken. It can be anticipated, however, that the language development of Hanna and Myriam will likely progress more quickly than that of students who do not use English at home.

Why isn't Hiroshi already fluent in English since his parents are? Why do they insist on using Japanese at home? (Likewise, in the case of Minji, since her aunt speaks English, why aren't they using English at home?) The families of Hiroshi and Minji are to be commended for facilitating their students' L1 abilities by using the first language in the home. Recall that we, as educators, want to support this decision and right for two important reasons: first, the skills learned in the first language transfer to the second language, and second, because the first language and culture of any student is and should be an important part of her or his identity development. Students whose parents are bilingual can benefit from their parents' abilities to assist them with assignments and clarify the meaning of various English terms and expressions, as well as engage their students in practicing and manipulating English orally. As a result, these students may acquire English a bit more quickly than students whose parents are not bilingual. However, this result does not always occur.

How can volunteers be used to assist Myriam in my classroom? Since the volunteer has been so successful in teaching Myriam to read, it is recommended that this work continue. After providing an early emphasis on the development of oral English language to ensure that the student can derive meaning from sentence-level text, the teacher can then provide high-quality, age-appropriate, lower-reading-level books that provide extensive visual support and are aligned with content curriculum for these sessions. This type of intentional alignment of supplementary materials will improve the connection between the tutoring and classroom activities, as well as ensure the student access to the curriculum. The tutoring sessions might also focus on writing development, since that is Myriam's lowest area of proficiency. Again, when this work addresses curricular content topics, all the better.

In the case of Oudry, how can parent communication be facilitated? Whose responsibility is it? Also, how can I get him to behave in the classroom? This challenge is a difficult conundrum, given that no interpreters for Oudry's language are available in the school district. However, it is the school district's responsibility to communicate with parents in a language that they can understand. It is recommended that teachers seek the assistance of educational agencies in their state or region in order to facilitate this process. Another option would be to connect with community organizations and members in order to find someone who can speak this family's language. A third potential source of assistance might be university students who could be fluent in the language. It is important to build an ongoing relationship between school and home to include parent-teacher conferences, parent updates on student progress by phone (these calls should focus on the positive whenever possible), invitations and reminders to parents to attend school events such as student concerts, Family Math Night, and so on.

Differentiating an Elementary Lesson

A unit ripe with opportunities for content and language development at the elementary level focuses on the topic of the rain forest. By first determining what language proficiency levels are represented in the classroom, teachers can design assignments/assessments according to students' language proficiency levels using the Differentiated Assignment/ Assessment Template. Based on this completed template that details needed student scaffolding and supports at various levels, teachers can then incorporate appropriate strategies. These strategies might include building appropriate background, pre-teaching vocabulary, gathering realia and pictorially supported texts, creating graphic organizers, and so on. Using a variety of interactive strategies, teachers can embed opportunities for the manipulation of language across domains according to student needs. Ultimately, using the leveled recommendations on the chart, teachers can differentiate both instruction and assessment to ensure student engagement and facilitate successful learning.

Table 8.1 illustrates how one lesson assignment on the topic of the rain forest might be differentiated. In this case, students are to write about features of the rain forest before and after deforestation. After the assignment was devised for native English-speaking students, the student descriptors and the teaching and assessment strategies on the chart were consulted in development of the differentiated assignment, first for Level 5, then for Level 4, working back to Level 1. It should be noted that this same assignment could be differentiated in other ways, according to instructional needs; there is not one single "correct" differentiation of an assignment. The key to successful differentiation is to align expectations with the descriptors and strategies provided on the chart.

The template is filled out with general guidance for students at each of the proficiency levels. Given that the students in this hypothetical 3rd grade class (as in many real classrooms) exhibit different levels of proficiency in different language domains, teachers may pull strategies from more than one column for a given student. This is an opportunity for educators to engage in reciprocal mentoring by sharing and combining their individual areas of expertise for the benefit of their students. The most critical consideration for the actual writing assignment, though, is to match the expectations to each student's level of writing proficiency, as indicated by test data. Teachers are urged to push students to higher levels of performance, particularly given that each of the proficiency levels represents a range of abilities, but the suggested language-based expectations listed in the template are in concert with the student descriptors for writing on the chart.

Of course, language is not the only topic that informs teachers of ELLs about appropriate instruction and assessment of students. Information from students' entire background profiles should be considered when designing instruction and assessment. With that consideration in mind, we offer some additional guidance regarding the individual ELLs who are a part of this fictitious elementary classroom:

Table 8.1 An example of a Differentiated Assignment/Assessment Template for elementary students: The assignment is to compare and contrast features of the rain forest before and after deforestation (in writing)

Level 1	Level 2	Level 3	Level 4	Level 5	Fully English Proficient
Language-Based Expectations:	*Language-Based Expectations:*	*Language-Based Expectations:*	*Language-Based Expectations:*	*Language-Based Expectations:*	*Language-Based Expectations:*
Copy three words or phrases describing	Write three simple sentences using occasional content/academic vocabulary describing	Write three short paragraphs using some content/academic vocabulary and simple/complex sentence structures describing	Write a three-paragraph essay using some content/academic vocabulary and complex sentence structures that describe	Write a three-paragraph essay demonstrating a variety of content/academic vocabulary and complex sentence structures that describe	Write a three-paragraph essay using grade-level vocabulary and sentence structures that describe

Standards-Based Content or Topic (from the curriculum):

features of the rain forest before and after deforestation

Copyright © 2010. Caslon, Inc. All rights reserved. The first purchaser may photocopy this page for classroom and personal use.

Scaffolding and Support:	Scaffolding and Support:	Scaffolding and Support:	Scaffolding and Support:	Scaffolding and Support:	Scaffolding and Support:
using	using	using	using	using	using
• experiences gained in a field trip to a botanical center, • word and picture cards featuring pre-taught vocabulary (to be used when labeling a Venn diagram), • a chant to assist students in remembering key phrases and vocabulary • a Venn diagram, • a think-aloud demonstration of labeling, • pictorially supported rain forest texts, • realia related to rain forest products (e.g., fruit, medicinal plants, wood carvings), and • photographs of forestation and deforestation to guide writing.	• experiences gained in a field trip to a botanical center, • pretaught vocabulary, • a Venn diagram, • a chant to assist students in remembering key phrases and vocabulary • a think-aloud demonstration of paragraph writing, • academic sentence frames posted in the classroom, • pictorially supported rain forest texts, and • photographs of forestation and deforestation to guide writing.	• experiences gained in a field trip to a botanical center and • a Venn diagram to guide writing	• experiences gained in a field trip to a botanical center and • a Venn diagram to guide writing	• experiences gained in a field trip to a botanical center and • a Venn diagram to guide writing	• experiences gained in a field trip to a botanical center and • a Venn diagram to guide writing

265

Copyright © 2010. Caslon, Inc. All rights reserved. The first purchaser may photocopy this page for classroom and personal use.

Student	Guidance
Hanna	Ensure that she is positioned in the classroom so that she can hear. Make sure that every aspect of the field trip is wheelchair accessible. Share assignments with her parents and the tutor.
Hanna, Myriam, and Oudry	Bear in mind that this assignment will be more demanding for these students who cannot read or write in their first languages than for students who can transfer L1 literacy skills to English.
Hiroshi and Minji	These students' first languages are very distant from English and, as a result, English is more difficult for them to learn than it is for other students who have first languages less distant from English (refer to Chapter 1 for further information on language distance). Since both of these students are literate in their L1s, the teacher could ask them to brainstorm ideas in the first language before writing in English. Another option would be to have them write about the field trip in their first language. (Bear in mind that bilingual students should not be expected to do more work than their monolingual peers, but whenever the first language can be used to support the learning of English and whenever it can be celebrated and encouraged, it should be.) These students come from more collectivistic cultures, so they may feel more comfortable with a collaborative approach to the assignment.
Oudry	Since this student is completely new to formalized schooling, teaching may need to initially focus on "school survival skills" (e.g., how to hold a pencil, how to negotiate the lunch line). A paraeducator or trained volunteer could help with this. His refugee experiences have undoubtedly impacted him; allowances need to be made while he adjusts to his new homeland.

A Middle School Example

Similar to the elementary level, when explicitly considering lesson design to meet the needs of a variety of ELLs functioning at various proficiency levels across all four domains in the classroom, teachers are reminded to integrate meaningful instruction, interactive activities, and appropriate assessment strategies, based on students' language proficiency levels; content knowledge, skills, and abilities; and, importantly, individual background profiles.

Middle School Student Scenarios

Our middle school class includes the following 7th grade students:

> **Martha** arrived in the United States three years ago as a refugee from Sudan through the United Nations High Commissioner for Refugees (UNHCR). A speaker of Dinka and English, Martha is often called upon to translate for her grandmother. Martha never attended school in Sudan and is not literate in her native language. After fleeing the war to Kenya, she and many others lived in a crowded refugee camp. Martha now lives with her grandmother, a respected elder in the African community. She is quickly becoming westernized by pop culture, taste in fast food, and the influence of her peers. Martha is trying out her new independence and exhibits behaviors in school that cause her teachers to think she might be in need of special education services. **L=4, S=4, R=3, W=2**

Martha's teachers are likely to be fooled into thinking that she is fully English proficient and that any lack of academic success can be attributed to laziness. In fact, while Martha scores well in both listening and speaking as a result of her social language ability, the development of her academic language and her literacy skills depends upon insightful and targeted instruction at school to scaffold her toward proficiency. Clearly, Martha will not receive supplementary instruction at home, since only Dinka is spoken there. As for her experimental behavior, teachers, counselors, and others can provide opportunities to talk about typical teen issues in safe settings (e.g., a girls' discussion group). It is not unusual for ELLs to "try on" the behaviors, attitudes, language, and styles of others. In so doing, they may exhibit behaviors that are not considered to be typical of their heritage cultures.

> **Irina** is a recent adoptee through a program that pairs Russian children with potential families during a summer exchange program. Irina is fluent and literate in Russian and now lives with an American family that includes three other siblings. She reads well in Russian and is rapidly expanding her verbal communication skills in English. **L=3, S=3, R=2, W=1**

On grade level at her Russian school, Irina is poised for success in acquiring English relatively quickly and transferring her knowledge of content and concepts to English readily. In addition, Irina will benefit greatly from interactions with her three English-speaking siblings, which will hasten her oral proficiency. Irina's low writing proficiency is not surprising, given that she initially learned to write in another alphabet and that she has been enrolled in American schools for only a short time.

Regardless of the current status of language speakers in the home, internationally adopted students should always be considered for potential participation in English language development programming, based on what their first language actually is. The fact that the student's new home is exclusively English speaking does not negate the fact that the first language heard by the student, which can have long-term impact on language learning, was not English. As a result, it is important for teachers to know not only what language is currently spoken in the home, but also what language was first heard and used by the student.

> **Jesús's** Mexican family owns a successful local restaurant that employs extended family members. Though his sister came to the United States with her father five years ago, Jesús and his mother arrived in the United States last year when, after interrupted schooling, he started to attend middle school. **L=3, S=2, R=2, W=2**

Because Jesús had stopped attending school in his rural Mexican hometown, he arrived at his U.S. middle school with unique learning needs. The interruption in his schooling resulted in gaps in content, literacy skills, and academic language development. Therefore, Jesús is not prepared to fully engage with the middle school curriculum. Because of his ongoing lack of academic success, he has struggled to get motivated to participate in school and seems to put a lot of energy into finding ways to avoid engaging in activities and assignments. At the same time, unsavory influences provide temptations for Jesús.

Knowing that Jesús needs to experience success in school in order to become motivated to participate, his teachers must work to facilitate this process in a variety of possible ways: implementing instructional and assessment strategies appropriate to his language proficiency levels across domains (based on the chart), utilizing an engaging reading program, providing a trained volunteer or paraeducator (under the direction of a teacher) dedicated to literacy instruction, embedding reading and writing topics that include personal interests, incorporating service learning at venues relevant to the student, including opportunities for student choice, and partnering the student with a mentor.

> **Claudia** is a migrant student from California. Her family moves frequently, always starting the school year in the same community, but moving after only two months. Claudia is a good student who enjoys school. Her parents are not very literate in Spanish, their first language, and rely on Claudia for translation, after-school care of younger siblings, and household responsibilities. **L=4, S=4, R=3, W=3**

Since Claudia and her family return annually to this community, along with other migrant families, community organizers now anticipate their arrival by hosting a welcome picnic in the city park, collecting furniture and clothing, donating food pantry items, and encouraging community residents to rent housing to the migrant families. Claudia's teachers are urged to welcome her return enthusiastically and assure her that they will help her to build critical skills by working hard together.

> **Karol's** entire family immigrated to the United States two years ago to reunite with his grandmother. On grade level in Poland, Karol exhibits signs of giftedness and has learned English extremely quickly. Karol has quickly adopted American culture, styles, and music. Karol's father is a long-distance truck driver and is often gone for extended periods; Karol has been testing his mother's patience during his father's absences by associating with a group of students who negatively influence his behavior. **L=proficient, S=proficient, R=proficient, W=5**

Academically, Karol is positioned to perform very well. This school district has developed assessments and checklists that identify ELLs for participation in gifted and talented (GT) programming without requiring standardized test scores that tend to preclude ELL participation. As a result, Karol has already been participating in the GT program for a year. Karol scores proficient in three language domains; his only area of "weakness" is writing, where he scores a 5. It is not unusual for ELLs to develop writing proficiency last. His score may be similar to a native-English-speaker's score on the English language proficiency test; some districts exercising local control might elect to stop providing a student with Karol's language proficiency profile with English language development services.

Karol, like all ELLs, is a student who will benefit from explicit information and counseling about long-range planning, college options, goal-setting, financial aid, and so on.

Teacher Questions, Concerns, and Responses

The 7th grade teacher who serves these students in her language arts/social studies class has several questions regarding how to best meet the needs of these diverse learners.

Is it okay for me, as the teacher, to be a cultural informant in order to clarify what may be helpful for school success? Definitely! Sometimes ELLs display behavior that may not be in their best interest. The reason for this behavior could be that they are emulating other students, that they are unaware of cultural norms followed in the school, or for other reasons. It is certainly appropriate for *any* teacher to provide guidance to ELLs regarding what constitutes appropriate behavior in the school setting.

Should Irina be exempted from writing activities since she's at Level 1? No. She will likely not be able to move to Level 2 or higher in writing if she is not engaged in writing activities that are matched to her current level of proficiency and that scaffold her toward the next higher level. Though it may take a bit of "thinking outside the box" in order to differentiate writing assignments for her, such scaffolding is a must. The completed templates at the end of this section offer guidance in this regard.

Since Jesús has gaps in his educational background, why is he placed in 7th grade? As stated in Chapter 1, it is important to place students in a grade that is within two years of their age-appropriate grade. Even if Jesús were to be placed in 5th grade, he might still have gaps, particularly (and obviously) in the area of American history. Further, putting him in a grade below his same-age peers might alienate him at an age when peer interaction is a priority. Teachers must address educational gaps possessed by ELLs in the same way that they would address content gaps for students who grew up speaking English: through differentiated instruction. It may be that a paraeducator or trained volunteer could assist in this endeavor for Jesús.

Why do migrant workers, such as Claudia's family, come to our community for such a short period of time and then leave? Since I can't accomplish much with her in the short period of time that she's here, why invest my time and energy into catching her up? (I have so many other students that need help and will be here all year.) Claudia needs an advocate: a teacher who will help her to be successful so she can maintain her interest in and enjoyment of school. She, like any other student, deserves benefit from high-quality instruction and teacher concern. For many ELLs, one special teacher who recognizes their value that can make all the difference. Every teacher can be that encouraging and welcoming teacher who helps students to value themselves, set goals, and reach their full potential. Again, a paraeducator or trained volunteer (possibly a classroom peer or a student from the high school) whom the teacher takes the time to find may be just the key to making school success possible for the student. Another potential resource would be college education majors who might need practicum hours or who want to gain experience to add to their résumés (if the school is near a college).

On a practical note, school districts will receive federal funds for each ELL in their district at a fall cutoff date, the following school year, whether the student remains a full school year or not. Such funding helps districts to provide services and materials for families that do seasonal work in American companies. In addition, migrant funds and programs should be explored by districts that have migrant students.

Karol's language skills are better than some native speakers—what about that? Why should he receive any additional support in writing when many students who grew up speaking English don't write as well as he does? This is an excellent question. However, if Karol is still entitled to English language development services, he should receive them. Further, if his level of language proficiency indicates that accommodations are necessary, they should be provided. The tests used to determine English language proficiency and the criteria that determine when ELLs are no longer provided with English language development services may need to be revisited if a large number of currently entitled ELLs are outperforming their native English-speaking peers.

Differentiating a Middle School Assignment

The middle school assignment exemplified here asks students to create and present speeches on different cultures using multimedia software. Drawing upon the real and motivating aspect of this expectation allows students to learn more about their own backgrounds and to share with peers. This assignment provides teachers many opportunities for facilitating language development in listening, speaking, reading, and writing. Thus this language-rich assignment offers an ideal format for a range of imaginative differentiation possibilities.

In terms of scaffolding to support students, teachers can choose from the variety of suggestions listed on the chart. Strategies such as making connections to previous experiences and learning, providing new experiences, creating a word or language wall supported by pictures, and posting academic sentence and discourse frames are just a few of the possibilities. As always, teachers must intentionally embed a multiplicity of interactive opportunities for students to manipulate and practice language.

Table 8.2 is a completed Differentiated Assignment/Assessment Template for this speech-making assignment. Readers are reminded that individual assignments can be differentiated in a myriad of ways; this is

Table 8.2 An example of a Differentiated Assignment/Assessment Template for middle school students: The assignment is to create and present a speech about an assigned country using multimedia technology

Level 1	Level 2	Level 3	Level 4	Level 5	Fully English Proficient
Language-Based Expectations:	*Language-Based Expectations:*	*Language-Based Expectations:*	*Language-Based Expectations:*	*Language-Based Expectations:*	*Language-Based Expectations:*
Create a 3–4-slide presentation using provided content/academic words and phrases	Create and present a 5–6-slide speech using occasional content/academic vocabulary and simple sentences	Create and present a 6–8-slide speech using some content/academic vocabulary and simple/complex sentence structures	Create and present a 10-slide speech using some content/academic vocabulary and complex sentence structures	Create and present a 10-slide speech using a variety of content/academic vocabulary and complex sentence structures	Create and present a 10-slide speech using grade-level vocabulary and sentence structures

Standards-Based Content or Topic (from the curriculum):

about an assigned country

Level 1	Level 2	Level 3	Level 4	Level 5	Fully English Proficient
Scaffolding and Support:	*Scaffolding and Support:*	*Scaffolding and Support:*	*Scaffolding and Support:*	*Scaffolding and Support:*	*Scaffolding and Support:*
using	using	using	using	using	using
• 3–4 sample PowerPoint slides on America (picture or clip art plus key word[s]),	• An outline of required speech components,	• An outline of required speech components,	• An outline of required speech components,	• An outline of required speech components,	• An outline of required content components,
• videos describing various countries,	• videos describing various countries,	• videos describing various countries,	• videos describing various countries,	• videos describing various countries,	• videos describing various countries,
• a think-aloud review of making a PowerPoint presentation,	• a think-aloud review of making a PowerPoint presentation,	• a think-aloud review of making a PowerPoint presentation,	• a think-aloud review of making a PowerPoint presentation,	• a think-aloud review of making a PowerPoint presentation,	• a think-aloud review of making a PowerPoint presentation,

Copyright © 2010. Caslon, Inc. All rights reserved. The first purchaser may photocopy this page for classroom and personal use.

• teacher-selected Web sites for clip art and pictures, • PowerPoint technology, • assistance from a "prepared and skilled" buddy, • assistance from the teacher or a bilingual paraeducator, • the student's own culture as a topic, • terminology in English and the student's first language • word and picture cards featuring pretaught vocabulary, • a think-aloud demonstration of making a PowerPoint presentation, • pictorially supported texts, • cultural artifacts, • photographs of native country, and • presentation made to buddy, teacher, or small group (ESL class), if possible	• teacher-selected Web sites for clip art and pictures, • PowerPoint technology, • assistance from a "prepared and skilled" buddy (as needed), • assistance from the teacher and/or a bilingual paraeducator, • the student's own culture as a topic, • academic sentence frames posted • word and picture cards featuring pretaught vocabulary, • pictorially supported texts, • cultural artifacts, • photographs of native country, and • presentation made to buddy, teacher, or small group (ESL class), if possible	• teacher-selected Web sites, • PowerPoint technology, • the student's own culture as a topic, • academic sentence frames posted, • cultural artifacts, and • photographs of native country	• teacher-selected Web sites, • PowerPoint technology, and • academic sentence frames posted, as needed	• teacher-selected Web sites, and • PowerPoint technology	• teacher-selected Web sites, and • PowerPoint technology

Copyright © 2010. Caslon, Inc. All rights reserved. The first purchaser may photocopy this page for classroom and personal use.

simply one example with many, many ideas for support and scaffolding (designed to alert readers to the many options for this particular assignment). Again, the key to successful differentiation is the alignment of expectations with the descriptors and strategies provided on the chart.

This template includes ideas aligned with the chart in terms of student abilities and appropriate scaffolding and support at each level of proficiency. Students may be at different levels in writing and speaking, the two skills required to complete the speech. Therefore, guidance for different proficiency levels may be drawn upon to support a single student. Further, teachers are reminded to push students within a given level of proficiency toward the next level. While the expectations outlined in the table are appropriate for each level of proficiency (according to the student descriptors found in the chart), educators must remember that these levels are broad and that a student whose test data list one given level may be on the cusp of the next level and should be pushed toward that level. Alternately, a given student may be at the lower end of the continuum for his or her particular proficiency level and may struggle to meet the assignment demands for that level. The needed "micro-differentiation" for these sorts of students is, of course, at the discretion of the teacher and is part of the art of teaching. Sorting out when and how to perform this micro-differentiation can be achieved through reciprocal mentoring in which content and language teachers and paraeducators collaborate to share their expertise and insights.

In addition to the linguistic abilities of one's students, other student factors will inform the teaching and learning process of individual students. Guidance for the particular ELLs in this hypothetical class is offered next.

Student	Guidance
Martha	This student's lack of literacy in her L1 may likely mean that it takes her longer to write in English than Level 2 writers who are literate in their first languages. This fact must be borne in mind as students are given time to work.
	In addition, this student's desire to be like "American" students can be used to help with her motivation to do the assignment.
Irina	Irina can be supported by her family in the labor-intensive process of writing the outline for the speech, if need be. However, this possibility does not excuse the teacher from providing needed scaffolding during in-class work times. A paraeducator or trained volunteer could be an excellent source of support for Irina.

Irina, Jesús, and Karol	It may be that this would be an appropriate time to allow Irina, Jesús, and Karol to do the assignment in their first languages. This is not recommended as a daily course of action, since improved English is the goal, but allowing students to use their first languages in the classroom *is* encouraged; it would be a pity if any of these students were to lose her or his first language (a particular concern with Irina, since she was adopted by an English-speaking family). All three of the students could give the speech in their first languages, allowing the rest of the class to understand what it feels like to sit in a classroom where the language is unfamiliar. Further, their first languages and cultural insights would be honored if they were to present about their countries of origin in their first languages. This opportunity could also serve as a motivating factor for Jesús, who has struggled as a result of gaps in his schooling.
Claudia	Perhaps Claudia could present on the culture of the world of migrant farm workers. Of course, this culture would represent a mix of the cultures of the countries of birth represented within the migrant communities and the cultures of their employers. This could be a particularly interesting speech, assisting non-migrant students to understand the realities of migrant workers and assisting Claudia in understanding herself a bit better.

A High School Example

Similar to both the elementary level and middle school levels, when explicitly considering lesson design to meet the needs of a variety of ELLs functioning at various proficiency levels across all four domains in the classroom, teachers are reminded to integrate meaningful instruction, student interaction, and appropriate assessment strategies based on students' content knowledge, skills, and abilities; language proficiency levels; and, importantly, individual background profiles.

High School Student Scenarios

Our example sophomore Cultural Issues class includes the following students:

> **Mercy** is a Liberian student who arrived with her cousin five years ago. She witnessed atrocities against her family and experienced violence herself. She has been plagued by mental health issues, including post-traumatic stress disorder.

> Though her first language is English, the variety of language and the cultural differences combine to qualify her for ESL program services. As a student, Mercy has difficulty with long-term projects and she tends to isolate herself. **L=5, S=proficient, R=3, W=3**

Mercy needs a very caring approach because of her background. Teachers who work with refugee students must become aware of the psychological effects of violence, torture, and rape on victims. They also need to be familiar with community resources available to assist students in dealing with the aftermath of trauma. However, cultural sensitivity must be exercised when dealing with such issues.

Mercy's teachers should assign "buddies" to ensure that she is not isolated in the classroom or during lunch. Buddies, paraeducators, or trained volunteers might also work with her on breaking down long-term projects in order to make them more doable. While Mercy is proficient in speaking, she will also benefit from targeted instruction and assessment, particularly in the areas of reading and writing.

As for her language proficiency, her high level of speaking ability is not entirely surprising, given that a variety of English is her first language. Special focus must be given to developing her academic English skills, particularly in reading and writing.

> **Kumar** is a 15-year-old student from Nepal. He suffered from polio as a child and, as a result, depends on a crutch for his mobility. Because of this disability, he was never allowed to attend school (though his older brother was). His immature behavior since arriving only a short time ago has shocked teachers who are not sure how to proceed. **L=1, S=1, R=1, W=1**

In some countries, children with disabilities are not afforded educational access, but, rather, may be kept at home. This lack of formal schooling may result from a variety of factors, depending upon the culture. These reasons may include lack of the availability of appropriate services and resources to serve potential special education students or cultural attitudes about disabilities that cause family embarrassment. Regardless of the reason for limited formal schooling, such children must be afforded the same access to educational opportunities as their native English-speaking peers. It is critical to enact immediate meaningful early literacy instruction, despite the fact that this student is older than students who usually receive literacy instruction at an introductory level. Enrolling pre-literate students, particularly in advanced grades, requires school districts to energetically embrace their responsibility to afford equal access to the curriculum to all students and to ensure that appropriate literacy development instruction is available to ELLs with limited or underdeveloped literacy skills. This undeniable mandate must be seized and acted upon in an intentionally goal-oriented long-range plan; such students depend on it for their survival and future quality of life.

> **Manivone** is the 16-year-old daughter of a Laotian woman and her Vietnamese-American stepfather. Vietnamese is spoken in the home. Before marrying her husband last year when he made a return visit to Vietnam, Manivone's mother was living in a small Vietnamese village where she worked farming rice. Manivone's mother only completed 3rd grade and could not afford to send her to school in Vietnam. However, she has taken steps to ensure her daughter receives educational opportunities since they arrived a year ago as a new family of three. **L=3, S=2, R=1, W=1**

Never is the need for explicit and rich literacy instruction more imperative or crucial than it is now, at the high school level, for a student with limited literacy skills in the first language such as Manivone. As is the case with Kumar, Manivone's teachers must devise a comprehensive program that will support her in acquiring literacy in English that is both at grade level and age appropriate. If such instruction does not happen, Manivone is likely to add to the alarming dropout statistics related to female ELLs in the United States.

Manivone would likely benefit from a variety of social supports, such as assigned "buddies," a peer tutor, a counselor who meets with her, a mentor, or a bilingual advocate.

> **Yasir** is a recent refugee student from Afghanistan. He arrived with his widowed mother and four siblings to enroll in school three months ago. Yasir's father was a high-ranking dignitary before his untimely death in Afghanistan. Through an interpreter, Yasir's mother shares that he is "different" from her other children and that she did not send him to school with his siblings. He is unable to remember facts or concentrate on tasks for an extended period of time. **L=1, S=1, R=1, W=1**

One of the most important pieces of data regarding Yasir is the input from his mother that he is "different." Obviously an ELL, Yasir must be evaluated carefully in order to determine the extent of his seeming disabilities. This process does not need to be postponed until he is proficient in English. Rather, it should be initiated immediately. Excellent guidance for this process is provided in *Special Education Considerations for English Language Learners* (Hamayan et al., 2007).

In the meantime, teachers must enlist the assistance of paraeducators, trained volunteers and peer mentors, or others who can help provide this student with appropriate instruction. Note that these individuals may require very explicit guidance from ESL and special education teachers in how to work with Yasir.

> **Victor** came to the United States from El Salvador three years ago. After working odd jobs for six months, he was informed that he could attend school. He immediately enrolled in high school and applied himself with uncommon energy while continuing to work fulltime. Victor is on track to graduate in the top 3% of his class. L=proficient, S=proficient, R=5, W=5

Victor is a highly motivated and self-directed student who regards his access to education as a privilege. Since his parents still live in rural El Salvador, Victor is driven by the desire to make his parents proud of him and to help support his family. In class, Victor often appears to be dozing, but he works the night shift and comes to school with only a few hours of sleep. He would benefit from a discreet application for free or reduced-cost breakfast and lunch and information about free health clinics and other services in the community. Since Victor is proficient in listening and speaking, his language-based instructional and assessment needs focus on reading and writing. Although he is a senior, he is only now taking this sophomore-level Cultural Issues class because of scheduling issues that relate, in part, to his arrival at this high school only three years ago. In a partnership with a local medical school, medical student tutors have volunteered to spend time mentoring high school ELLs in chemistry and math. This program has benefitted Victor greatly, both academically and socially.

Teacher Questions, Concerns, and Responses

The Cultural Issues teacher has a number of questions regarding appropriate service for these unique students.

If Mercy's first language is English, why does she qualify for ESL services? Although English is Mercy's first language, the variety of English that she learned in Liberia is a type of dialect that resulted in English language proficiency test scores that qualified her for English language development services. Further, Mercy's unfamiliarity with U.S. schools and U.S. culture position her as a student in need of guidance regarding how to negotiate the intricacies of U.S. academic settings, which English language development programs optimally address. As such, this type of support is entirely appropriate for Mercy.

Why shouldn't Kumar and Yasir both be immediately put in a special education classroom?   Kumar has never experienced formal schooling. This fact alone is not indicative of cognitive impairment; Kumar should not be assumed to have a cognitive disability. However, given the information provided by Yasir's mother, it seems that he may, in fact, possess a cognitive disability. Evaluation may be appropriate for Yasir, though a very thoughtful approach will be required, given that he does not speak English yet. Again, *Special Education Considerations for English Language Learners* (Hamayan et al., 2007) is recommended for its clear guidance.

Why is Manivone placed in a high school Cultural Issues class, given her lack of school experience and literacy skills?   When ELLs enroll in high school, they cannot typically spend the entire day in a program designed to teach them English. As a result, these students must enter content classes even at beginning levels of English proficiency. (In fact, this is the case with students in elementary and middle school, as well.) Given that ELLs represent many cultures from around the globe, a cultural issues class is a good starting point for their matriculation. Teachers at the high school level who have ELLs in their classrooms can use the chart and the guidance in this book to differentiate their expectations for ELLs at all levels of proficiency, thereby sheltering their instruction and teaching English language through their content. Further, the opportunities for interaction with classmates will support oral language development.

Why is Victor in ESL, given that he is performing above many of his native English-speaking peers?   This issue was also raised with Karol. According to the school, district, and state guidelines, Victor is apparently still entitled to participate in English language development programming. However, the criteria for entitlement may need to be revisited if Victor's involvement in this programming seems unnecessary.

What are Victor's educational options after high school? Should I be helping him fill out college applications?   Victor is an undocumented student, and, as such, he will not be eligible for any federal financial aid.[2] His unauthorized status basically precludes his attending college unless he can pay for it himself. Even if he can somehow afford to pay for college, obtaining an appropriate job following graduation could be problematic

---

[2] While it is inappropriate to inquire about immigration or citizenship status, teachers may learn about student situations and be asked for advice. Teachers should be prepared to refer students to the appropriate resources.

because of documentation requirements for employment. Teachers are reminded that such impossible outcomes begin to dawn on some ELLs at early ages, particularly at the middle and high school levels, and can have a negative impact on motivation for academic achievement or staying enrolled in school.

Differentiating a High School Lesson

Nothing facilitates speedier language acquisition than engaging students in authentic, real-life applications that contribute to enhanced student motivation. In keeping with this observation, the differentiated high school lesson plan focuses on developing panels of students to present information on relevant cultural issues to local civic groups, the school board, and other schools as part of a school wide service learning initiative. The ELLs in this class will focus their efforts on their own experiences as students in a new country, highlighting their academic accomplishments and extracurricular activities. The focus of the presentation was developed through a collaboration of the Cultural Issues class teacher and the ESL teacher as a way for high school ELLs to inform the school board of their progress and to show gratitude for the support that they have been given by the district, which has been working to improve services to diverse learners. Requiring preparation, organization, and practice, this assignment easily incorporates the development of all four domains of language. Further, the final product, the public presentation, incorporates authentic skills needed beyond school settings. This assignment, like the previous two examples at the elementary and middle school levels, serves double duty as an ideal assessment when accompanied by an accurate and well-thought-out scoring rubric.

The Differentiated Assignment/Assessment Template presented in Table 8.3 outlines expectations for this assignment tailored to all five levels of English language proficiency. Teachers are reminded that this is simply an example and are encouraged to differentiate in their own innovative ways, remembering that the key to successful differentiation is the alignment of expectations with the student descriptors and strategies provided on the chart.

Since the ELLs in this class represent different levels of language proficiency in different domains, teachers may need to think broadly when offering scaffolding and support. That is, a given student may have skills in one domain (e.g., speaking) that enable him or her to easily address the core assignment, but may not necessarily be able to take advantage of all of the scaffolding unless it is differentiated for a lower proficiency level in another domain (e.g., writing). Fortunately, the example template provides ideas regarding different levels of scaffolding that can be applied to any student. This assignment offers an example where reciprocal mentoring, in its various forms, would be very useful; content and language teachers and paraeducators could collaborate to ensure the successful completion of the assignment by all students.

In addition to issues of language, other relevant student factors must also be considered in supporting the students in successfully completing the differentiated assignment. Some ideas focusing on the individual students in this hypothetical high school class are offered here.

Student	Guidance
Mercy	Since Mercy struggles with long-term projects, this assignment will likely need to be broken down into parts for her. (This strategy would likely support all the students, but it is critical for her.)
	Mercy's tendency to isolate herself means that the teacher may need to continually encourage her to participate with other group members in preparing the panel presentation. Perhaps she could be encouraged to develop her part of the panel presentation in concert with Manivone, with the two of them sharing their stories as a team.
Kumar and Yasir	Since these two students are both new to school, extra guidance will likely need to be provided to them regarding how to work as part of the group on this academic task.
	These students likely come from more collectivistic cultural backgrounds and may feel very nervous about being singled out to introduce the group. Allowing them to work as a team may help ease this nervousness.
	Remembering all the information needed in order to make introductions may be a challenge, given that traditional notes would not work for either of these students. In addition to pictorial notes, teacher prompts during the presentation may be needed.
Manivone	This student may be very soft-spoken, in accordance with cultural expectations. Extra support and guidance will be needed in order to help her to feel comfortable in speaking to a large group with sufficient volume to be heard.
	Manivone's culture is also more collectivistic. For this reason, she may want to work together with Mercy to prepare and even to tell her story. (Perhaps they could share ideas in a "back-and-forth" team effort—e.g., each student explains when she arrived in the school district, then each student explains her relevant academic accomplishments, then each student speaks to the issue of extracurricular activities.)
Victor	With his linguistic strengths, Victor seems to be in the position to take on a leadership role in the panel presentation. His high level of motivation and academic accomplishment supports this view.
All Five Students	These students may need assistance in understanding appropriate attire for this event and in obtaining it.

Table 8.3 An example of a Differentiated Assignment/Assessment Template for high school students: The assignment is to highlight academic and extracurricular accomplishments in a short oral presentation to the school board

Level 1	Level 2	Level 3	Level 4	Level 5	Fully English Proficient
Language-Based Expectations:	*Language-Based Expectations:*	*Language-Based Expectations:*	*Language-Based Expectations:*	*Language-Based Expectations:*	*Language-Based Expectations:*
Introduce self and other presenters using appropriate conventions of public speaking, talking very briefly (e.g., eye contact, volume, content, expression, body language)	Develop and deliver a mini-presentation using occasional content/academic vocabulary and simple sentences and using appropriate conventions of public speaking (e.g., eye contact, volume, content, expression, body language)	Develop and deliver a brief oral presentation using some content/academic vocabulary and simple/complex sentence structures and using appropriate conventions of public speaking (e.g., eye contact, volume, content, expression, body language)	Develop and deliver a short oral presentation using some content/academic vocabulary and complex sentence structures and using appropriate conventions of public speaking (e.g., eye contact, volume, content, expression, body language)	Develop and deliver a short oral presentation using a variety of content/academic vocabulary and complex sentence structures and using appropriate conventions of public speaking (e.g., eye contact, volume, content, expression, body language)	Develop and deliver a short oral presentation using grade-level vocabulary and sentence structures and using appropriate conventions of public speaking (e.g., eye contact, volume, content, expression, body language)

Standards-Based Content or Topic (from the curriculum):

about academic and extracurricular accomplishments

Level 1	Level 2	Level 3	Level 4	Level 5	Fully English Proficient
Scaffolding and Support:	*Scaffolding and Support:*	*Scaffolding and Support:*	*Scaffolding and Support:*	*Scaffolding and Support:*	*Scaffolding and Support:*
using:	using:	using:	using:	using:	using:
• information gleaned from a visit to the location where school board meetings are held;	• information gleaned from a visit to the location where school board meetings are held;	• information gleaned from a visit to the location where school board meetings are held;	• information gleaned from a visit to the location where school board meetings are held;	• information gleaned from a visit to the location where school board meetings are held;	• information gleaned from a visit to the location where school board meetings are held;

Copyright © 2010. Caslon, Inc. All rights reserved. The first purchaser may photocopy this page for classroom and personal use.

• a Post-it note brainstorm strategy (students write ideas on Post-it notes); • a categorization activity wherein students organize the Post-it notes on a T-chart graphic organizer according to academic and extracurricular accomplishments; • the T-chart as a springboard in order to generate language to introduce the other students; • videos of school board meetings, diagrams, and pictures (to build background); • pretaught vocabulary; • pretaught and modeled conventions of public speaking; • provided language frames for introductions; • pictorial notes; • assistance of a paraeducator or trained volunteer; and • practice.	• a Post-it note brainstorm strategy (students write ideas on Post-it notes); • a categorization activity wherein students organize the Post-it notes on a T-chart graphic organizer according to academic and extracurricular accomplishments; • the T-chart as a springboard in order to generate sentences to describe their accomplishments; • videos of school board meetings, diagrams, and pictures (to build background); • pretaught vocabulary; • pretaught and modeled conventions of public speaking; • provided academic sentence frames; • notes; and • practice.	• a Post-it note brainstorm strategy (students write ideas on Post-it notes); • a categorization activity wherein students organize the Post-it notes on a T-chart graphic organizer according to academic and extracurricular accomplishments; • the T-chart as a springboard in order to generate sentences to describe their accomplishments; • videos of school board meetings, diagrams, and pictures (to build background); • pretaught vocabulary; • pretaught and modeled conventions of public speaking; • provided academic sentence frames; • notes; and • practice.	• a Post-it note brainstorm strategy (students write ideas on Post-it notes); • a categorization activity wherein students organize the Post-it notes on a T-chart graphic organizer according to academic and extracurricular accomplishments; • the T-chart as a springboard in order to generate sentences to describe their accomplishments; • videos of school board meetings, diagrams, and pictures (to build background), as needed; • pretaught and modeled conventions of public speaking, as needed; • provided academic sentence frames, as needed; • notes, if needed; and • practice.	• a Post-it note brainstorm strategy (students write ideas on Post-it notes); • a categorization activity wherein students organize the Post-it notes on a T-chart graphic organizer according to academic and extracurricular accomplishments; • the T-chart as a springboard in order to generate sentences to describe their accomplishments; • notes, if needed; and • practice.	• a Post-it note brainstorm strategy (students write ideas on Post-it notes); • a categorization activity wherein students organize the Post-it notes on a T-chart graphic organizer according to academic and extracurricular accomplishments; • the T-chart as a springboard in order to generate sentences to describe their accomplishments; • notes, if needed; and • practice.

283

Copyright © 2010. Caslon, Inc. All rights reserved. The first purchaser may photocopy this page for classroom and personal use.

Differentiated Scoring of Differentiated Assignments/Assessments

Of necessity and in fairness, the scoring of the preceding differentiated assignments/assessments must also take into consideration students' language proficiency levels. Based on test data in students' cumulative folders, teachers understand where language learners fall along the continuum of language proficiency. This knowledge allows educators to design appropriate assignments and assessments for individual students who are not yet proficient in English. As students strive to meet expectations set according to their levels of language proficiency, teachers must assign grades accordingly.

For example, if a Level 3 student has met all the expectations set forth by the teacher, the student should be graded bearing in mind those differentiated expectations. That is, students at each level of proficiency should be able to achieve success and corresponding good grades. Further, these students should be graded in terms of the extent to which they have met the expectations set by the teacher, rather than in comparison to a fully English proficient student. It should be possible for both students to receive top grades, though the ELL's report card may include a notation clarifying that data-driven accommodations were used in adapting curriculum.

Developing a differentiated scoring rubric, like developing differentiated assignments/assessments, involves the use of the *chart* in order to ensure that expectations are appropriate.

Developing a Differentiated Scoring Rubric

The process of creating a rubric that differentiates expectations according to students' language proficiency needs is similar to rubric creation for other contexts. The additional step is the adjustment of expectations for students at different levels of language proficiency.

Differentiated rubrics require specific details rather than global descriptions. Rather than using more general holistic rubrics, teachers must break down each level to discrete and specific benchmarks. In so doing, teachers and students have a clear understanding of the overall expectations and student progress toward success. The steps for developing this type of detailed (analytic) rubric that is differentiated for students at different English proficiency levels follow.

1. Determine what criteria will be graded (e.g., content, organization, or grammar and mechanics). It is recommended that three to five criteria be selected; choosing a greater number results in a cumbersome grading process. (If many criteria must be graded, perhaps some can be merged under umbrella terms such as "mechanics" rather than separate categories of capitalization, punctuation, and spelling.)

2. Determine what performance levels will be incorporated (e.g., below basic, basic, proficient, advanced). Note that three to six levels are recommended; when using more than six levels, differentiating between the performance levels can become difficult (e.g., "What's the difference between a 5 and a 6 in an 10-level scale?").

3. Set up a seven-column table (as in Table 8.4) with the English language proficiency levels listed across the top and the performance levels listed down the side.

4. Copy this table for each of the criteria that will be graded (e.g., content, organization, and grammar and mechanics). Label the tables accordingly (one for content, one for organization, etc.). Further, note that the criteria can be weighted differently. For example, content may be afforded twice the value of grammar in a science term paper. Make decisions about weighting according to the emphasis on each criterion in the classroom and in real life.

5. Using the chart, write appropriately differentiated descriptions of performance expectations in each cell. (Teachers may determine that some criteria will not be extensively differentiated across language proficiency levels if those criteria are not language-related—e.g., volume in an oral presentation.)

6. Employ parallel language and facets (aspects of a given criterion, such as sentence structure within grammar) across performance levels.

7. Use positive language to the extent possible.

8. Ensure that expectations in the cells do not overlap within the expectations for a given proficiency level.

Table 8.4 Rubric layout

	Level 1	Level 2	Level 3	Level 4	Level 5	Fully English Proficient
Advanced						
Proficient						
Basic						
Below basic						

Copyright © 2010. Caslon, Inc. All rights reserved. The first purchaser may photocopy this page for classroom and personal use.

Though this sounds like considerable effort, it is an essential aspect of the use of differentiated assignments/assessments. (Why differentiate expectations and then grade all assignments using the same set of expectations?) To minimize the demands on their time (and in order to assist students in internalizing requirements), we recommend that teachers create a few standard rubrics that are used consistently throughout the year (e.g., one for essay writing, one for presentations). In order to tailor such rubrics to specific assignments, teachers might add a criterion or two for scoring. In this way, teachers will be consistent in their expectations, and students will be able to internalize these expectations, rather than working throughout the year to meet the "moving target" of expectations that differ for each assignment. Further, teachers do not have to invest extensive time in creating scoring schemes for each assignment. This is a "win-win" solution to the grading conundrum.

As with the development and differentiation of assignments/assessments, there is not one "perfect" way to create a differentiated rubric. Teachers must rely on their own expertise to determine what criteria are included in the rubric. The key is to ensure that the language demands of the assignment/assessment are scored or graded in accordance with reasonable expectations for students at the various English proficiency levels.

Table 8.5 is an example of a differentiated rubric designed for scoring or grading content-based writing. It is not meant to be a perfect representation of how to grade ELLs across proficiency levels; rather, it is meant to offer food for thought and a starting place for teachers to develop their own differentiated rubrics. Readers will notice that some language-related criteria are either not graded at all for students at lower proficiency levels or are graded more "gently" (e.g., no Ds or Fs for students at Level 1, since their language development does not allow much production; there are data-based reasons for not requiring Level 1 or 2 students to produce grammatical work).

Conclusion

Teachers who incorporate differentiation according to student language proficiency levels support English language learners in essential ways. These teachers recognize that their ELLs bring rich resources to the classroom and that bilingualism, or multilingualism, is a cognitive

Table 8.5 Example of a differentiated writing rubric with three parts: content, organization, and grammar and mechanics

For Content:

	Level 1	Level 2	Level 3	Level 4	Level 5	Fully English Proficient
A	3–4 main ideas	4 main ideas	4 main ideas	4 main ideas	4 main ideas	4 main ideas
B	2	3	3	3	3	3
C	0–1	2	2	2	2	2
D		0–1	1	1	1	1
F			0	0	0	0

For Organization:

	Level 1	Level 2	Level 3	Level 4	Level 5	Fully English Proficient
A	Ideas in sequence	Ideas in sequence	Ideas in sequence with some connectors used	Logical organization with good use of basic connectors	Strong organization facilitated by use of a wide variety of connectors (a few minor errors may be present)	Exemplary organization facilitated by use of a wide variety of connectors
B	Ideas generally in sequence	Ideas generally in sequence	Some sequence and connector problems	Logical organization with some use of connectors	Logical organization with a number of connectors	Strong organization facilitated by a wide variety of connectors (a few minor errors may be present)

For Organization:

C	Out of sequence	Significant sequence and connector problems	Some breakdowns in organization and use of connectors	A few breakdowns in organization and use of connectors	Noticeable problems in organization and use of connectors
D	N/A	Serious problems	Significant breakdowns in organization and use of connectors	Noticeable breakdowns in organization and use of connectors	Serious problems in organization and use of connectors
F	N/A	N/A	Serious breakdowns in organization and use of connectors	Serious breakdowns in organization and use of connectors	Lack of organization

For Grammar and Mechanics:

	Level 1	Level 2	Level 3	Level 4	Level 5	Fully English Proficient
A	N/A	N/A	Well-formed simple sentences, some errors in more complex sentences, basic mechanics in place in simple sentences, errors only occasionally obstruct meaning	Well-formed simple sentences, complex sentences used with general accuracy, mechanics generally accurate, errors rarely obstruct meaning	Well-formed simple sentences, more complex sentences rarely include errors, accurate mechanics, errors do not obstruct meaning	Grade-level expectations in terms of sentence construction and grammar and mechanics

(continues)

The comparative nature of the performance descriptions within each column is intentional because it allows for variable performances (e.g., strong simple sentences but very weak mechanics *or* some errors in both areas) to be eligible for a given grade. This kind of "compensatory" approach may not be preferable to all educators; readers are reminded that this is merely an example of a differentiated scoring rubric.

Copyright © 2010. Caslon, Inc. All rights reserved. The first purchaser may photocopy this page for classroom and personal use.

Table 8.5 *Continued*

For Grammar and Mechanics: Continued

	Level 1	Level 2	Level 3	Level 4	Level 5	Fully English Proficient
B	N/A	N/A	A few problems with Level 3 sentence structure and mechanics	A few problems with Level 4 sentence structure and mechanics	A few problems with Level 5 sentence structure and mechanics	Grade-level expectations in terms of sentence construction and a few problems with grammar / mechanics **or** Simpler sentence construction than dictated by grade-level expectations and strong grammar and mechanics
C			Noticeable problems with Level 3 sentence structure and mechanics	Noticeable problems with Level 4 sentence structure and mechanics	Noticeable problems with Level 5 sentence structure and mechanics	Noticeable problems with sentence construction **or** with grammar/ mechanics **and** A few problems with the other area

Copyright © 2010. Caslon, Inc. All rights reserved. The first purchaser may photocopy this page for classroom and personal use.

D	N/A	N/A	N/A	Significant problems with Level 4 sentence structure and mechanics	Significant problems with Level 5 sentence structure and mechanics	Noticeable problems in sentence construction and with grammar and mechanics **or** Serious problems with either sentence construction or grammar and mechanics and a few problems with the other area
F	N/A	N/A	N/A	N/A	Serious problems with Level 5 sentence structure and mechanics	Serious problems with sentence construction **and** with grammar and mechanics

Copyright © 2010. Caslon, Inc. All rights reserved. The first purchaser may photocopy this page for classroom and personal use.

asset. When supported by appropriate instruction, students demonstrating ability in more than one language are positioned for academic and professional success. Teachers who collaborate and differentiate according to language proficiency levels clearly embrace their shared responsibility to provide academic parity through access to the curriculum for every student in the classroom. They recognize that language imposes an obstacle that can be surmounted. These teachers understand that learning language is an incremental process and that language proficiency levels will advance only with appropriate instruction. They take steps to remove barriers and to validate students for what they *do* know, building opportunities to allow all students to demonstrate their knowledge, skills, and abilities, even without language mastery. Similar to teaching a child to ride a bicycle using training wheels, these teachers provide supports and scaffolds for learning, gradually reducing them until the student achieves full proficiency in content and language. In the end, teachers are uniquely positioned to make a world of difference in the lives of English language learners. It is to that worthy goal that we dedicate our efforts.

Professional Development Activities

Activity 8.1   Applying the Differentiated Assignment/Assessment Template to Students Within the Book

Select a group of ELLs from scenarios in other chapters, changing their ages to those represented by students in your classroom. (Be sure to choose students that represent a range of proficiency levels and backgrounds, as applicable to your context.) List them in the following table, along with the page number of each student scenario.

Next, using the Differentiated Assignment/Assessment Template, adapt the assignment for the proficiency levels represented by the students that you selected.

Then, based on the scaffolding and supports listed in your completed template, design instruction (based on content and language objectives) to ensure that your group of ELLs can complete the assignments. Use any lesson planning template or layout that you prefer.

Finally, consider the individual needs of the students that you selected in terms of the following topics discussed in Chapter 1:

- Educational background
- Immigrant and refugee status
- Cultural background
- Prior difficult experiences
- Age
- Language distance
- Social distance
- Psychological distance

Write guidelines for consideration in tailoring the assignment to those students in the following table.

Assignment

Students must read a short story and draw connections to their lives in a group discussion.

My focal students

Student	Scenario Page No.	Guidance

Copyright © 2010. Caslon, Inc. All rights reserved. The first purchaser may photocopy this page for classroom and personal use.

Differentiated Assignment/Assessment Template

Assignment: Read a short story and draw personal connections in group discussion

Level 1	Level 2	Level 3	Level 4	Level 5	Fully English Proficient
Language-Based Expectations:	*Language-Based Expectations:*	*Language-Based Expectations:*	*Language-Based Expectations:*	*Language-Based Expectations:*	*Language-Based Expectations:* Read and discuss (using grade-level vocabulary and sentence structures) personal connections to

Standards-Based Content or Topic (from the curriculum):

a short story

Scaffolding and Support:	*Scaffolding and Support:*	*Scaffolding and Support:*	*Scaffolding and Support:*	*Scaffolding and Support:*	*Scaffolding and Support:* using strategies explained by the teacher.

Copyright © 2010. Caslon, Inc. All rights reserved. The first purchaser may photocopy this page for classroom and personal use.

Suggested Ways to Differentiate This Assignment

Note that this completed template represents only one way to differentiate this assignment. There are many appropriate ways to accomplish this purpose; the key is to align teacher expectations and actions with what students at different levels of proficiency are capable of, as outlined in the chart.

Differentiated Assignment/Assessment Template

Assignment: Read a short story and draw personal connections in group discussion

Level 1	Level 2	Level 3	Level 4	Level 5	Fully English Proficient
Language-Based Expectations:	*Language-Based Expectations:*	*Language-Based Expectations:*	*Language-Based Expectations:*	*Language-Based Expectations:*	*Language-Based Expectations:*
Read and discuss (using provided words and phrases) personal connections to	Read and discuss (using occasional content/academic vocabulary and simple sentences) personal connections to	Read and discuss (using some content/academic vocabulary and simple/complex sentence structures) personal connections to	Read and discuss (using some content/academic vocabulary and complex sentence structures) personal connections to	Read and discuss (using a variety of content/academic vocabulary and complex sentence structures) personal connections to	Read and discuss (using grade-level vocabulary and sentence structures) personal connections to

Standards-Based Content or Topic (from the curriculum):

a short story

(continues)

Differentiated Assignment/Assessment Template Continued

Assignment: Read a short story and draw personal connections in group discussion

Level 1	Level 2	Level 3	Level 4	Level 5	Fully English Proficient
Scaffolding and Support: For reading: • that uses minimal language, includes visual support, and focuses on a familiar topic, • using strategies explained by the teacher, • with reading assistance from a paraeducator or trained volunteer For discussion: • using pretaught words and phrases, • using everyday language, • where appropriate, repeating teacher cues.	*Scaffolding and Support:* For reading: • that uses simplified language, includes visual support, and focuses on a familiar topic, • using strategies explained by the teacher, • with reading assistance from a paraeducator or trained volunteer For discussion: • using pretaught language that is part of environmental print (e.g., on a language wall), • using everyday language.	*Scaffolding and Support:* For reading: • that uses simplified language, uses visual support, and focuses on a familiar topic, • using strategies explained by the teacher, • with reading assistance from a paraeducator or trained volunteer For discussion: • using pretaught language (including some content/academic language) that is part of environmental print (e.g., on a language wall).	*Scaffolding and Support:* For reading: • that is on grade level but includes visual support, • using strategies explained by the teacher, For discussion: • using pretaught academic language that is part of environmental print (e.g., on a language wall).	*Scaffolding and Support:* For reading: • that is on grade level, • using strategies explained by the teacher. For discussion: • using pretaught academic language that is part of environmental print (e.g., on a language wall).	*Scaffolding and Support:* For reading: • that is on grade level, • using strategies explained by the teacher. For discussion: • using pretaught academic language that is part of environmental print (e.g., on a language wall).

Activity 8.2   Applying the Differentiated Assignment/Assessment Template to Your Own Context

Select a group of students from your teaching context that spans all five proficiency levels. (If you do not have students at all five levels, that is fine. Further, you may have more than one student at a given level.) List your students in the following table.

Next, using the Differentiated Assignment/Assessment Template, create an assignment or assessment. Differentiate it for the proficiency levels that your students represent.

Then, based on the scaffolding and supports listed in your completed template, design instruction (based on content and language objectives) to ensure that your group of ELLs can complete the assignments. Use any lesson planning template or layout that you prefer.

Finally, consider the individual needs of the students that you selected in terms of the following topics discussed in Chapter 1:

- Educational background

- Immigrant and refugee status

- Cultural background

- Prior difficult experiences

- Age

- Language distance

- Social distance

- Psychological distance

Write guidelines for consideration in tailoring the assignment to your students in the following table.

My focal students

Student	Scenario Page No.	Guidance

Copyright © 2010. Caslon, Inc. All rights reserved. The first purchaser may photocopy this page for classroom and personal use.

Differentiated Assignment/Assessment Template

Assignment: _____

Level 1	Level 2	Level 3	Level 4	Level 5	Fully English Proficient
Language-Based Expectations:	*Language-Based Expectations:*	*Language-Based Expectations:*	*Language-Based Expectations:*	*Language-Based Expectations:*	*Language-Based Expectations:*

Standards-Based Content or Topic (from the curriculum):

Scaffolding and Support:	*Scaffolding and Support:*	*Scaffolding and Support:*	*Scaffolding and Support:*	*Scaffolding and Support:*	*Scaffolding and Support:*

Copyright © 2010. Caslon, Inc. All rights reserved. The first purchaser may photocopy this page for classroom and personal use.

Professional Development Resources

ELL Differentiation Communiqué for Teachers

Educators' names: _____ _____ _____

Class: _____   For the week of: _____

ELLs' Names and language proficiency levels:

_____ L= ___ S=___ R=___ W=___

_____ L= ___ S=___ R=___ W=___

_____ L= ___ S=___ R=___ W=___

_____ L= ___ S=___ R=___ W=___

_____ L= ___ S=___ R=___ W=___

_____ L= ___ S=___ R=___ W=___

Content objectives (to be completed by classroom/content teacher):

Language objectives (to be completed by ESL teacher and/or classroom/content teacher):

Targeted vocabulary (to be completed by classroom/content teacher and/or ESL teacher):
Content vocabulary: Cross-curricular academic vocabulary:

Activities/assignments/assessments (to be listed by classroom/content teacher):

Differentiation ideas based on the chart (to be completed by ESL teacher and/or classroom/content teacher):

Student Names →	Level 1	Level 2	Level 3	Level 4	Level 5
Connections to prior experience and learning					
Instructional strategies					
Supplementary materials					
Assessment strategies					

Copyright © 2010. Caslon, Inc. All rights reserved. The first purchaser may photocopy this page for classroom and personal use.

Resource 8.2 Differentiated Assignment/Assessment Template

Differentiated Assignment/Assessment Template

Assignment: _____

Level 1	Level 2	Level 3	Level 4	Level 5	Fully English Proficient
Language-Based Expectations:	*Language-Based Expectations:*	*Language-Based Expectations:*	*Language-Based Expectations:*	*Language-Based Expectations:*	*Language-Based Expectations:*

Standards-Based Content or Topic (from the curriculum):

Scaffolding and Support:	*Scaffolding and Support:*	*Scaffolding and Support:*	*Scaffolding and Support:*	*Scaffolding and Support:*	*Scaffolding and Support:*

Copyright © 2010. Caslon, Inc. All rights reserved. The first purchaser may photocopy this page for classroom and personal use.

For Further Reading

On Assessing ELLs

Fairbairn, S. (2007). Facilitating greater test success for English language learners. *Practical Assessment, Research & Evaluation, 12*(11). Available online: http://pareonline.net/getvn.asp?v=12&n=11

Gottlieb, M. (2006). *Assessing English language learners: Bridges from language proficiency to academic achievement.* Thousand Oaks, CA: Corwin Press.

On Collaboration

Jones-Vo, S., Fairbairn, S., Hiatt, J., Simmons, M., Looker, J., & Kinley, J. (2007). Increasing ELL achievement through reciprocal mentoring. *Journal of Content Area Reading, 6*(1), 21–44.

On General Topics Pertaining to ELLs

Iowa Department of Education. (2007). *Educating Iowa's English language learners: A handbook for administrators and teachers.* Des Moines: Author.

Wong-Fillmore, L. (2000). Loss of family languages: Should educators be concerned? *Theory into Practice, 39*(4), 203–210.

On Gifted Education for ELLs

Castellano, J. A., & Diaz, E. (2001). *Reading new horizons: Gifted and talented education for culturally and linguistically diverse students.* Boston: Allyn & Bacon.

Iowa Department of Education, & The Connie Belin and Jacqueline N. Blank International Center for Gifted Education and Talent Development. (2008). *Identifying gifted and talented English language learners: Grades K–12.* Des Moines: Iowa Department of Education.

On Issues of Culture

Axtell, R. (1997). *Gestures: The do's and taboos of body language around the world.* New York: John Wiley & Sons.

Delpit, L. (1995). *Other people's children: Cultural conflict in the classroom.* New York: New Press.

Dresser, N. (2005). *Multicultural manners: Essential rules of etiquette for the 21st century* (rev. ed.). Hoboken, NJ: John Wiley & Sons.

Trumbull, E., Rothstein-Fisch, C., Greenfield, P. M., & Quiroz, B. (2001). *Bridging cultures between home and school: A guide for teachers.* Mahwah, NJ: Lawrence Erlbaum.

Valdes, G. (1996). *Con respeto: Bridging the distances between culturally diverse families and schools.* New York: Teachers College Press.

On Knowing Your Individual Students

Flaitz, J. (Ed.). (2003). *Understanding your international students: An educational, cultural, and linguistic guide.* Ann Arbor: University of Michigan Press.

Flaitz, J. (2006). *Understanding your refugee and immigrant students: An educational, cultural, and linguistic guide.* Ann Arbor: University of Michigan Press.

On Literacy Instruction

Algozzine, B., O'Shea, D. J., & Obiakor, F. E. (Eds.). (2009). *Culturally responsive literacy instruction.* Thousand Oaks, CA: Corwin Press.

Cappellini, M. (2005). *Balancing reading and language learning.* York, ME: Stenhouse.

Fountas, G. S., & Pinnell, I. (1996). *Guided reading: Good first teaching for all children.* Portsmouth, NH: Heinemann.

Kauffman, D. (2007a). *What's different about teaching reading to students learning English? Study guide.* McHenry, IL: Delta.

Kauffman, D. (2007b). *What's different about teaching reading to students learning English? Trainer's Manual.* McHenry, IL: Delta.

Knox, C., & Amador-Watson, C. (2000). *Responsive instruction for success in English (RISE): Participant's resource notebook.* Crystal Lake, IL: Rigby.

Peregoy, S. F., & Boyle, O. F. (2008). *Reading, writing, and learning in ESL: A resource book for teaching K–12 English learners.* Boston: Pearson.

On Special Education Programming for ELLs

Hamayan, E., Marler, B., Sanchez-Lopez, C., & Damico, J. (2007). *Special education considerations for English language learners: Delivering a continuum of services.* Philadelphia: Caslon Publishing.

Roseberry-McKibbin, C. (2008). *Multicultural students with special education needs.* Oceanside, CA: Academic Communication Associates.

On Students with Limited Formal Schooling

Freeman, Y. S., & Freeman, D. E. (2002). *Closing the achievement gap: How to reach limited-formal-schooling and long-term English learners.* Portsmouth, NH: Heinemann.

On Vocabulary Instruction

Blachowicz, C., & Fisher, P. J. (2006). *Teaching vocabulary in all classrooms.* Upper Saddle River, NJ: Pearson, Merrill Prentice Hall.

Bravo, M. A., Hiebert, E. H., & P. D. Pearson. (2007). Tapping the linguistic resources of Spanish-English bilinguals: The role of cognates in science. In R. K. Wagner, A. E Muse, & K. R. Tannenbaum (Eds.), *Vocabulary acquisition: Implications for reading comprehension* (pp. 140–156). New York: Guilford Press.

Folse, K. (2004). *Vocabulary myths: Applying second language research to classroom teaching.* Ann Arbor: University of Michigan Press.

Fry, E. B. (2004). *The vocabulary teacher's book of lists.* San Francisco: Jossey-Bass.

Snow, C. E., & Kim, Y. (2007). Large problem spaces: The challenge of vocabulary for English language learners. In R. K. Wagner, A. E Muse, & K. R. Tannenbaum (Eds.), *Vocabulary acquisition: Implications for reading comprehension* (pp. 123–139). New York: Guilford Press.

References

American Educational Research Association (AERA), American Psychological Association (APA), & National Council on Measurement in Education (NCME). (1999). *Standards for educational and psychological testing.* Washington, DC: American Educational Research Association.

Anderson, N. (1999). *Exploring second language reading: Issues and strategies.* Boston: Heinle & Heinle.

August, D., & Shanahan, T. (Eds.). (2006). *Executive summary–Developing literacy in second language learners: Report of the national literacy panel on language-minority children and youth.* Mahwah, NJ: Lawrence Erlbaum Associates. Retrieved March 6, 2010, from http://www.cal.org/projects/archive/nlpreports/executive_summary.pdf

Axtell, R. (1997). *Gestures: The do's and taboos of body language around the world.* New York: John Wiley & Sons.

Bachman, L. F., & Palmer, A. S. (1996). *Language testing in practice.* Oxford, UK: Oxford University Press.

Bailey, A. L. (2007). Introduction: Teaching and assessment students learning English in school. In A. L. Bailey (Ed.), *The language demands of school: Putting academic English to the test* (pp. 1–26). New Haven, CT: Yale University Press.

Bernhardt, E. B. (1991). A psycholinguistic perspective on second language literacy. In J. H. Hulstijn & J. F. Matter, (Eds.), *AILA Review, 8,* pp. 31–44.

Bonfils, N. (2009, February). *Reaching out to ESL families.* Session presented at the Iowa Culture and Language Conference, Des Moines, IA.

Capps, R., Fix, M., Murray, J., Ost, J., Passel, J., & Herwantoro, S. (2005). *The new demography of America's schools: Immigration and the No Child Left Behind Act.* Washington, DC: Urban Institute.

CAST. (2008). *Universal design for learning guidelines version 1.0.* Wakefield, MA: Author.

Castellano, J. A., & Diaz, E. (2001). *Reading new horizons: Gifted and talented education for culturally and linguistically diverse students.* Boston: Allyn & Bacon.

Chamot, A. U., & O'Malley, J. M. (1994). *The CALLA handbook: Implementing the cognitive academic language learning approach.* White Plains, NY: Longman.

Chiswick, B. R., & Miller, P. W. (2005). Linguistic distance: A quantitative measure of the distance between English and other languages. *Journal of Multilingual and Multicultural Development, 26*(1), 1–11.

Cook, H. G. (2008, June). *Effects of native language and context factors on the learning trajectory of English language learners: A growth model approach.* Paper presented at the CCSSO Student Assessment Conference, Orlando, FL. Retrieved December 11, 2009, from http://www.ccsso.org/content/PDFs/106_Cook.pdf

Cummins, J. (2001). The entry and exit fallacy in bilingual education. In C. Baker & N. H. Hornberger (Eds.), *An introductory reader to the writings of Jim Cummins* (pp. 110–138). Buffalo, NY: Multilingual Matters.

Curtis, J. L. (2006). *Is there really a human race?* New York: Joanna Cotler Books, an imprint of HarperCollins Books.

Delpit, L. (1995). *Other people's children: Cultural conflict in the classroom.* New York: New Press.

deOliviera, L. C., & Athanases, S. Z. (2007). Graduates' reports of advocating for English language learners. *Journal of Teacher Education, 58*(3), 202–215.

Dresser, N. (2005). *Multicultural manners: Essential rules of etiquette for the 21st century* (rev. ed.). Hoboken, NJ: John Wiley & Sons.

Dressler, C., & Kamil, M. (2006). First- and second-language literacy. In D. August & T. Shanahan (Eds.), *De-

veloping Literacy in Second-Language Learners: Report of the national Literacy Panel on Language-Minority Children and Youth (pp. 197–238). Mahweh, NJ: Lawrence Erlbaum.

Echevarria, J., Vogt, M., & Short, D. (2008). *Making content comprehensible for English learners: The SIOP model* (3rd ed.). Boston: Pearson Education.

Education Week. (2009, January 8). Teaching ELL students. [Electronic version.] *Education Week, 28*(17), 26.

Elliott, D. (2004). *And here's to you!* Cambridge, MA: Candlewick Press.

Everson, M. E., & Kuriya, Y. (1998). An exploratory study into the reading strategies of learners of Japanese as a foreign language. *Journal of the Association of Teachers of Japanese, 32*(1), 1–21.

Fairbairn, S. (2006). English language learners' performance on modified science test item formats: A pilot study. *Dissertation Abstracts International,* DAI-A 68/01. (Publication No. AAT 3248008.)

Fairbairn, S. (2007). Facilitating greater test success for English language learners. *Practical Assessment, Research & Evaluation, 12*(11). Available online: http://pareonline.net/getvn.asp?v=12&n=11

Fairbairn, S. B., & Fox, J. (2009). Inclusive achievement testing for linguistically and culturally diverse test takers: Essential considerations for test developers and decision makers. *Educational Measurement: Issues and Practice, 28*(1), 10–24.

Fitzgerald, J., & Graves, M. (2004). Reading supports for all. *Educational Leadership, 62*(4), 68–71.

Flaitz, J. (2006). *Understanding your refugee and immigrant students: An educational, cultural, and linguistic guide.* Ann Arbor: University of Michigan Press.

Fountas, G. S., & Pinnell, I. (1996). *Guided reading: Good first teaching for all children.* Portsmouth, NH: Heinemann.

Fox, M. (1997). *Whoever you are.* San Diego: Voyager Books, Harcourt.

Franco, L. (2005, June). *What's different about teaching reading to English language learners?* Workshop presented for Heartland Area Education Agency, Des Moines, IA.

Freeman, D. E., & Freeman, Y. S. (2000). *Teaching reading in multilingual classrooms.* Portsmouth, NH: Heinemann.

Freeman, Y. S., & Freeman, D. E. (2002). *Closing the achievement gap: How to reach limited-formal-schooling and long-term English learners.* Portsmouth, NH: Heinemann.

Freeman, Y. S., & Freeman, D. E. (2009). *Academic language for English language learners and struggling readers: How to help student succeed across content areas.* Portsmouth, NH: Heinemann.

Garcia, S. B. (2008, February). *A culturally and linguistically responsive approach to implementing response-to-intervention (RTI) models: Realizing the promise for all students.* Workshop presented for Heartland Area Education Agency, Johnston, IA.

Goodman, K. (1994). Reading, writing, and written texts: A transactional sociopsycholinguistic view. In R. B. Ruddell, M. R. Ruddell, & H. Singer (Eds.), *Theoretical models and processes of reading* (4th ed.) (pp. 1093–1130). Newark, DE: International Reading Association.

Gottlieb, M., Carnuccio, L., Ernst-Slavit, G., Katz, A., & Snow, M. A. (2006). *PreK–12 English language proficiency standards.* Alexandria, VA: Teachers of English to Speakers of Other Languages (TESOL).

Grognet, A., Jameson, J., Franco, L., & Derrick-Mescua, M. (2000). *Enhancing English language learning in elementary classrooms: Trainer's manual.* McHenry, IL: Delta Publishing Company.

Hamayan, E., Marler, B., Sanchez-Lopez, C., & Damico, J. (2007). *Special education considerations for English language learners: Delivering a continuum of services.* Philadelphia: Caslon Publishing.

Harper, C., & de Jong, E. (2004). Misconceptions about teaching English-language learners. *Journal of Adolescent & Adult Literacy, 48,* 152–162.

Hindley, J. (1996). *In the company of children.* York, ME: Stenhouse Publishers.

Hinkel, E., & Fotos, S. (2002). From theory to practice: A teacher's view. In E. Hinkel, & S. Fotos (Eds.), *New perspectives on grammar teaching in second language classrooms* (pp. 1–15). Mahwah, NJ: Lawrence Erlbaum Associates.

Hoffelt, J. E. (n.d.). *We share one world.* Bellvue, WA: Illumination Arts.

Hofstede, G. (1991). *Cultures and organizations: Software of the mind.* London: McGraw-Hill.

Iowa Department of Education. (2007). *Educating Iowa's English language learners: A handbook for administrators and teachers.* Des Moines: Author.

Iowa Department of Education, & The Connie Belin and Jacqueline N. Blank International Center for Gifted Education and Talent Development. (2008). *Identifying gifted and talented English language learners: Grades K–12.* Des Moines: Iowa Department of Education.

Jones-Vo, S., Fairbairn, S., Hiatt, J., Simmons, M., Looker, J., & Kinley, J. (2007). Increasing ELL achievement through reciprocal mentoring. *Journal of Content Area Reading, 6*(1), 21–44.

Kauffman, D. (2007a). *What's different about teaching reading to students learning English? Study guide.* McHenry, IL: Delta.

Kauffman, D. (2007b). *What's different about teaching reading to students learning English? Trainer's Manual.* McHenry, IL: Delta.

Kinsella, K. (2007, May). *Rigorous academic vocabulary development to bolster language and literacy for protracted adolescent English learners.* Workshop presented at the International Reading Association Annual Convention, Toronto, Canada.

Knox, C., & Amador-Watson, C. (2000). *Responsive instruction for success in English (RISE): Participant's resource notebook.* Crystal Lake, IL: Rigby.

Koda, K. (1996). L2 word recognition research: A critical review. *Modern Language Journal, 80*(iv), 450–460.

Kouritzin, S. G. (2004). Programs, plans, and practices in

schools with reputations for ESL student success. *Canadian Modern Language Review, 60,* 481–499.

Krashen, S. (1982). *Principles and practice in second language acquisition.* Oxford: Pergamon Press.

Krashen, S., & Terrell, T. (1983). *The natural approach: Language acquisition in the classroom.* Hayward, CA: Alemany Press.

Lapp, D., Fisher, D., Flood, J., & Cabello, A. (2001). An integrated approach to the teaching and assessment of language arts. In S. R. Hurley & J. V. Tinajero (Eds.), *Literacy assessment of English language learners* (pp. 1–26). Boston: Allyn & Bacon.

Lau v. Nichols, No. 72–6520, Supreme Court of the United States 414 U.S. 563 (1974).

Lenski, S. D., & Ehlers-Zavala, F. (2004). *Reading strategies for Spanish speakers.* Dubuque, IA: Kendall/Hunt.

Lightbown, P. M., & Spada, N. (1999). *How languages are learned* (2nd ed.). Oxford, UK: Oxford University Press.

Moll, L. (1992). Bilingual classroom studies and community analysis: Some recent trends. *Educational Researcher, 21*(2), 20–24.

National Center for Education Statistics. (n.d.). Language minority school-age children. In *Participation in education: Elementary/secondary education.* Retrieved December 24, 2009, from http://nces.ed.gov/programs/coe/2009/section1/indicator08.asp

National Clearinghouse for English Language Acquisition and Language Instruction Educational Programs (NCELA). (2007, Oct. 19). What are the most common language groups for ELLs? In *NCELA FAQ.* Retrieved March 18, 2009, from http://www.ncela.gwu.edu/expert/faq/05toplangs.html

Office of English Language Acquisition, Language Enhancement, and Academic Achievement for Limited English Proficient Students (OELA). (2007). *The growing numbers of limited English proficient students: 1995/96–2005/06.* Retrieved June 13, 2009, from http://www.ncela.gwu.edu/files/uploads/4/GrowingLEP_0506.pdf

Ormrod, J. (2008). *Educational psychology: Developing learners* (6th ed.). Upper Saddle River, NJ: Merrill Prentice Hall.

Patrick, E. (2004). US in focus: The US refugee resettlement program. In *Migration information source: Fresh thought, authoritative data, global reach.* Retrieved June 29, 2009, from http://www.migrationinformation.org/USfocus/display.cfm?ID=229

Payne, R. (2008). Nine powerful practices. [Electronic version.] *Educational Leadership, 65*(7), 48–52

Peregoy, S. F., & Boyle, O. F. (2008). *Reading, writing, and learning in ESL: A resource book for K–12 teachers* (5th ed.). Boston: Allyn & Bacon.

Plyler v. Doe, No. 80–1538, United States Court of Appeals for the Fifth Circuit. 457 U.S. 202 (1982).

Schumann, J. H. (1978). *The pidginization process: A model for second language acquisition.* Rowley, MA: Newbury House.

Snow, C., Burns, M. S., & Griffin, P. (Eds.). (1998). *Preventing reading difficulties in young children.* Washington, DC: National Academy Press.

Solano-Flores, G. & Trumbull, E. (2003). Examining language in context: The need for new research and practices paradigms in the testing of English-language learners. *Educational Researcher, 32*(2), 3–13.

Ting-Toomey, S. (1999). *Communicating across cultures.* New York: Guilford Press.

Tomlinson, C. A. (2005). *How to differentiate instruction in mixed-ability classrooms* (2nd ed.). Upper Saddle River, NJ: Merrill Prentice Hall.

Trumbull, E., Rothstein-Fisch, C., Greenfield, P. M., & Quiroz, B. (2001). *Bridging cultures between home and school: A guide for teachers.* Mahwah, NJ: Lawrence Erlbaum.

UNHCR. (2007). *The 1951 refugee convention: Questions and answers.* Geneva, Switzerland: Author. Retrieved February 9, 2009, from http://www.unhcr.org/basics/BASICS/3c0f495f4.pdf

Vann, R. J., & Fairbairn, S. B. (2003). Linking our worlds: A collaborative academic literacy project. *TESOL Journal, 12*(3), pp. 11–16.

Wiggins, G., & McTighe, J. (2006). *Understanding by design* (expanded 2nd ed.) Upper Saddle River, NJ: Pearson Education.

Wong-Fillmore, L. (2000). Loss of family languages: Should educators be concerned? *Theory into Practice, 39*(4), 203–210.